TWELVE AGAINST THE GODS

WILLIAM BOLITHO

DIVERSION
BOOKS

Diversion Books
A Division of Diversion Publishing Corp.
443 Park Avenue South, Suite 1004
New York, NY 10016
www.DiversionBooks.com

For more information, email info@diversionbooks.com

First Diversion Books edition September 2018
Print ISBN: 978-1-63576-539-7
eBook ISBN: 978-1-63576-504-5

LSIDB/1809

Contents

WILLIAM BOLITHO:
A Memoir

BY WALTER LIPPMANN

WHEN A MAN OF Bolitho's quality dies in his youth it is a subtle temptation to exalt him above his works. His friends who had sat with him and talked with him and apprehended the resources of his spirit must naturally find it hard not to dwell upon his promise at the expense of his achievement. They have felt how abruptly his time was limited, and it is in the nature of their affection that they should wish others to let faith in the man fill out the uncompleted record of his writings.

What affection and faith authorize, a gentle vanity quite readily exploits: I could find in my own feelings when the invitation came to me to write this memoir a disguised wish to imply that no mere reader of Bolitho can appreciate his stature, and thus to claim membership in the privileged circle of those who might truly say they understood him. This temptation to make a private cult is a strong one. For Bolitho was a radiant person. In his company ordinary things were transfigured, acquiring the glamour of mystery and great import. His talk had a quality which belonged to one who dwelt familiarly, so it seemed, with the hidden elements of man's life and with the infinite permutations of his affairs. In his presence it was easy to believe that one had a private revelation of those great concerns which in prosaic living seem verbal and remote; with him one walked quickly through portals, that are usually closed, into the statelier mansions of the soul. He was an eager guide. Whoever happened to be there, he took with him in his explorations, not pausing to ask whether his companion had the wit or the courage for such adventures. He was lavish in his talk. He belonged to what he once called the smaller class of those who are the givers rather than the takers, the fountains rather than the wells. He gave his immediate best profusely to anybody without reserve to economize his strength. His only defenses were his own unstinted gift of self-expression. It is said of Copeland of Harvard that he once remarked when he was asked whether he had enjoyed a tea party that "if I had not been there I should have been very much bored." Bolitho in public gatherings was a little like that. Against the destructive impact of tedious autobiography and self-justification, he protected himself by seizing command of the discussion and transporting it quickly to regions where even the most debilitating bore was too uncertain of himself to do anything else but listen. Yet it was expensive. When Bolitho left New York for the last time, he was weary, not from the effort of his work, for being an artist, working refreshed him, but from the strain of keeping himself at concert pitch. He could not be insensitive, and he did not relax by taking things for granted; he had that unremitting responsiveness which is a faculty of genius and one of its burdens. In any company he took the floor at the beginning of the evening and held it until the end, thus saving himself and the rest of the party much weariness. Because he was so instantly aware of all who were present, seeing them not as silhouettes but in the round and often clairvoyantly, he made them all share the excitement which he had in exploring his own thoughts. They would go home feeling, not only that they had heard a brilliant performance, but that they had been rather uncommonly brilliant themselves. The echoes of his voice are still about us. Thus for a little time the spell of his presence cannot fail to obscure the less immediate expression in his printed works; and it is natural that only by making the special effort of reading his books as things divorced from the man who was in New York last year will his friends overcome the feeling that they knew a promising artist rather than a writer whose place is certain among those who have been mirrors to this age. I have read again as much of his work as I could lay my hands on, making the effort to read as one would read who had not known him: the selection of his essays for the *World* now republished under the title *Camera Obscura*; the earlier essays in the same vein called *Leviathan*; his *Murder for Profit*; and the manuscript of his play *Overture* which will have been produced in New York when this edition of *Twelve Against the Gods* appears. There are no certainties in these matters of taste and preference; I can express only my own conviction that among these writings there is much which will persist. What Bolitho would have done had he lived longer is another question. He would almost certainly not have gone on to do a little better and a little better the things he had already done. What he wrote up to the age of thirty-nine is the achievement of a young man in the full phase of his powers. The quality of his essays is intrinsic, authentic and entirely his own. Every paragraph he wrote has the signature of his own spirit upon it. Had he lived longer, I cannot believe that he would have gone steadily forward on the path he had taken; he would in the nature of things have taken some other path as his powers altered with maturity and his imagination took hold of new aspects of existence.

The essays we have are in themselves completely done, and they were done, too, as I happen to know, with unstinted care. Although most of them were written for newspapers and magazines, he never wrote with the sense that, because tomorrow's column will be forgotten the day after, it is not prudent to spend too much time upon it. He was not content to skim the top of his mind in order to fill a column; he labored ultimately to satisfy an ideal audience, which was himself, devotedly in moods of intense concentration and passionate absorption. He respected his own powers too much to exploit them; the feeling that his talents were no mere personal possession precluded any compromise with the naïve theory that a young writer can do potboilers now in order to gain time and leisure for masterpieces in his middle age.

The intense honesty of Bolitho's work came from something besides the wisdom which knows that first rate abilities cannot stand the effects of doing second rate things, from something more than a conscientious wish to give full measure, from something more than that capacity to take pains which is often set down as the hall-mark of genius. His artistic integrity was an inseparable quality of the very special sort of artist that he was. He expended such unreserved energy on a daily column in a newspaper, or even on talk at a dinner table, because the circumstances of his life had rendered him peculiarly immune to the calculations of the careerist in an established society. He travelled through the world with very little baggage. The people he met, the books he read, the events he witnessed, did not encumber him. They were objects of interest, not possessions which clouded his faculties.

So among accumulating memories he preserved an invincible innocence of the eye. He did not come to see new things in remembered patterns, or to respond to them defensively and offensively as portents of his own worldly fortunes. Few of us are as free as this. We are for the most part immersed in our memories; they are the habits of our perception, they are standards of loyalty to which new experience must conform. Bolitho was unentangled. Thus his awareness often seemed preternatural. His mind was unmortgaged. He had no need to face two ways—towards the verities and toward his loyalties—but he could seize experience, and making it wholly his own, manipulate what he perceived into gorgeous and original shapes.

For Bolitho was a visitor in this western civilization, and to the end he remained, in spite of his many friends, like the anonymous figure in Santayana's dialogue, a stranger in all his dwelling places. He was a British subject. He had been a British soldier. Yet he chose to live in Provence making excursions from Montfavet as his base to places like London, Paris, Berlin, New York and Chicago, where the latest manifestations of the western culture were manifesting themselves. He went to observe and to understand, never as an immigrant and settler.

He did not share, therefore, the tacit assumptions upon which our civilization operates, its contemporary style, its accepted purposes, its historic ethos. All of these, which for most of us lie below the threshold of our awareness, he saw in their external perspective. The modern western ways of living did not impose upon him the internal illusion that, like wind and weather, they are indefectible, and he never became habituated to look upon them blankly and with dull familiarity. He knew well the arts and institutions of the west, seeing them as a sympathetic visitor might see them, as portentous, exotic, and contingent.

Thus Bolitho moved through our world enjoying the privileges of a native and the freedom of an alien. He did not have the corporate feeling that the fortunes of that world were the whole human destiny. Its fortunes were one among the many spectacles which historic circumstance has presented. He was without the illusion of permanence or that incredulity of well-established people that for them too there are wilder possibilities. Bolitho knew that our civilized establishments are a crust of ordered assumptions resting uneasily upon convulsive and implacable forces.

He had more than an idly curious eye for the outcroppings of elemental things. His studies of murderers, conquerors, libertines, and adventurers, were the work neither of a collector of bizarre odds and ends, nor yet the objective record of a sober historian, but the poetic vision of a man who had intuition of how near to the surface of our conventions lie monstrous energies. Because our conventions did not possess him, he never mistook the short octave of our accepted values for the whole scale of experience; thus his work attempts vast complicated rhythms in which those whose ears are alert can hear the undertones of man's savagery and the clear notes of his occasional raptures and mystic joys.

To the expression of his sense of life he brought, as all who have read him know, the gifts of competence and intelligence. Bolitho could tell a story as well as any good novelist, he could expound ideas or report events as well as any journalist of his time. But such ordinary talents will not convey so extraordinary a vision as Bolitho had. Thus I have often wondered whether his peculiar genius could be fitted to the limitations of the prose essay; he had, it seemed to me, a method of seeing which in my own experience at least I have not met before in writers of prose. It was a capacity for intense and unimpeded realization of the object as such, a capacity for such intrinsic awareness that in the act of seeing the normal associations fell away and something undreamed of was revealed. Often it has seemed to me that his prose gives evidence of strain under the effort to put into discursive sentences a quality of perception to which his language would not conform. Beautiful as much of his writing is, there are moments when his words resist him. These moments are often those when his realization is most intense, and they suggest the possibility that he was seeking to take hold of his material in a form to which the analytical discourse of the prose essay was inadequate.

It may well be that the evidence of conflict with his medium foreshadowed what might have been the next phase of his work. I think it likely, though in such matters there are no proofs conceivable, that he would soon have turned from the prose essay to some other medium, to some form of expression like the poetic tragedy, in which instead of having to expound it, he could have projected his sense of the troubled destiny of man. On some such voyage of exploration he was perhaps compelled by the demands of his nature to set forth, and in the months before he died I think he knew that the time had come when he was leaving the plateau of his successes to ascend the peaks of his genius.

Introduction

ADVENTURE IS THE VITAMINIZING element in histories, both individual and social. But its story is unsuitable for a Sabbath School prize book. Its adepts are rarely chaste, or merciful, or even law-abiding at all, and any moral peptonizing, or sugaring, takes out the interest, with the truth, of their lives.

It is so with all great characters. Their faults are not mud spots, but structural outcroppings, of an indivisible piece with their personality. But there is a special reason for the inveterate illegality, or if you prefer, wickedness, of your true adventurer, which is inherent in the concept of Adventure itself. Adventure is the irreconcilable enemy of law; the adventurer must be unsocial, if not in the deepest sense anti-social, because he is essentially a free individualist.

This is what boys—those natural judges of the matter—have been trying to mutter for centuries, when fobbed off with lives of missionaries, or generals, where varied incident in vain ornaments an essentially unadventurous character. A feat, a danger, a surprise, these are bonbons adventure showers on those who follow her cult with a single mind. Their occurrence even repeated does not constitute a life of adventure.

Here also we renounce utterly the comfort of Mr. Kipling, who believes commuting, and soldiering in the British Army, and buying English country houses, adventurous; and Mr. Chesterton, who is certain that a long walk on Sunday and a glass of beer set one spiritually in the company of Alexander, and Captain Kidd and

Cagliostro. All this amiable misconception is as touching as the children's wish for a good pirate, for bloodshed in which no one gets hurt, and roulette with haricot beans. Tom Sawyer knew better. The adventurer is an outlaw. Adventure must start with running away from home.

But in the mere fact that the essentially socially-minded, the good, the kind, and the respectable long to adopt the adventurer, it is clear that the opposition set between adventure and order, between the adventurer and society, is not exterior to humanity, but an inner antithesis, which divides our will.

The adventurer is within us, and he contests for our favour with the social man we are obliged to be. These two sorts of life are incompatibles; one we hanker after, the other we are obliged to. There is no other conflict so deep and bitter as this, whatever the pious say, for it derives from the very constitutions of human life, which so painfully separate us from all other beings. We, like the eagles, were born to be free. Yet we are obliged, in order to live at all, to make a cage of laws for ourselves and to stand on the perch. We are born as wasteful and unremorseful as tigers; we are obliged to be thrifty or starve, or freeze. We are born to wander, and cursed to stay and dig.

And so, the adventurous life is our first choice. Any baby that can walk is a splendid and typical adventurer; if they had the power as they have the will, what exploits and crimes would they not commit! We are born adventurers, and the love of adventures never leaves us till we are very old; old, timid men, in whose interest it is that adventure should quite die out. This is why all the poets are on one side, and all the laws on the other; for laws are made by, and usually for, old men.

It is this doublemindedness of humanity that prevents a clear social excommunication of the adventurer. When he appears in the flesh indeed, he can hope for no mercy. Adventure is a hard life, as these twelve cases will remind you. The moment one of these truants breaks loose, he has to fight the whole weight of things as they are; the laws, and that indefinite smothering aura that surrounds the laws that we call morals; the family, that is the microcosm and whip lash of society; and the dead weight of all the possessors, across whose interwoven rights the road to freedom lies. If he fails, he is a mere criminal. One-third of all criminals are nothing but failed adventurers; they usually get a stiffer sentence than the rest, the imbeciles and the hungry. It is when he imposes himself and gets out of reach of the police that society's reaction is most curious. No one cares to say that Napoleon, or Alexander, or Cæsar, were worse men, before any fair court, than Deadwood Dick and Jesse James; we try to digest them. The consequences of their actions are turned into motives; boys are urged to imitate some version of their lives from which all their disgraceful, but practicable and necessary, stepping-stones have been carefully removed.

To these perjuries and frauds, the respectable can plead "crime passionnel." It is violently unpleasant to send a Napoleon to prison—though when they had to, they did it. But in another aspect of the social problem of adventure, the deliberate trickery of the adventurous into lawfulness, the altered signpost and the camouflaged cage, "we of the virtue" are harder to defend. These booby traps are always set; the recruiting sergeant is always waiting at the first corner for the runaway to sell him a uniform or a flag, but in unsettled times, when the drive to adventure becomes too general and fierce for any ordinary method of society to contain, law and order do not hesitate to descend to special ruses. So the wild riders of the Middle Ages were embrigaded into that flattest of enterprises, knight errantry, shipped off to the dull and most legitimate wars of the Crusades, or bamboozled into being a sort of blue police of the great highroad.

No, the adventurer is an individualist and an egotist, a truant from obligations. His road is solitary, there is no room for company on it. What he does, he does for himself. His motive may be simple greed. It most often is, or that form of greed we call vanity; or greed of life, which is no more admirable, after all. But beware of underestimating this motive. Greed has been loaded with almost as many stupid insults as that other fundamental, sexual instinct; yet it would be gratitude for us at least, the adventurous race by definition, the insatiable Europeans, the conquistadores, to think of it as a virtue, a manurial virtue, out of which our difference from and supremacy over the contented breeds has demonstrably proceeded. God help the ungreedy...that is, the Australian blacks, the poor Bushmen of South Africa, those angelic and virtuous Caribs, whom Columbus massacred in the earthly paradise of Haiti, and all other good primitives who, because they had no appetite, never grew.

At the beginning of most careers stands an adventure, and so with states, institutions, civilizations. The progress of humanity, whatever its mysterious direction, is not motored by mere momentum. Let ethics make what it can of it. There is therefore a sociological rôle of adventure; necessarily an accidental one, since it is in itself non-social. History is jolted along with great breaches of law and order, by adventurers and adventures. From the flint-jabber age to standing room in the subway, from a cave at Les Eyzies to the plumbing of New York, we have come by two forces of effort, not one; the guard and the search, made by the home-stayer on the one hand, and by the bold affronter of the New on the other. That is, by the adventurer as well as by the citizen. By law, but also by those who leaped outside its protecting palisade, caring nothing if they damaged it in the action, and augmented the treasures of the race by courage and not thrift. The first adventurer was a nuisance; he left the tribal barricade open to the risk of the community when he left to find out what made that noise in the night. I am sure he acted against his mother's, his wife's, and the council of old men's strict orders, when he did it. But it was he that found where the mammoths die and where after a thousand years of use there was still enough ivory to equip the whole tribe with weapons. Such is the ultimate outline of the adventurer; Society's benefactor as well as pest.

On the strength of this sociological rôle then, the adventurer may depart on his high and lonely quest with some of our sympathy restored to him. He, our alternative self, has need of it, for the odds are against him. His first enemy we know, the mechanical, interlocking weight of law, social and moral. The second is the Unknown itself. In so far as the nature of all living things is conditioned by their enemies, the adventurer is defined by his fight with Order, and his fight with Chance. The first he may win—if he does not, he will go to prison. The second he cannot beat, for it is a manifestation of the universal. This book contains no invitation to the life of adventure: that has the same end as all the rest. I do not mean that in our material categories an adventurer cannot be successful. Some, though not the greatest, have died of old age, on heaps of that they set out to get. There is a more subtle tragedy that waits for adventurers than ruin, penurious old age, rags, contempt. It is that he is doomed to cease to be an adventurer. The law of his morphology is that, setting out a butterfly, he is condemned when his development is ripe to become a caterpillar. The vocation of adventure is as tragic as that of Youth; its course is parabolic, not straight; so that at a certain point it leads back to the cage again. The greatest adventurer that ever lived ended as a nervous, banal millionaire.

The secret of this ultimate tragedy of adventure is psychological; it hides in the nature of the adventurer's motive, swinish and god-like. It is interwoven in his personality. For this greed they have in all their five senses, for gold, for power, for vainglory, for curiosity, even at their highest moments, the greed for life itself, is dual. It contains the urge to keep, as well as to grab. It is retentive as well as prehensile. One of the fascinations of watching these lives is to follow the beautiful interplay of static and active greed in them, the slow advantage of conservation creeping upon acquisition, the sudden incursion of fear, the fear to which even Alexander sacrificed in his tent, when he knew he had won too much and the adventure was over, which is the sign of conservation's progress within him, and the inevitable deadening of its complement that follows.

For these are men betrayed by contradiction inside themselves. Their mixture differs from ours only in its proportions; in them too is a social man at war with a free man, miser as well as spendthrift, stay-at-home as well as rolling stone, hoarder and gambler, shepherd and hunter. It is his own social self that trips up the adventurer, and strangles him.

Above these closely related sociological and psychological struggles of the adventurer there is another, sublimely interesting, transcendent to both: the fight, which is like a wooing of the unknown, whose names are also chance, danger, inexhaustible container of everything that is new. It is with desire of her, herself inseparable from her gifts, that he is greedy. It is her perfidy—here is her majesty and cruelty—that loads him with prizes, that muffles him with the veils of her benevolence, to chain him with gold and victories so that he dares not go on, to change him from a lover into a slave. It is when the pirates count their booty that they become mere thieves.

So much for the main outline, sociological, psychological and in a sense mystical, of adventurer and adventure, which I hope these twelve practical researches that follow will fill in with many curious and interesting variations. Among them there will be found two or three women, out of the few that so far have clearly merited to be in the sublime company by the size and originality of their fate. During the interminable age (which however seems just ending), in which marriage was the career of women, it might be defended that every woman's life contained an adventure; and that every woman of marriageable age was an adventuress, just as married women are society's irreducible bodyguard. This is the old novelists' thesis—the stereotype of that adventure and its banality puts it outside our scope. But now that times are changing, the once purely speculative question as to whether women, outside the simple limits of their economic dependence on man, could feel and follow adventure has become important, and any light the study of undoubted woman-adventurers (adventuresses is a question-begging epithet) of the past can throw on this, and any evidence for or against a different morphology of the sexes in adventure will be interesting.

It is evident that the varying resistances of the three formative elements, that is, the social complex, the field, and the psychology of the adventurer, alter not only adventure's features—since every age produces its peculiar type, conquerors in antiquity, discoverers in the Middle Ages, prospectors in the nineteenth century—but its quantity and incidence, at any rate from the point of view of the historian. Of these we must neglect the third, supposing it constant since we cannot estimate it. But it is obvious enough that the influence of the other two can be expressed in a simple law: that adventure is harder, rarer, and less important, according to the strength of the social tie, and to the narrowing of the field of the unknown. Both these adverse conditions are in operation today. We are far from an international government, but we already have an international police, with cables, posts, aeroplanes and a general similarity of codes and understanding at its service, which would make short work today of the adventurous lives of a Cellini, a Casanova, a Cagliostro. This ecumenical civilization, as Keyserling calls it, allows less and less space for the individual. Concurrently the field has cramped with the mapping of the world. The geographical unknown, the easiest of access and the most naïvely alluring, has gone. There is a telephone wire to Lhassa, flags on each Pole, and though from time to time a few indomitable ladies try to convince us that the Sahara is not commonplace, and romantic Travels to places in Asia—to which the tourist agencies will sell you a ticket—still dribble from the press, in the gloomy schoolboy commonplace, "exploration is worked out." Is adventure, with these handicaps, a thing of the past?

I have already discarded the comfort of those writers and poets, who in the difficulty try to palm off as adventure what is only "interesting" and often only mildly interesting at that. Without descending to the adulteration of good notions, adventure does still exist, and even the adventurer, in his fortunate and aesthetic form, with a fate out of contact with sordidness, is no rarer than he has always been. There have been lean seasons for adventurers before, the eighteenth century notably, when everything seemed owned, done, mapped. In such times the new is to be sought inwards, not in immutable Nature, but in the ever renewed flux of human life. Geography has become banal, but topography is inexhaustibly original.

It is there that immortal adventure has taken refuge in our days, in the deserts of high finance, the jungles of business among the innumerable savage tribes that our great cities have disguised and not exterminated, in the human world, where there are greater spaces than between the stars. In the titanic works and events of our day there is the same hostile co-operation of runaway and stay-at-home, the same cult-struggle with the same enigmatic goddess, who asks all and gives all. History has always treasured a catalogue of adventurers—she has not changed her ways, though she may not, for business reasons, be allowed to publish it.

As for the adventure-feat, the Atlantic flights, the polar journeys, the Everest climb, that flowering of heroism and endurance above anything in humanity's past, perhaps, which is the panache of our times, it only secondarily concerns our subject. The heroes of these things are the soldiers of society, not adventurers; only a misunderstanding which these studies may clear up could make their friends claim for them the title. I shall have occasion to return to the matter.

What follows is intended, then, a little to elucidate history, more to illustrate it, to honour without hypocrisy the deeds of men and women whose destiny was larger, if not deeper than our own. Above all to shake loose the perception of the adventurer in us, and of us in the adventurer. To appreciate where I am not allowed to admire; neither to warn nor to encourage; in equal veneration for the insatiable spirit of man and for the inexhaustible mystery around him he preys on, depends on, and worships.

WILLIAM BOLITHO

I.

Alexander the Great

Then came the Fire, and burnt the Staff,
That beat the Dog,
That bit the Cat,
That ate the Kid,
That My Father bought,
For Two pieces of money.
A Kid! A Kid!

T HE JEWS, THOSE ETERNAL contemporaries, who have seen everything and remembered everything, have a sort of muttering nursery rhyme on world history. Right in its beginning, where I have quoted it, arrives Alexander, the Fire, who burned the Achaemenian Empire, that ruled the world with its Staff, that beat the cruel Assyrian Dog, that bit the wise Babylonian Cat, that ate the poor, pure Kid, the chosen tribe God purchased from Moses, that stands at the bottom of the cosmical process of munching, which is their interpretation of history. Now Fire is a good word for Alexander, who lived like Fire, fought like Fire and died young, burnt out.

He stands first in these studies, not only because of his date (356–323 B.C.) but because he is a compendium of the subject. Every adventurer resembles Alexander in some way and some of the great ones have consciously imitated him. And in him, more than anyone else, are contained the secrets of the growth and evolution of the character that unites them all.

This is partly due to the accident of his birth, that made him the son of a great man. Boys in this position have usually been psychological monsters, cast for the rôle of a bitter or ludicrous Hamlet. But Alexander drew from it some of that double-heated energy of reaction that Bacon noted in the cases of humpbacks and dwarfs. The chief phase of his development had to be opposition to his father, whose enormous personality blocked his horizon in all directions. All the other factors in his period of autoformation are linked to this: the influence of the tigerish witch-woman, his mother Olympias, who also hated Philip, by a different sort of jealousy; and that of Aristotle, his tutor, which his father imposed upon him.

This Philip had had an extraordinary career. Before he was out of his teens he was sold to his enemies, the Thebans, by a conspiracy of treacherous and ferocious mountain princelings who wished to exclude him from his father's throne. Even his rights as the head of such a court hardly seemed worth fighting for. From such a start, in twenty or thirty years Philip succeeded in making himself not only the King of a pacified and settled Macedonia, but the Captain General of all Greece, a feat to be compared in difficulty to a young Mexican's arriving against law and custom and racial feeling at the Presidency of the United States. Nevertheless Philip was no adventurer. His career had less adventure in it than a game of chess. It was a construction. He was an engineer of life. Every gain in his life was planned, and gathered ripe. Nothing but the affection of his son ever fell out of his hands.

When such a man is also good-humoured, with the temperament of a mountain and the health of a rock, infectiously gay at a party, keen as a schoolboy in sport, vain with the exuberant half-seriousness of a man more pleased at heart with life than with himself, with the grin as well as the game always on his side, he more than conquers, he oppresses. There is a passage in Plutarch that gives Alexander's secret away.

"Whenever news was brought that Philip had taken some strong town, or won some great battle, the young man, instead of appearing delighted with it, used to say to his companions, 'My father will go on conquering till there is nothing extraordinary left for you and me to do.' For he did not desire to inherit a kingdom that would bring him opulence, luxury and pleasure, but one that would afford him wars, conflicts, and all the exercise of great ambition."

But hero-hatred is as imitative as hero-worship, save that it works by opposition. Alexander was as limited by his furious desire to tear his personality from all likeness to Philip, as he would have been if he adored him, for he compressed himself into a series of contraries. Thus Philip's shrewdness was famous; Alexander chose recklessness, and the large gesture. Philip was eloquent. Alexander prided himself on a taciturnity which his boiling nature found hard to manage. Philip had the vanity to record his victories in the Olympic Chariot Race in the impression of his coins. Alexander on the other hand, when he was asked whether he would not run in the Olympic Race (for he was swift of foot), answered, "Yes, if I had kings for my antagonists." Against this sporting side of his father's character, with some precocious knowledge of its specific importance as the dominant feature of the popular feeling for him, Alexander was specially careful in contrariety, and drew a curious distinction between his father's tastes and his own. Thus Philip loved to watch boxing and wrestling. Alexander "professed a perfect detestation for the whole exercise of wrestling," which included under the name of the Pancratium a sort of boxing with knuckle-dusters.

The story of the taming of Bucephalus, still stocked by all Wild West romancers, is a sudden illustration of this hidden contest between the two. "When Philonicus, the Thessalian, offered the horse named Bucephalus in sale to Philip at the price of 13 talents (say 8,000 dollars), the king with the prince and many others went into the field to see some trial made of him. The horse appeared extremely vicious and unmanageable, and was so far from suffering himself to be mounted that he would not bear to be spoken to, but turned fiercely upon all the grooms. Philip was displeased at their bringing him so wild and ungovernable a horse, and bade them take him away. But Alexander, who had observed him well, said, 'What a

horse are they losing for want of skill and spirit to manage him!'
Philip at first took no notice of this; but, upon the prince often repeating the same expression, and showing great uneasiness, he said,
'Young man, you find fault with your elders, as if you knew more
than they, or could manage the horse better.' 'And I certainly could,'
answered the prince. 'If you should not be able to ride him, what
forfeiture will you submit to for your rashness?' 'I will pay the price
of the horse.' Upon this all the company laughed, but the king and
the prince agreeing to the bet, Alexander ran to the horse, and laying
hold on the bridle, turned him to the sun; for he had observed, it
seems, that the shadow which fell before the horse, and continually
moved as he moved, greatly disturbed him. While his fury lasted,
Alexander kept speaking to him softly and stroking him; after which
he gently let fall his mantle, leaped lightly upon his back, and got his
seat very safe. Then, without pulling the reins too hard, or using either whip or spur, he set him a-going. As soon as he perceived his
uneasiness abated, and that he wanted only to run, he put him at a
full gallop, and pushed him on both with voice and spur.

"Philip and all his court were in great distress for him at first, and
a profound silence took place; but when the prince had turned him,
and brought him straight back, they all received him with loud ac-
clamations, except his father who kissed him and said, 'Seek another
kingdom, my son, that may be worthy of thy abilities, for Macedonia
is too small for thee.'"

The faint irony of this remark, from the shrewdest horse-coper of
a nation of horsemen, to a young man who has just assisted a dealer
to sell him a vicious nag at an exorbitant rate has escaped good
Plutarch. But it was certainly mixed with a part of genuine pride.
Giants envy their fathers, only pigmies their sons. Philip's dominant
attitude to Alexander was an amused pride, the pride of a fancier
mixed with that of a father, which subsisted under the most violent
of his rages against his son's sulks and insolence.

So the secret of Alexander's personal code—that species of ath-
letic asceticism, which has had almost as much educative influence
on the world as a codified religion, which to this day in a queerly

doctored and patched eighteenth century form, labelled "English Gentleman," is the ideal of part of the world—possibly lies, as its typical idiosyncrasies show, in this opposition of Alexander to his father. Its foundation is the wilful converse of a sensual, boisterous, still half-savage mountain laird, which Philip until his death remained. But on that rigid foundation Alexander built one of the most attractive ideals of conduct for himself that the Aryan youth can find. Its prohibitions and permissions are much more than a series of whims, and just as far from being derived from any religion or metaphysics. It is true that his central contempt for the body and its pleasures has been claimed by various Greek schools as their instigation. As a doctrine it had just before Alexander's time been developed by the dogged Antisthenes from that saw of Socrates, "Virtue is Knowledge," into the "bad manners as an end in themselves," that gave his school the name of Cynics, or as we should say "Snappers." And Antisthenes's impudent friend, the ex-coiner Diogenes of Sinope had given the school much personal publicity. Alexander was undoubtedly attracted by what he heard of these people, at the age when every intelligent youth is looking for theoretical backing for his likes and dislikes. But beneath and beyond any influence their gloomy ratiocinations had on him was an instinctive complex, in which I fancy I see two communicating factors—the urge to self-deprivation, and that, not purely calculating, nor purely disinterested, to realize the cult conditions of Adventure, in the first moments her inviting gesture becomes clear. That is, coarsely put, Puritanism, and Training.

The first is here none of my business, if its very existence in Alexander, as in the rest of humanity, were not commonly unsuspected. It might clarify our understanding of all biographies, and particularly of these that follow, if instead of assuming lightly that the natural bent is only towards "pleasure"; that any dislike of any young man for feather beds, wine, and roses, was supernatural, or at any rate only to be explained by the influence of some inspiring moral doctrine, it were remembered that man is pulled to deprive himself as well as to enjoy himself; at certain ages often more strongly and irrationally; that "pleasure" is a question-begging term; in short that there are as many misers as gourmets in the world.

But in young Alexander this innate fondness for hoarding himself is doubled by a premonitory desire to cut away everything that can hamper in the adventure. Every encumbering habit, every compromising fondness. To Alexander, as soon as he has perceived the lineaments of his future, the pleasures of bed and table are not sinful, not unworthy, though at one moment with his head full of Diogenes's nonsense he may have used the word, but in the last sincerity, nothing but dangerous handicaps. Let him explain his morality, when his success had rather blunted the edge of its necessity, in his own words, "Sleep and commerce with the sex are the things that make me most sensible of my mortality."

The second human influence on this fiery, comfort-hating, father-jealous boy was his mother, the terrible Olympias. The third is the more slippery factor of Aristotle, his tutor from the age of thirteen, the universal philosopher; and the woman and the sage curiously interweave their traces on the boy.

This Olympias, even in the blurred and misunderstood outline that the historians have left of her, is a magnificent creature. She hated Philip, for the commonest reasons as well as for the most complex, which we shall need to examine later. To the Greeks of the city-states, the court of Philip of Macedon was somewhat wild and primitive. But Olympias, the Queen, was born a princess of Epirus, that is, the inner mountains of Albania, where they are always five hundred years behind the calendar. She belonged to a time, indeed, far anterior to that sunset of the ancient world where her son and husband stood. In her there was the neolithic, the stone age, that vast and intricate culture, which never had or needed an historian, so that we are obliged to patch together our bald ideas of it from the hints of cromlechs and the Ju-ju of aboriginals.

The key to her, which for the sake of Alexander we must seek a little, is therefore in a view of her sex which has long been lost. She was a woman as they were while they still had the memory of the matriarchate, and of that tenderly nourished civilization that came while man was hunting; and still resented the change. In the Greek books they call her "witch-woman," and the peaceable Plutarch, who heartily wished that even the families of his heroes had been respectable, stammers when he has to discuss her. But it is not now her crimes that interest us, but her way of thinking, and that is, naturally, her religion. She was an ardent devotee and a high priestess of the Mysteries of Orpheus and Dionysus. Hear Plutarch on it: "They tell us that the women of that country, Epirus, were of old extremely fond of the ceremonies of Orpheus and the orgies of Dionysus, and that they were called Clodones and Mimallones because in many ways they imitated the Edonian and Thracian women about Mount Haemus, from whom the Greek word *threscuein* (to cast a spell) which signifies the exercise of extravagant and superstitious observances. Olympias being remarkably ambitious of these inspirations, and desirous of giving the enthusiastic solemnities a more strange and horrid appearance, introduced a number of large tame serpents, which often creeping out of the ivy and the mystic fans, and entwining about thyrsuses and garlands of the women, struck the spectators with terror."

And so it is whenever Olympias's name occurs in the histories, we are taken, hintingly and allusively, into this still incompletely explored background of archaic and supernatural secrets that lies behind the most luminous rationalizations of Greek life. The only pertinent side of these Mysteries, in which she was adept, is here the disproportionate part women played in them, out of all scale to their recognized political or even social rôle, and the character, if not precisely of internationalism, at any rate of intertribalism, and non-nationalism, which for some inexplicable reason (where all is inexplicable) was invariably linked with this. Whatever childish and brutal things Olympias and her fellows may have taught the boy under cover of these venerable hugger-muggeries, this non-nationalism was valuable and critically important to him. This confused and enigmatic polytheism had in its shrines a place for Isis as well as Attis. Cybele cohabited there with the Etrurian Priapus, the Persian Mithras with the Greek Orpheus. Not only could a wandering Jew or a Syrian or a Mede become a blood brother in their rites with a Greek or a Macedonian, but these societies were so many, their secrets so entangled, that the distinction between initiate and outsider, which might have been expected to produce its own sort of particularism, was in fact veiled by an infinite intercommunication of membership, and an indefinite shading of degrees of initiation. That Alexander was a member, initiated by his mother, of the mysteries of Orpheus would not prevent him from joining or being adopted into those of Egyptian Thebes, rather it would give him a half-footing in them.

So as a first consequence of his mother's influence Alexander loses the greatest encumbrance of the adventurer, an exclusive patriotism. In his most private affections a Persian could be his brother, and an Athenian an outsider. He could, that is, disengage himself from the most subtle manœuvre of Society, the adventurer's enemy—Nationalism itself. The socially minded man can forgive adventurers for anything rather than their inveterate unpatriotism. This patriotism, in fact, is in obscure intention an attempt to meet the adventurer half-way; to dress society, that old stay-at-home madame, in color; to persuade and entice the truant to stay in the ranks, by a sort of music; to make her allegiance not only a duty, but an excitement. And the repulse of this wile is felt, not as a man feels a blow, but as a woman feels a rebuff. Nevertheless patriotism, mass-adventure is an alternative to pure adventure, which is individual. The non-adventurous races (the French and the modern British) are precisely the most patriotic. And in the lives of the most typical and unmistakable adventurers, there is to be observed, parallel and concordant with their disregard of or hostility to law, social or moral, a more or less flagrant indifference to the sentiment of country. A patriotic adventurer is not certainly such a paradox as a law-abiding adventurer. But occasionally, and exactly in the highest instances, as here, there is a definite charge of unpatriotism against him, which his official biographers have difficulty in explaining away. So was it as you will see with Alexander. His adventure, the crown of Greek power turned into a vast betrayal of Greece, whose epoch ended with him.

The first lesson of Olympias is non-nationalism; the second is still less likely to be approved. Plutarch reveals that "the night before the consummation of her marriage, Olympias dreamed that a thunderbolt fell on her belly, which kindled a great fire, and that the flame extended itself far and wide before it disappeared. And some time after her marriage, Philip dreamed that he sealed up the queen's womb with a seal, the impression of which he thought was a lion. Most of the interpreters believed that the dream announced some reason to doubt the honor of Olympias, and that Philip should look closely into her conduct. But Aristander of Themesus said it only denoted that the queen was pregnant, and that the child would prove to be of a bold and lion-like courage. A serpent was also seen lying by Olympias as she slept, which is said to have cooled Philip's affections for her more than anything else... It is also said that he lost one of his eyes which was that he applied to the chink of the door, when he saw the god (Jupiter) in his wife's embraces in the form of a serpent. According to Eratosthenes, Olympias privately related to Alexander the secret of his birth and exhorted him to behave with a dignity suitable to his divine extraction."

The "Jupiterism" of Alexander is placed by this story on a very different plane, from the crazy vanity, whipped up by the wild compliments of Orientals, which some commentators have tried to make of it. In the first place it arises external to himself, in the collaboration of Philip and Olympias, in the second, its origin is somewhere—ingenious Freudians from the serpent and thunderbolt might guess closer—in the earliest relations of the two, and at the beginning of their ill-feeling. The boy believed he was a god, long before his conquest of Persia, possibly before he thought of that conquest. Olympias in any case knew of it, and perhaps she fostered it, and used it as an instrument of her peculiar education. Even if this latter is not true, and Plutarch hesitates, the world the boy kept her company in could not fail to favour the idea. This extravagant mother and hating wife lived as a primitive and an Orphic in a world peopled with godhood. The first words her initiation taught his soul to say were, "I am a son of Earth and Heaven." The last words engraved on the amulets the dead adepts held in their hands were, "I have flown out of the circle

of life." And, "O blessed and happy one, thou hast put off thy immortality and shalt become divine."

But leaving the question of its origin and growth, there is the
practical one of its effects upon him, both in his personal evolution,
and as a psychological instrument in the unheard-of feats he was to
perform. First of all, he could organize with it the depths of his basic
rebellion against his father's personality. He could protect himself
against the worst spiritual hardship sons of great men in his position
have: the heredity of his father and the reproach, from without and
within, that all they do is simply their father's blood working in
them. And once in company with so potent a fiction, once having
persuaded himself with the help of his mother, his needs, her world
of wonders and mysteries, to faith, there was hardly any end to its
advantages for him. If a new William James would celebrate the
pragmatic Lie, the generous Mephistopheles man must ever turn to
from the stingy truth, the stately fiction that works all social constitutions, and the homely private romance about ourselves, whose
presence is the unacknowledged secret of all happiness, if not of all
success, and whose departure is the adequate cause of all sane suicides! Believing he was a god, Alexander conquered the civilized
world, and in the end was worshipped on his throne; if he had stayed
at being a hero, he would not have gone so far. But meanwhile
Aristotle? The "father of them that know," the genius of the matter
of fact, whom Philip at the boy's most plastic age had brought in
against the witch-mother? It is time to look at the influence of such
a tutor; if not positive—these experiments in the education of the
great by the great are always disappointing—at any rate, as a correc-
tive. As for the first, it is soon told. The canny Macedonian seems to
have made no great effort to force schooling on the boy. He had a
philosophical garden made on his arrival on the most pleasant
Athenian models, grassy walks shaded by rare trees, stone seats, and
terraces for discussion and teaching when the heat of the day is past;
and when Alexander wished he sauntered there and asked questions.
His former teachers were a grotesque courtier named Leonidas, and
a still more burlesque local man named Lysimachus, and by these, or

in spite of these, Alexander had learned to love the Iliad. He explained to Aristotle with the solemnity of fourteen that this was "because it was a portable treasury of military knowledge," and Aristotle assented and gave him a copy corrected and annotated by his own hand that he afterwards carried on all his campaigns. Alexander had a fitful enthusiasm for metaphysics, and later in life reproached Aristotle for publishing "the secret parts of logic" to the vulgar world, exactly as his mother would have reproached a religious teacher for divulging the secrets of his lodge. Nevertheless the boy-god learned to have a respect for philosophers, and even for poets, though Aristotle had no interest to teach him that. In one curious field, he held Alexander's enthusiastic attention: that of medicinal botany. Alexander may have been disappointed that his tutor could tell him next to nothing of their magical properties, the shriek of the mandragore, the anti-demoniac scent of vervaine, the merits of hyssop gathered at the full moon, but he delighted in even the soberer stories of the first scientist, and made teas and potions and doctoring his friends his life-long hobby.

A lesser philosopher would perhaps have attempted and perhaps have succeeded in eradicating the two tremendous ideas Alexander drew from Olympias; the unpatriotism of the Mysteries, the Jupiterism that was pressing him to his destiny. But being Aristotle it is more likely that his view was not so simple. It must have been almost with fright that he saw this wild prince, after scrambling with his crazy mother over god knows what miles of unauthorized sheep tracks of thought, had arrived, not at nonsense, but on the very summits of Aristotle's own doctrine, where though the whole of his logic bears him up, he himself feels a vertigo to stand. For this phantasy of Alexander of a state to be made, where nationalities, cities, tribes, are only elements ruled by a man-god, is a clear corollary of the extreme, almost esoteric limit of Aristotle's political doctrine; that the true King is a god among men, bound no more than Zeus by country or law, "because himself is the Law."

So in the rearing of Alexander everything seemed accomplice; every factor coincided to the greatest, almost unattainable advantage that can come to a man ambitious of any undertaking, but especially of adventure: the unification of the will. Which when it is purged of contradiction, and then alone, can set about a great business. It remained only to direct it; and here, too, Alexander's fate was single-minded. Every goal but one was blocked by the extended personality of his father. It was impossible for the boy-god to desire to be merely a magnificent king, the leader of Greece. Popularity, strength, statesmanship, all these things had been achieved by his father, and Alexander's will was fixed on the necessity to out-do and other-do him. One object remained, that by its size and impossibility had escaped Philip's ambitious, much more his universal success. The conquest of the Achaemenian Empire by a Greek could not enter any mortal imagination; but to the boy who believed himself an invincible god while he was still using a half-size spear, it was simple and inevitable. As all his education tended to unite his will, so all his circumstances, personal and exterior, swept him towards this single enterprise. Not for the Macedonians, still less for the Greeks—a single will means a single egotism—but for himself.

In mere geography this vast antagonist, or prize, that Alexander chose, was in this sense the world, that is, it was its core, the hub of the three old continents. For at its greatest extent it held Thrace in Europe, and its rulers had the waters of the Danube, the Nile and the Indus brought and mingled in a cup in their palace as a symbol of their possession. The old names for its components give a better idea of its power, for the lands of Persia, Palestine, Afghanistan, Asia Minor, Iraq, have lost even the memory of their ancient fertility. The Empire, then, had absorbed and held the lands of its august predecessors: Egypt, Babylon, Assyria, the country of the Carians, the Lydians, the Phrygians, the Armenians, the Jews, the Hyrcanians, Parthians, Bactrians, with their capitals, their gods and their wealth, and much more. It extended from the Upper Nile to the Indus, from Samarkand to Babylon and beyond, from the Caspian to the Red Sea. It was the greatest visible power the world had yet seen, comparable in strength and riches and stability to any the world ever saw until the rise of our swollen nineteenth century. For hundreds of years before Alexander an uncountable population had enjoyed more security and fruitful peace within its scope than had ever existed in the world before. It was the oasis of governmental civilization, as contemptuously ignorant of the China that was being born across its north-east deserts as of the weak and infinitely divided Brahmanic kingdoms south-east of its mountain barrier. On its punitive expeditions—it was too great to make wars—it could, as is recorded of Xerxes, mobilize and transport over thousands of miles a million soldiers of a hundred different languages and styles of fighting.

Something of awe and regret still seizes poets and historians at the trace of its ruins, more even than those of Rome or Old Egypt can inspire. We have to decipher its look from the books of its unscrupulous enemies, the Greeks, ever mean in victory, and the Jews, who hated everything human but themselves. Nevertheless, even in their accounts this Empire makes a grand figure. Its rulers were beautiful and humane, its laws were celebrated for their objectivity and tolerance; its wealth was boundless, and wealth is the human standard for states. Over the world into which Confucius, Buddha and Plato were born, it threw the shadow of the greatest social achievement of humanity, summing up the Golden Age. To me at this unbridgable distance it seems that it may have been the most promising of all those achievements, which if it had prospered only a few more centuries might have saved humanity in Europe as well as in Asia the long stagnant centuries of their separation.

Beside this colossus that leaned across its narrow seas, Greece cut something the same figure as the Jews next to Pharaonic Egypt, that is, a small, waspish people, important because of their intelligence rather than their power, hardy borderers, never to be despised, but often forgotten. To the great Persian lord of the interior, the Greek soldier was better known and esteemed than the Greek artist or philosopher; thousands of them went into mercenary service in the Empire, usually to stay and be absorbed. Their religion was respected, the laws were light and equal, and salaries plentiful and regular. These handsome, evil-tempered, blond troopers, who fought, according to their cities and social standing, with spear, sword or ax, were

the most intelligent soldiers the world has ever seen, and though religion, or injustice, can make illiterates and boobies fight to the death
on occasion, the professional fighting man's worth varies according
to head. In remote market places in Baluchistan, or in the irrigated
paradise behind Babylon, these Spartans, Athenians, men from the
Isles and Macedon, were familiar sights to the women, stalking
among the black-avised, moody Medic bowmen, and all the mixed
races which the Great King collected under his sceptre, like demi-
gods, ever in a quarrel or an argument, or an amour, the men most
intensely alive.

From such of these as returned, and from the encyclopaedic
Aristotle, Alexander would eagerly learn of the wonders of Persia.
When he was fifteen his father began with anxiety and care to prepare the dangerous crown of his career: a raid on the opposite coast
ports of the Empire. The reports of spies massed themselves in his
archives, and from them Alexander would learn, if he cared, solemn
data on this secretly elected antagonist, the names and temperaments
of governors, distances and routes and garrisons. It is more probable
that the colored narratives of returned mercenaries, and even the
speculations of his tutor, interested him more. There is no evidence
that Alexander in fact ever planned his conquest, in the sense that
Philip planned his raid. The one was a scheme, the other an adventure, which would have been hampered by any other than a spiritual
preparation. There are no lines of communication in an adventure.

But without one construction of Philip, the Macedonian Army,
even Alexander could have done nothing. This instrument is set beside the Median cavalry of Cyrus, the janissaries of the Sultan, the
troopers of Gustavus Adolphus. Its heart was Macedonian peasantry,
the foot companions, or *pedzetairoi*, in a loose phalanx, armoured in
bronze, armed with the *sarissa*, the great Macedonian pike, fourteen
feet long. Because of its more open order and incomparably greater
speed in the field made possible by a discipline as stiff, yet elastic, as
steel, it was able to beat, whenever it met it, the Greek phalanx which
had no other rival in the world. As a satellite to this body, was the
corps of royal footguards, yeoman farmers more lightly armed, and

equipped with burnished silver-bronze greaves, helmets, pikes and shields. Out of these again Philip had chosen a shock battalion of 1,000 men quicker over everything but made roads than cavalry itself.

The Macedonian cavalry was in the main composed of needy, arrogant, rash country gentlemen, material worthy of Philip's genius for psychological engineering. Out of these he extracted the essence of all their qualities and useful faults in the small but terrible squad of the "king's companions," "the last defence and the head of the attack." In this Alexander took his place as soon as he could lift a regulation sword.

It is not likely that Alexander ever breathed of his intention to his father. If he had, the veteran would have set it aside as talk. A natural anecdote of Plutarch lights up here, both the respectful view Alexander himself had of the Empire and the bitter and complicated family background behind him. "Pexodorus, the Persian governor in Caria (that small province at the south-western corner of Asia Minor, south of Ephesus and Smyrna), being desirous to draw Philip into a league, defensive and offensive, by means of an alliance between their families, offered his eldest daughter in marriage to Aridaeus, son of Philip (and half-brother to Alexander), and sent Aristocrates into Macedonia to treat about it. Alexander's friend and his mother infused notions into him again, though perfectly groundless, that by so noble a match, and the support consequent upon it, Philip designed the crown for Aridaeus." If the prospect of a marriage into the family of one of its subordinate officers could so rouse him, what must have been his sober estimation of the full power of the Empire?

We know little more of these growing years. When Alexander was sixteen he took part in some hill-fighting. The next year he headed the charge of the "king's companions" that broke the Sacred Band at Chaeronea, Philip's last great battle. When he was eighteen, the family drama took a new turn. Olympias was suspected of having drugged young Aridaeus, so that from "being of a proud and swelling spirit," he became a half-wit. Philip decided to repudiate her, on account of this, and no doubt of her age and temper, and married Cleopatra, one of his court beauties.

"While they were celebrating the nuptials, Cleopatra's uncle Attalus, intoxicated with liquor, desired the Macedonians to entreat the gods that this marriage might produce a lawful heir to the crown. Alexander, provoked at this, said, 'What, dost thou take me for a bastard?' and at the same time he threw his cup at his head. Hereupon Philip rose and drew his sword, but fortunately for them both, his passion and the wine he had drunk made him stumble, and he fell. Alexander, taking an insolent advantage of this circumstance, said, 'Men of Macedon, see there the man who is preparing to pass from Europe to Asia. He is not able to pass from one table to another without falling.'"

Philip had little time left to live. We do not know if Alexander had any share in his assassination. We know that he profited by it; and that that theological snake-charmer, his mother Olympias, hired the obscure bravo who stabbed Philip at the end of a feast two years later. The women of Epirus were very dangerous.

So at last—he was only twenty years old, but he had been waiting an age—the boy-god had the army; the only part of kingship that interested him. Little else indeed was left of the fortune of Philip. The Captain-Generalship, the ordered realm, the treasure, all melted away in the first days. A spontaneous revolt, from the city-states of the south to the hillsmen of the north, split the structure Philip had spent a lifetime to build. The army, three or four old generals, Parmenio, Perdiccas, the inner ring of the young roisterers of the court, Hephaestion, Clitus, Craterus, Ptolemy, and a sullen and unpromising loyalty of Philip's administrators, these were all Alexander could count on. It was enough. In the events that followed, the wonder of his raging impatience almost eclipses the memory of his extraordinary achievement. His sole feeling against the rebellion, which was more formidable perhaps than anything that had threatened his brilliant father, was neither fear, nor resentment, nor anything than the passion and elemental energy aroused by being delayed. He rushed first upon the wrong end of the enterprise. Instead of meeting the organized armies of the Greek States, he turned north to burn the revolting highlanders out of their heather.

The Romans, the Turks after him, with all their resources, never completely subdued this Balkan wasps' nest. Alexander ended the resistance in a month. His phalanxes forced the Shipka Pass. His cavalry, riding outwards from the line of march like the spokes of a wheel, rushed the defiles, and in a zig-zag of fire, he burnt and massacred, as if he was dealing with herds of wild sheep, and not the dourest rebels in the world on their ground.

At the end of his dominions and march was the Danube. Beyond that was the mystery of darkest Europe. Alexander reached it at night, and waited till dawn, peering across. Somewhere, unguessably far off, at this time men were building Stonehenge, worshipping in the gaunt alleys of Karnak, perhaps still adding an inch a year to the middens of Denmark. Prehistoric Europe. Alexander hesitated. Not for the last time the main current of the world was in that stream. Everything was possible that night; Alexander could not decide. The next morning, with a gesture, he moved his whole army across. Philip's machine needed no more than a finger to move it, when it was new. There was a village of some poor savage devils the other side, Germans, Kelts? Who knows? Behind them on the vast plain his scouts in an hour's ride could see nothing. So Alexander burnt their village and by evening moved back again, leaving the mystery to another thousand years.

Then, through what is now Yugo-Slavia, at a speed no army before or after has attempted, he appeared before the walls of Thebes, the head of the coalition, centre of civilization and order, the city of Pindar. In a few days this place was a smouldering rubbish heap; 6,000 of its fighting men dead, 30,000 sold for slaves. Only the house of Pindar was spared, to remind the world that the destroyer was a lettered man and the pupil of a philosopher.

Nor must any apologist dare to say that these were the crimes of an inconscient being, without any more discernment than fire. In all his crimes Alexander was responsible; they were necessary to his adventure, but he knew what he was doing, and could feel remorse. He executed his father's assassin, and searched more or less earnestly for his accomplices. And he, no more than Greece, suddenly quiet, never got over that Theban day. "The calamities he brought on the Thebans gave him uneasiness long after, and on that account he treated many others with less rigor. It is certain he imputed the murder of Clitus, which he committed in his wine, and the Macedonians' dastardly refusal to proceed on the Indian expedition, through which his wars and his glory were imperfect, to the anger of Bacchus, the avenger of Thebes. And there was not a Theban who survived the fatal day that was denied any favor he requested of him."

Now he was recognized again as Captain-General and even received grudging contingents from the city armies (except the Spartans) to bring his troops up to 30,000 footmen and 5,000 horse.

Then with continuity of the same momentum, he set himself to the East. First, with a perfect knowledge of what such an adventure required of him, he set himself to destroy his lines of retreat. He divided up all that he and the monarchy owned, lands, revenues, monopolies, and gave to his friends, to one a farm, to another a village, to this the revenue of a borough, and to that of a post. When in this manner he had disposed of his possessions, Perdiccas seriously asked him what he had reserved for himself. Alexander answered "Hope." In reality, he reserved for himself Life, and life as a god, as Homer described it, an endless game of fights with a good poet to describe it. Lacking the latter, he took his Homer with him, "the casket copy" that Aristotle had annotated for him.

We know very exactly how he looked when he leapt off the pontoon on the further shore of the Bosphorus. He was red-haired, with that illusive appearance of openness that goes with the colour, sunburnt. The turn of his head, which leaned a little to one side, and the quickness of his eye, were best hit off, we are told, by the sculptor Lysippus. He was not tall, nor heavy. He usually fought with the cavalry, and his mounting was always the signal for the charge. His favourite weapon was a light sword with a razor edge. In set battles Aristander, his soothsayer, rode beside him in a white robe, with a gold crown, to point out the omens in the skies. When he began, he wore no other armour than a quilted coat, and an iron helmet that was polished like silver.

His first act when he landed was, naturally, to go up to the ruins of old Troy and sacrifice to Minerva and Achilles. In honour of the hero he anointed the pillar on his tomb with oil and ran round it with his friends naked, as was the custom.

The Leviathan Empire was slow to react. Hardly a quiver seems to have reached its brain far east in Susa. A local police action, entrusted to the governors of the invaded territory, seemed to the somnolent monster sufficient. A force about equal to his own slowly drifted towards Alexander's encampment, composed mainly of mercenaries of his own nation. This was enough to trouble old Parmenio, trained in the very different spirit of Philip, and he suggested to the astonished and amused Alexander to manœuvre for a while, at any rate until the month, which was May and unlucky by Macedonian tradition, was out. Alexander suggested they should change the name of the month.

The battle began late in the afternoon. The enemy had taken up a good, regulation position on the banks of the Granicus, a small fierce stream, whose banks were steep on Alexander's side, and muddy on the other. The older officers thought the position unfavourable. But while they were still deliberating, Alexander charged the stream with thirteen troops of horse. The Persian bowmen sent a drooping punishing volley on them in the water, and as soon as they crossed, mercenary cavalry, officered by the two Persian grandees, Rhoesaces and Spithridates, charged them in the mud. Alexander was picked out by his helmet and the huge crest of white feathers he had placed on it, and for some minutes had to defend himself single-handed. Under such a leadership the battle resembled a hard football match rather than an operation of war; the seasoned and serious leaders were at sea with an opponent who ignored any tactics they had ever heard of. Young Rhoesaces and Spithridates caught the infection and leaving their squadrons to command themselves, entered on a personal fight with Alexander. Spithridates succeeded in getting home with his battle-axe on the helmet of the Greek, and cut the feathers clean away. Clitus, Alexander's friend, transfixed him with his pike.

While this horseplay was hottest, the machine came into action. The Macedonian phalanx crossed and smashed into the formations of bowmen—who ran away. Only the Greek mercenaries remained at the end of ten minutes. These collected in good order on a slope and sent a message to Alexander that they would surrender. But the prince in his excitement refused and without a pause charged his horsemen, who had mechanically re-formed, at them. His horse was killed, and this useless and inglorious end of the battle lasted for hours, until the mercenaries were all killed or down.

The campaigns of Alexander from this point have absorbed an enormous amount of learned ingenuity. In any success there is a discoverable structure, but the word "plan" should be reserved for a definite anterior conception; in this sense it is hard to admit that Alexander in his armed wanderings, which cover the map like the scribblings of a child, had one. He did the right thing, because it pleased him; that is, he spent the remainder of the year in one of his immense zig-zags, looking for battle, which happened to be good strategy. No further large attempt came to expel him; the Empire waited. Where he came the inhabitants either accepted him with roses and wine, or fought and were beaten. He preferred the latter.

But after a year of this mad, gay marching in Asia Minor, the Emperor Darius saw that Alexander would not be absorbed for a long time, nor retire of his own account. He collected one of those monstrous armies which empires that have lost the military sense have recourse to, a steam roller of an army, that could scarcely move a couple of miles a day, the inevitable defence of sheer numbers of the peaceful herd against the beast of prey. The smallest battalion in it represented a larger power than Macedonia; it was composed of levies from every warlike or unwarlike tribe in Hither Asia. This human tide rolled slowly westwards until it reached the Mediterranean at the Issus, opposite Cyprus.

Meanwhile Alexander had had at any rate one year's life as a god, a fight or a siege weekly, triumphal entries monthly, long days of muscle-kneading fatigue on the dusty roads, nights broken by the everlasting, cheerful noise of Greek encampments, and such Homeric feasts as that cutting of the Gordian knot in the coloured city of Midas. There was an ancient chariot in the temple tied with cords made of the bark of the cornel tree. A vast crowd came to see what Alexander would do with the puzzle, for it was the tradition "The Fates decreed the Empire of the world to him that should untie the knot." It was twisted so many ways, and the ends so artfully concealed within, that Alexander found he could do nothing with it. But though the most thorough believer in omens that was ever brought up by a snake-charmer, he had the habit of forcing them, if contrary, as he renamed the unlucky month in the beginning. So with a stroke of his sword, he slashed it through.

It did not immediately bring him luck. He was passionately fond of bathing (though he could not swim) and caught a chill in the icy waters of the river Cydnus just when his generals were worried at the news of the human landslide rolling towards them. While he was lying at the point of death he received a letter from the ever uneasy Parmenio: "To beware of Philip your Doctor, whom Darius has prevailed upon by presents of infinite value and the promise of his daughter in marriage to take you off by poison." Plutarch continues: "He put this letter under his pillow without showing it to any of his friends. The time appointed being come, Philip, with the King's friends entered the chamber, having the cup which contained medicine in his hand. Alexander received it without the least mark of suspicion and at the same time put Parmenio's letter in his hands. It was more interesting than any tragedy, the one reading while the other was drinking. The king, with an open and unembarrassed countenance, expressed his regard for Philip, who threw himself down beside him and entreated him to be of good courage and trust to his care. As it happened the medicine was so strong and overpowered his spirits in such a manner that at first he was speechless, but afterwards—in three days—it cured him."

As soon as he could stand, he broke camp and threw himself upon the slow monster that was feeling out on his flanks to envelop him. He attacked at night, far out off the wing, to avoid this danger, and by dawn the Imperial army was torn in pieces, Darius in flight and the roads for leagues around blocked by mobs of utterly disheartened fugitives. This was the famous battle of the Issus.

Neither Alexander nor any of his men felt any desire to follow it up at that moment. The Macedonians, pikemen and horsemen, settled down to the loot. Although Darius, to force on the rate of his march, had left the majority of his baggage in Damascus, enough remained to send the soldiery mad. He had left even his tent, even his harem behind. When Alexander came in the high pavilion of embroidered silk "and took a view of the basins, vials, boxes and other vases curiously wrought in gold, smelled the fragrant odours of essences, and had seen the splendid furniture of spacious apartments therein—the king's crystal bath, the huge enamelled censers that still smoked, for everything had been left in order and untouched, the table and vessels in which the satraps dined with the ruler of the world" he turned to his friends, and said, "This, then, it seems, it is to be a king."

After he had washed and supped, the ladies were brought to him. Here is placed the incident that more than any other has pleased humanity. Not only did he respect their feelings and virtue himself, but he protected them, and allowed them to have the same retinue as they were accustomed to. He used to say by way of a jest: "What eyesores these Persian women are," though among them were the most beautiful women in the Empire and not the least the Emperor's wife and two daughters.

We have examined in its beginnings this continence of Alexander, which at this period at any rate aroused almost as much astonishment in the world as his conquests. In eating, he was very temperate; but in drinking, especially after Issus, scarcely the same. This battle indeed made him rich, not on a Macedonian but on an Asiatic scale, and his style of life outwardly showed it. Instead of dried figs and bread, his officers and companions were asked nightly to banquets, the expense and profusion of which would have made his bonvivant father, Philip, gasp. After the meal the company would sit late talking, for Alexander loved company, "especially that of flatterers and court poets," of whom he had a great number, to the silent disgust of his friends.

At Damascus he fell in with the rest of the camp treasure, and set out for Egypt. He had the habit of sacrificing to local gods as he came across their shrines: it is highly probable that he visited the Temple of Yahweh at Jerusalem, though there is no clear tradition of it.

Tyre alone resisted him; and he was obliged to make one of those long and difficult sieges of which Semite military history is full. The Phoenician defenders resorted to a curious stratagem; having suspected, through the vision of a priest, that their god was playing them false in Alexander's favour, they loaded it with chains, and nailed its feet to the pedestal.

In Egypt nothing is remembered of his doings except the visit to Jupiter Ammon, and his foundation of the city named after him, Alexandria. It appears that he was pleased by the site, and by a quotation from Homer on city building he found apt. So without delay he ordered the streets to be laid out. His model was his short Macedonian cloak, that is, a semi-circle bounded by a straight line.

The priest of Jupiter Ammon, to see whom was quite possibly the principal motive of this vast side-conquest, pleased him enormously. "For being desirous to address Alexander in an obliging manner in Greek, the priest instead of saying 'O Paidon' (My son) in his barbarous accent made of it 'O pai dios,' that is O Son of Jupiter." The rest of the interview was between them alone. It is supposed to have turned on the question of Philip's assassination, but Alexander himself in the letter he wrote to his mother on that occasion is reported to have said only "He received certain private answers from the oracle, which he would communicate with her on his return."

Here, in Egypt, the morning of Alexander's adventure ends. Henceforth he is divided; Alexandria is his first possession and he is no longer free. His soldiers are no longer demigods, but merely rich men; his companions have become potentates who mark the change by the unheard-of vulgarity of their luxury. Such a one in the province that had fallen to him has camel loads of earth brought to him from Egypt, to rub himself when he went to the baths. Another has silver nails in his shoes. Philotas had hunting nets made a hundred furlongs broad. All of them had their grooms of the bath, their chamberlains, and some "made use of richer essences than oil" for friction after bathing. Alexander himself lived as hard as he had ever done, and sent all the treasures he captured to his mother and to his friends at home. But the weight of his success could not be lifted by mere personal asceticism. As he had done to Bucephalus, duty and responsibility saddled and mounted him, no gallop could henceforth throw them off. The adventure slipped with every gain deeper into the condition of a conquest.

It is the morbid interest of this degeneration, the slow smothering of the light and heat of him in the sheer bulk of his gains, the slow strangulation of success, that now fills the story.

It is not only his hope of renewing the adventure, but his clear interest, that impelled him to move his army in search of Darius. The unhappy Emperor, handsomest, tallest and most ineffectual of men, had collected a second army, the size and better than the quality of that butchered at Issus, and moved half-heartedly, westwards again. The Macedonian machine was built on a plan that the corruption of its materials could not derange; once more Alexander set it in motion, and found it as supple, as swift, after a year's rust as ever. But as if to reveal to the world the intimate, invisible change, Alexander did a simpleminded and strange thing. When he had come to scouts' distance of Darius, who was encamped in inertia at Gaugamela, a village near the site of ancient Nineveh, he with his soothsayer and spiritual confidant, Aristander, "performed some private ceremonies and offered sacrifice to Fear." Not, it is sure, to any physical or tangible Fear, but to Fear-Anxiety, Fear-Worry, the fear not of losing but of the responsibility; new and terrible companion of all his night watches henceforth.

It is related that the noise of the Persian camp in the distance was like the bellowing of an immense sea, and that the whole horizon that night seemed to be lighted with its innumerable camp fires. Parmenio particularly was depressed by the prospect of the next day, and with most of the staff generals came to Alexander and begged him to make a night attack as his only hope, as the darkness would hide from the phalanx the hugeness of their task. Alexander, fresh from his sacrifice, made the celebrated and stupid reply, which shows how much of the old spirit the nearness of battle had restored him, "I will not steal a victory."

Then he went to bed and slept more soundly than he had done since the Issus. Parmenio could not imitate him. At earliest dawn the old bear entered Alexander's tent and called him two or three times. "When he waked, Parmenio asked him how he could sleep like a man who had already conquered, when he had the greatest battle the world ever heard of to fight?"

The day started badly. Dense and never-ending clouds of Bactrian cavalry, the ancestors maybe of those light riding, demoniac Mongol horsemen which a thousand years later gave Genghis Khan the mastery of a larger but not greater world than Alexander's, beat away the wing where Parmenio commanded the cavalry. Parmenio sent a desperate message to Alexander to look to his retreat. Alexander, having yelled a contemptuous reply to the messenger, that all could hear, put on his helmet, and mounted. But for the first time in his life this was no signal to charge. He hesitated and rode slowly to the front of the silent reserves, and addressed them. He had not gone far in his exhortation before they began to shout, and stopping to listen, he found that "so far from needing any encouragement, they were striving to add to his confidence and to urge to attack at once." At this the son of Jupiter snatched a short javelin from the hands of a soldier and brandished it in the air calling on Jupiter to see the deeds of his son. Then waited again.

Meanwhile on the whole centre, the supreme trust of Darius, the army of chariots, had charged. The great mass, the terror of the old world, came on with the impetus of a dam-burst, watched down the slope by the hard, pale phalanx of pikemen. Behind the frenzied horses stood like men of stone or bronze the Medes of the monuments, muffled to the eyes, straining for the impact. They struck the light Macedonian javelinists and bowmen. These murdered their horses with accurate fire, and then when the front was in confusion charged the chariots, in the marvellous discipline which, while it allowed the freest play to each man, coordinated their efforts like a football scrum. In a few minutes the charge re-formed itself and came through the struggling mass. But not a tenth, not a fiftieth of those who had begun; the phalanx opened to meet them and let them pass through to be hamstrung in the rear. At this moment Alexander and his men perceived flying high an eagle, the bird of Jupiter, and he immediately gave the signal for the main action. The impetuosity of the phalanx carried it at once far into the heart of the Asiatics, and Alexander was thrown up against the bodyguard of Darius. Here there was the most desperate bravery; even when they were dying the Persians held on to the hoofs of their enemies' horses and tried to obstruct them with their bodies, which mounted in heaps. In the course of a very short time, during which Alexander and Darius may (as all traditions have it) have come to grips, a panic seized the Persians; they were heard shouting that their king was dead, that the gods were come out on them, and all ended in a great rout.

In the issue of this battle, the world changed masters. Alexander becomes henceforth an earthly god, treated with divine honours by all civilized men, not as he had dreamed, a bright, flashing god such as fought in his book, but an Oriental idol, condemned to squat on all the suspicions and responsibilities of the world. His days were taken with ceremonial, correspondence and the tedium of a world-wide administration. His nights were wearisome with the memories of the day's business. Three times, it is recorded in his lifetime he tried to return, to cease to be a conqueror and become a free adventurer again. The first was as follows.

When at last he came to Persepolis and sat on the throne of the Kings of Persia under a gold canopy, he gave a banquet. The whole of Greece seemed to have transported themselves to share in his fortunes, and the chief of this company, whether they were generals or poets or statesmen or courtesans or even buffoons, were invited. A famous courtesan of Athens, named Thais, who had attached herself to young Ptolemy, was there. After the meal, they all were extremely intoxicated and Thais got up on the table in front of Alexander and said, "I have undergone great fatigues in wandering about Asia, but this day has brought me a compensation by putting it in my power to insult the proud courts of the Persian kings. Ah, how much greater pleasure it would be to finish this carousal by burning the palace of Xerxes and set fire to it myself in the presence of Alexander." This typical proposition was greeted with outrageous uproar of acclamation; all strove to persuade the King to agree. At last he leaped from his throne, put a garland on his head, and with a torch in his hand led the way to the street. They all followed, shouting and dancing, and came to the palace. The soldiers, who had got wind of it, ran up with lighted tow and wood, and though marble and gold are hard to light, made a commencement of the thing. They had the idea, under their drunkenness it seems, that by burning this palace Alexander meant to show that he did not intend to remain in the country as its king, but to go back with the plunder to Greece. Plutarch adds briefly, "But all agree that the King soon repented, and ordered the fire to be extinguished."

In his pursuit later of the unhappy Darius, who fled north with a few faithful guards, Alexander came to Maracanda in the country of the Sogdians, in the extreme north, that is, to Samarkand. Here was the river Iaxartes, and here there was a curious repetition of what had happened in the first days of his adventure, on the Danube. Again he led his army across, as if pressed by an ungovernable impulse, and again he returned after burning a village. That way led the road to China, where at this moment Tsin was warring with the shadow emperors—an immense supplement to his adventure. But he turned back. His friend Clitus, who had saved his life once, was with him and at the feast that night at headquarters they quarrelled. There was a Greek buffoon, who had made smart verses against the uncouthness and vanity of the Macedonian soldiers, and at wine, when they were all warm, he had the King's permission to sing it. All but the Macedonians were loudly amused. Clitus and some of the older officers protested. The King said nothing to them, but told the buffoon to give it all over again. Clitus then shouted out, "It is these Macedonians, anyway, that made you great and saved you from the spear of Spithridates when you were turning yourself back, though now you give out that you are the son of Jupiter Ammon and disown your father, our Philip." A terrible argument between the two broke out, to end which Alexander turned to the company and said, "Do not the Greeks appear to you among these Macedonians like demi-gods among so many wild beasts?" Clitus retorted, "Say what you should, or do not invite freemen to your table, but slaves who will worship you without scruple." Alexander snatched an apple from the table at this and flung it in Clitus's face, and looked for his sword. But another of his friends had hidden it. He dragged himself loose from those who were trying to quiet him and rushed to the door and called out, in the Macedonian language, for his guards, saying there was a mutiny. There was a trumpeter standing on service in the ante-room, and he ordered him to sound the general alarm. The man hesitated, and Alexander fell upon him and beat him with his fists. Afterwards he was rewarded for having stopped the whole army from being roused. Clitus, who was now persuaded to leave, stood in the doorway and recited a mocking couplet, on boasters, from a drama. Then Alexander snatched a spear from one of the guards and as Clitus was pulling the curtain ran him through. He died at once.

This death Alexander ever regarded as one of his chief misfortunes. After it his sourness and his hardness of character increased. He became more and more obsessed by fears of rebellion and conspiracy among his countrymen: many serious revolts provided him with reasons. No one after Clitus was dead could be exempt from suspicion, to which in a most cruel way many of his companions fell victim; amongst them poor Parmenio, and Philotas, his son, whom he had put to the torture. While this Philotas was in the tormentors' hands he bewailed himself in such lamentable fashion that Alexander, who was hidden behind the curtains to hear such confession as he might make, burst out with "O Philotas, with all this unmanly weakness durst thou embark in so great and hazardous an enterprise?"

In 328 B.C. he made his most determined effort while he still possessed some of the affections of his men. While giving it out that he intended to explore the extreme east of his dominions, he planned a descent into India proper. The beginning of the expedition recalls that of the great days. "Seeing his troops were so laden with spoils that they could not march; therefore, early in the morning that he was to take his departure, after the carriages were assembled he first set fire to his own baggage and to that of his friends, and then gave orders that the rest should be served in the same manner." The orders were well received. On Alexander's route on this expedition and on the extremely tangled details of the running campaign against the tribes that lay on it, there is a whole literature. The mere facts, that he brought his army practically intact across the Hindu Kush and through the Khyber Pass in less than a year, through a labyrinth of mountains inhabited by the fierce ancestors of the Pathans and Afghans, are perhaps more impressive. Among the strangest sights that fell their way on this march was the tomb of Cyrus the Great, the founder of the Empire two hundred years before, Alexander's equal as a conqueror, though not as an adventurer. On it was inscribed in Persian: O MAN WHOSOEVER THOU ART AND WHENSOEVER THOU COMEST FOR COME I KNOW THOU WILT: I AM CYRUS THE FOUNDER OF THE PERSIAN EMPIRE. ENVY ME NOT THE LITTLE EARTH THAT COVERS MY BODY.

Alexander stayed a long time looking at this, and ordered the tomb to be repaired.

As soon as he arrived at the Indus he defeated the first of the Maharajahs, Porus, or Paurara, and by his generosity made him his friend. Among his captives were certain old apostles of the Jains, the clothes-hating sect, contemporaries and rivals of the first Buddhists, who also have lasted until our day. When his troops mutined and refused to go further, and he knew that the adventure was finished, to distract himself he had ten of these brought before him to be questioned, promising them that the one who answered worst should be killed and the rest left free. Of his questions and their answers, with the uneasy light they throw on his intimate thoughts, a few will suffice. Of the first he asked, "Which are the most numerous, the living or the dead?" The Jain answered: "The living, for the dead no longer exist." The fifth man seems to have dared to be ironical. Alexander asked him, "Which is oldest, the day or the night?" The sage replied, "The day, by one day." Alexander seemed surprised at this answer, on which the man observed, "Abstruse questions must have abstruse answers." "How," said Alexander to the next, "can a man become a god?" "By doing what is impossible for a man to do." The last question he put was, "How long is it good for a man to live?" "As long," said the naked philosopher, "as he does not prefer death to life." The king loaded them all with presents and dismissed them.

He returned by the thirsty road through Lower Baluchistan, to Babylon, where he died. At the end of the march the soldiers threw off their discipline and respect in a wild Bacchanal. "In the whole company there was not to be seen a helmet or spear, but instead of them cups, flagons and goblets of precious metal. These the soldiers dipped in huge vessels of wine and drank to each other as they marched along, and others seated themselves by the way. The whole country resounded with flutes and songs, and with the dances and riotous frolics of their women. This dissolute and disorderly march was closed with very immodest figures and with all the licentious ribaldry of the Bacchanals."

In his last period he lived in his pavilion outside the walls of Babylon, amusing himself with sailing up and down the Euphrates. One day a strange incident occurred. "Alexander had finished playing a game of ball. His servant who had gone in to fetch his clothes came back and said that there was a stranger seated on the throne. Alexander hurried there and saw a man on his throne seated in profound silence, wearing his royal robes and with the diadem on his head. They questioned him and he said that his name was Dionysus, and a native of Greece. He had fled from his country for a debt, and had been imprisoned in Babylon. That day the god Serapis had appeared to him, freed him from his chains, brought him there and ordered him to put on the robe and crown and sit there in silence."

Alexander was not enraged, but on the advice of the soothsayers he had the man put to death. This and several other omens preyed on his mind. He believed that his death was at hand, but thought it would come from a Macedonian conspiracy. His temper became terrible. A man named Cassander, a nobleman of Macedonia, who had come to do homage, was so astonished by the solemnity of the Court reception and especially of the courtiers prostrating themselves before the king, that he laughed aloud. Alexander leapt off his throne and seized him by the hair and dashed his head against the wall. This man afterwards became King of Macedonia, and master of all Greece. But the interview made such a lasting impression on him that he could never pass a statue of Alexander without being seized with trembling.

So in smoke and ashes the greatest adventurer of the world ended. After a drinking bout which had lasted a night and a day, he insisted on going to bathe. He caught a fever which rapidly developed, since he would take no care of himself. In the fourteenth day of his illness the Macedonian soldiery heard rumours of his condition and came to the palace gates, raising a great clamour, threatening the generals and officers, so that they were forced to admit them. Alexander was lying on his bed speechless and they filed past him paying their last respects with tears. He died next day at the age of thirty-three.

His death was the signal for the partition of the Empire amongst his generals. Of these and of those who had known him intimately, Ptolemy almost alone was fortunate. His dynasty ruled Egypt until the Roman conquest. Olympias had her throat cut. Alexander's wife Roxana and her infant son suffered the same fate. Of his work, nothing in a few years remained; his influence on Asia was almost confined to the fashion which all Kings thenceforward followed of claiming deity and divine honours. The arts and sciences of the Greeks disappeared in a few centuries from Asia like water in a desert, but to this day there is a trace of Greek influence in the statues of Buddha they make in China. His personality and mode of life, as has been said, by the route of Plutarch had a great influence in English education. His name, distorted to Iskander, or Askander, figures in countless folk-tales of the East. But he must be judged as a finder, not a holder, as a destroyer of old roads, not a maker of new. In this case he made the history of the world; if the bad results are to be charged to him, the separation of Asia and Europe, the loss in history of a central uniting Empire, the path cleared for the Romans and all that followed, so in justice some part of the good, of the immense history that branched from him, should also stand to his credit.

II.

Casanova

Tʜᴇ ᴜʟᴛɪᴍᴀᴛᴇ ᴘʀᴏʙʟᴇᴍ ᴏF character can only be settled by omnipotent experiment: if some Shakespearean god indulged his spite by resetting Shakespeare as the son of a prosperous English Labor leader, or Napoleon Bonaparte, to be brought up in the ice cream trade at Brooklyn, and attentively watched their wriggles for a life time. Without such a vivisection it is impossible to cut the acquired moulding of education, surroundings, and the very accidents of a career, from the nucleus of personality, the I, which is our insatiable curiosity. Nevertheless it has always tempted presumption to make biographical parallels between heroes, to imagine what Alexander would have made of Cæsar's life, or Casanova with Christopher Columbus's; or even more naturally to wonder what they would have done with our shoes, we with theirs. Such comparisons depend on the unprovable hypothesis that behaviour is a direct manifestation of unchangeable personality; that, in other circumstances, Alexander would go on being rash and successful; that Cæsar would take his icy courage with him; and so beg the question. The speculation would be more profitable if (leaving ourselves out) the two lives to be compared were as widely different in setting, circumstance, and scope as possible; and not as near. To fancy the interchange of two military conquerors, or two poets, or two explorers and pirates, is to lose oneself in a confusion of shadings. There must be contrast near black and white, to shake out any plausible, or simply interesting differences and similarities, to help our understanding of personality, and life. In bringing this Venetian, Giacomo Casanova, alongside that Macedonian Alexander, there is no intended humor. Anything the chaste, painstakingly noble demigod of Asia has in common with the disreputable card expert, whose summit was an escape from jail, whose memoirs of necessity remain unpublishable in their entirety in the safe of Brockhaus in Leipzig as long as there is the least censorship of the obscene, must belong to the essentials of the quality of adventurer which alone they shared. As you will observe, this community is not only one of spirit, in the quasi-physical sense of life-force, but still more significantly of trajectory. Missiles shot through the organic tissue of society, they had not only the same ruthless directness, that is, the same incorruptible egoism, and though they certainly did very unequal amounts of damage, the same range, but the same mysterious law of fatal ballistics made them repeat the same psychological and personal tragedy.

Giacomo Casanova was the eldest son of a futile and charming fellow, an actor of Venice with a cuckoo's idea of rearing a family.

In the family tree were runaway nuns, soldiers of fortune, pamphleteers, an unlucky companion of Columbus, gentlemen devoted to love, war and literature, fast women, and precocious children. This Gaetano, Casanova's father, ran away from a shabby-genteel home after a little slut named Fragoletta, who played soubrette in a wandering troupe of comedians. He learned small rôles, which he played badly. When Fragoletta tired of him, he came back to Venice with a company, who played in the San Samuele Theatre. Opposite his lodgings was a respectable shoemaker, Farusi, with a vivacious stage-struck daughter, Zanetta, aged fifteen or sixteen. Gaetano Casanova persuaded her to elope with him. Her father promptly died of mortification.

But they married and her mother forgave them. Giacomo, our man, was the eldest. He saw little of his father, who died when he was far off his teens, nothing of his mother, who developed into a practical, intriguing little person, and finally found her fortune in a life engagement in the Dresden State Theatre. Without pain, even with a sort of amused pleasure, when he afterwards reflected on it,

of plebeians, but too tired to check claims to title; heartless, but universally in love; hostile to adventure, but with the gambling fever; in despair, but enjoying itself more wholeheartedly than Europe has ever dared to do; cruel and sentimental; superstitious and atheist, in the image of beauty with a mask.

His poor old grandmother taught him hardly more than to dress himself and walk. The first influence in his life was the patrician Baffo, by birth a full member of the class that ruled Venice. He had a generous heart, was frightfully ugly, famous for his pornographic verses and prudish conversation. He taught the child his letters, and it was on his advice that Casanova was sent to school in the healthier air of Padua, on the mainland, at the age of nine.

The mistress of this school was a frightful Serb, who left her charges unwashed, half-fed and untaught. It is rare for children in such hands to rebel, and Casanova was sickly. Yet, feeling his way, starting by the passive opposition of small thefts, stealing sausage ends and crusts of bread when Signora Squeers was asleep, he progressed until he arrived at the thought "that it was ridiculous to be oppressed" and with prudence and courage managed to save himself by bringing about the intervention of Baffo.

Then, lean, ragged and perpetually hungry (but with the self-confidence of the first escape) he was put in charge of the learned, innocent Doctor Gozzi.

Gozzi had a good table, a better library and a heart. Casanova used them all with tremendous appetite. He grew like a wolf cub in spring; in a few years he was the first draft of that swarthy giant—six foot one—muscled like a porter, acrobatically agile, which all the courts and jails of Europe were one day to know. This appetite that he found in a verminous kindergarten never left him while he had teeth. He was indeed to die of it. It did not exclude (and probably abetted) an equally healthy voracity for learning, which all the books and teaching of Gozzi could hardly supply. He ate the classics— Horace, chief poet of the unpoetical, the tidbit—as if they were fresh-baked bread. Nothing rebuffed his palate, mathematics, the natural sciences, history, poetry, plays, French and Italian, and fatally in that age of Reason, when the marvellous is most sought because of its rarity, the arts of magic, astrology, the Cabbala, alchemy. When he had exhausted the somewhat short range of the Doctor's books on these last subjects, he turned to their respectable cousin, theology. He learned to play the fiddle, and Bettina, a minx of thirteen, took it on herself to give him long and complicated lessons on the complicated and idyllic personality of a born coquette.

In this way he acquired the only education that makes a man interesting, without which the greatest specialist is only a walking factory: an omnivorous autodidacticism, nourished, but not directed, by a learned man. In those days nimble wits were still the chief passport to mathematics, the sciences were richer in hypotheses that opened the imagination than experiments, and the great poets had not been appropriated by grammarians. Casanova, before he was out of his teens, had the elements of the best talker in Europe (save Voltaire). Only experience of life—the anecdote—was lacking.

On this he now entered. His first step seems burlesque, without its somewhat subtle historical reasons. He received the tonsure of the minor orders from the Patriarch of Venice, and thus after the custom of the day became in title and dress, a parson. The Abbé Casanova. In all such times in history, when the Church for its own reasons chooses brains rather than virtue to direct it, its constitutional rôle in society becomes more important than its teaching. Thus, in the mineralized Europe of that day, it was the only organic tract of society that remained; where there was still movement, and where a career could grow.

Consequently towards this one free channel the current of all the ambitions and energies of the age, from the ever boiling lower strata of society, the rich in nothing but brains, like Casanova, tended to flow. It was no more extraordinary that a Casanova should take orders in that century than that the infusoria of the Gulf of Mexico drift towards the Gulf Stream. A recommendation—he had it from Baffo—and an education were all that was required of him. He entered the service of the Church without the least idea of giving more.

With these facts in view, one must not see either contradiction (let

alone vice), in the coincidence of this ordination, with his entrance
and not exit from the world, and his first essays in love. From this
point the passion, pursuit, and worship of women becomes the high
road of his memoirs, never long left for the most fascinating excursions in other adventure. Without attempting an apology, which he
himself in his cowardly old age shrank from, except in the sense that
all explanations are apologies, some obvious, if little known features
of this principal activity of the most active man of his times seen
from his own point of view, and more particularly of the secrets of
his successes, must be set out. A rationale of seduction, indeed, is
only to be attempted by sniggering old men like Ovid, though if it
were based on the wisdom and practice of this maligned Casanova it
might have the result of frightening the majority of amateur wom-
an-hunters from the chase. The only part of the immense burdens
social life has laid on the relation of the sexes that Casanova shirked
was constancy, which, whether it is expressed in marriage or in the
often more adhesive *union libre*, is only at bottom its economics,
however ornamented. Both the mystical coating and the business
core Casanova repudiated, or ignored. Yet love to him was no more
on a footing with any other pleasure than a ruby is with a garnet. A
sweetheart was not a post-prandial dish nor any other of the inadequate things the pseudo-libertine makes of her: a trophy, a prey, or
an instrument. His love for every one of the thousand was as real as
any that led to holy matrimony; only it did not last. So he escaped
both alimony and the gluey years. But his women were not cheated
out of their sacred due, for he gave them everything he possessed and
his whole self, in one single payment. Casanova was neither a bilker
nor a gigolo. If all the subtle psychologists who have speculated on
the mystery of his "sex magnetism" had realized this we should have
been spared much ingenious nonsense. Casanova paid. His love
making had nothing more esoteric in it than what every woman who
respects herself must demand; all that he had, all that he was, with
(to set off the lack of legality) the dazzling attraction of the lump sum
over what is more regularly doled out in a lifetime of instalments.
How many times he unmetaphorically beggared himself for the par-

amour of a week, how many times at the height of his fortune he threw himself without hesitation or regret down into the gutter for a new charmer; and without any thought of a bargain, this for that. Let those envy his amours who can imitate him in this; and those who can add to it his real tenderness, that never forgot the name of one of his light of loves, or how beautiful she was, the irresistible riches of the talk of the man, the prestige of his shoulders, his neck and his eyes, dare to emulate him. As for his censors, only those have the right to damn him who are quite certain the promise of life-companionship of a man, however poor and tedious, outweighs all Casanova gave.

The prime direction of Casanova's adventure, therefore, is the forbidden country of women. In the rise of his trajectory his will is as single as Alexander's. Riches and honors mean scarcely more to him, the son of a strolling player, the devotee of good eating and drinking, when they conflicted with his true goal, than to the puritan heir of the captain-general of Greece.

Such bizarre equivalences encourage a search for another parallelism: of their initial renunciations, as it were their ritual entry into adventure. Had Casanova his Bosphorus transit, his solemn propitiation of Chance by sacrifice of his line of retreat?

There was a certain Senator Malipiero, rich, handsome, a bachelor, and eighty years old. After forty years' enjoyment of the highest offices of the State of Venice, he had retired to his magnificent palace to nurse his gout, and continue platonically his passion for beautiful women. The first benefit of Casanova's new status of abbé was an introduction to this man. Malipiero was so pleased with him that he took him under his protection, and put a room at his disposal. He shared Malipiero's exquisite luxury and through his influence could hope for a brilliant career. The star or the moon of the Senator's harem at this time was the youthful daughter of an actress, named Therese Imer, on whose beauty, affected modesty, and talents, Malipiero jealously doted. The young abbé out of gratitude to the old sybarite and also because he was occupied in the first enthusiasm of his first amour with the two sisters, Nanette and Marton, more than by prudence, steeled himself for as long as he could against this delicious Therese. But after a period, in which the friendship of the powerful Senator gave ever more promise to his future, the inevitable moment arrived when Therese showed her pique for the overdone coldness of Casanova towards her. Notwithstanding his knowledge of the ever wakeful suspicion of his benefactor, the treachery of the servants, and the penalty of almost inevitable discovery, Casanova plunged into the risk—with the dash of Alexander distributing his kingdom; and was ignominiously caught, thrashed, and thrown out of the Palace. Instead of a powerful friend, on the doorstep of his life, he had made a deadly enemy of Malipiero.

He had to begin again, and at a very different level. The quick road to fortune was barred to him; he entered a humble seminary, where the only prize in sight was some poor parish priesthood. But even this unattractive prospect soon disappeared. He fell innocently into a seedy scandal where his pride and obstinacy led to another beating, in public this time, and another expulsion. He found himself without money, family or friends, or even a roof.

So far we have seen a boy, who, except for one fault which his youth might excuse, calls for no hard names. In the next act enters the true Casanova, whose individualism by no means stopped at breaches of the moral code: Casanova the swindler. With perfect spontaneity, and no more hesitation before the laws of the penal code than those of the church, he proceeded to sell for his own pocket the few sticks of furniture his father had left by will to the rest of the family.

A lawyer named Razetta intervened, and had him locked up in the prison fortress of Saint André on the Lido. In this supreme misfortune the rest of the traits appear on the portrait; the full man is before us in characteristic reaction, resolute, revengeful, daring, and lucky. He escaped from the fortress one night, returned to Venice by gondola; after a short hunt comes upon Razetta, smashes three of his teeth, breaks his nose and throws him into the canal. Returns in time for a prearranged alibi. The whole operation conducted with the precision of a trench raid, or the professional hold-up of a bank.

Its very success super-heated the hostilities to him in Venice. He resolved not to wait for the riposte of Razetta or for some still more redoubtable move from Malipiero—brave's dagger or state prison—and as soon as a quibble in the law arranged his release, Casanova left the city.

In his stay with the cultured old epicure, Casanova had learnt two Latin saws, which were to be for the rest of his life his gospel and his policy: *Fata viam inveniunt. Volentem ducit, nolentem trahit.* As we may say: *Fate finds the way,* and *Life leads its lover, betrays its rebel.* The one handed down from the Stoics through Epictetus and Seneca; the second a translation by Cicero of a line in a lost tragedy of Euripides. There is no better epitome of the purest tradition of adventure, with all the comfort of fatalism without its enervating effects; no better summary of the mystical doctrine of adventure. Casanova held to them like a Calvinist to his Bible, and repeating them to himself, set out on his next adventure in good spirits.

A few months before, in the time of his good fortune, he had received a letter from his mother at Dresden, with a recommendation to an obscure monk whom she claimed to have had presented to a bishopric in the south of Italy. When Malipiero was his friend, Casanova had no need of this Brother Bernardino, Bishop of Martirano, "by the Grace of God, the Holy Father and my mother." Now, he did not think the journey of almost the entire length of the peninsula too much to find him.

He intended to go round to Rome by sea, and booked a passage in a coasting vessel. But at Chiozza, a few leagues from Venice, his education progressed a new stage; he accepted an invitation to a card party from a one-eyed monk, who claimed to have heard of his fame as a versifier, and lost every penny and every shirt the first night. The road Fate indicated therefore had to be done on foot.

Had it not been for the shameless cunning of another monk, a certain red-haired rogue named Stephano, worthy to figure in Gil Blas or the galleys, our worshipper of Fate and woman would certainly have died of starvation and misery, before he had gone halfway.

The protégé of Malipiero does not spare hard words on his companion, who he recalls was foully dirty, utterly ignorant, brutal, naïve, lazy, a beggar always, thief sometimes, and not above an occasional murder. But with many quarrels, by profiting by his instructions and sometimes of the fruits of his industry, Casanova arrived at Rome.

The bishop had long ago left for his diocese, and Casanova set out to follow him; on the savage and little frequented road southwards. At Portici his fate, as if pleased with his indomitable persistence, began to be a little kinder. He met a rich Greek merchant, a trader in mercury, at Portici, and succeeded in selling him a device for the adulteration of his wares with lead and bismuth. In return the Greek only half cheated him. Out of this typical deal Casanova had enough to complete the journey in better style.

At Martirano the worst disappointment of all awaited him. The bishop was there, an unhappy disappointed man, of mediocre talents and ambitions, but too high for his post and his prospects. The population was much as it is today, poor, mean, and rustic; the sea was not a prize but a prison or an exile. Casanova with the remaining sequins of the Greek still lining his pockets summed up the situation in a single night.

The next morning he told the good prelate that he did not feel the vocation to die a martyr, after a few months in his distressful town. "Give me, I added, your benediction and leave to go; or rather come with me, I give you my word we will make our fortune elsewhere." This proposition made the bishop laugh heartily several times during the rest of the day. But if he had accepted it, he would not have died, as he did, two years after, in the flower of his age.

This decision, this speech perhaps is worth any of Alexander. The bishop gave him a letter of credit for sixty ducats drawn on a merchant of Naples. Casanova in return pressed on him an enamelled case "worth at least the same sum," which he had cajoled from his fraudulent Greek, and set out, neither disappointed nor tired.

His condition had so changed that he is now distrustful of his company in the stage coach, who do not appear to him to have the appearance of honest men. At Naples he is received with open arms by the banker, who tells him "the bishop has written of you that you are positively sublime." He accepted his hospitality and by him is introduced to the best society of Naples; and his first great conquest, Donna Lucrezia, a beauty of birth, riches and importance.

After a short but brilliant stay, he proceeds, once more fate's favorite, to Rome. This second visit is a contrast which pleases him and makes him think almost sentimentally of his first introducer, Brother Stephen.

Thanks to his Neapolitan relations, he obtains a post of private secretary to Cardinal Acquaviva, the "protector" of Spain and Naples at the Vatican, a European personality, in whose suite he approaches and is noticed by the Pope himself, Benedict XIV. The great world found the tall young abbé fascinating company; he learns eagerly their ways and especially the vital difference between discretion and dullness. The way seems clear to an even greater career than Malipiero could offer, and he has the inner satisfaction of knowing it was opened to him by his wits and destiny alone. Perhaps the summit of this prosperity was the famous picnic at Tivoli, where he outdid in ingenuity and outrageous success, at the expense of the too modest husband of Lucrezia and brother-in-law of Angelica, the most celebrated tales of the Decameron.

But his goddess, Chance, as if anxious not to lose this promising catechumen so early, soon demanded of him the same sacrifice that he made to Therese Imer. Naturally the catastrophe came about through a girl, a certain Barbara Dalacqua, daughter of a professor whom the Cardinal had engaged to improve Casanova's French. Casanova here plays, almost for the first time, the noble rôle; not that he had abandoned his anti-social code of morals, which would have brought the greatest confusion into his life and excluded him from the list of great adventurers, but by the necessary hazard, which only a perfect parallelism could exclude, that here the divergent lines coincided. For once, that is, Casanova's notion of a good action was that of society, tradition, and religion.

This poor, silly Barbara had plunged into a passionate love affair with a young Roman noble, with interesting and visible results, to mend which they planned a midnight elopement. Casanova, who had watched the development of the affair with indulgence, was lodged in the Cardinal's palace. The police, incited by the family of the young nobleman, surprised the couple as soon as they had left her lodgings, in spite of her disguise—she had put on the cassock and shovel hat of an abbé—and chased her to the very door of Casanova, where in her frightened selfishness she fled. They did not dare to enter, but kept watch all night. Casanova did not hesitate, though he was aware of the risk, and had no other interest in the girl but humanity; he yielded his bed to her and in the early morning smuggled her out to safety through a secret door.

The affair caused a scandal, which the Cardinal, though no puritan, either for himself or others, could not tolerate. He sent for Casanova and in a speech full of nobility and kindliness told him that "Rome believes that the wretched girl is either your mistress or mine." He agreed that to turn her away in her distress would have been an action "unworthy of a man of heart." But he was obliged to ask Casanova not only to leave his service, but Rome itself.

Casanova makes no attempt to conceal that this dismissal plunged him into a "sombre despair." Ruin meant something more definite to him than when he risked the siesta hours in Malipiero's library with Therese Imer, and the horrible tramp world of Brother Stephen, the vermin of wayside inns, the icy nights and dusty days on the road that he had half forgotten, rushed back into likelihood. Nevertheless the measure of the youngster is in the answer he made to the Cardinal's pressing offer to give him a letter of recommendation to any other capital city that would enable him to make a new if less brilliant start elsewhere. Constantinople. The equivalent of Timbuctoo, or I don't care a damn. As he would give no other answer the Cardinal shrugged his Spanish shoulders and replied. "I thank you for not having named Ispahan, which would have embarrassed me." Next day Casanova received a passport for Venice, and a

sealed letter addressed to the High and Noble Lord, Osman
Bonneval, Pacha of Caramani, at his Palace in Constantinople. With
this a purse of seven hundred sequins, which with what he had already, made up the thousand—say two thousand dollars. The con-
templation of this round sum and the queer name on his letter
already consoled him a little. *Volentem ducit nolentem trahit.* He went
to say good-bye to Lucrezia. She had heard of his disgrace and refused to see him. The next day he hired a place in a post-chaise for
the north. The only other occupants were a lady and her daughter.
"The girl was ugly. It was a boring journey."

So ends the apprenticeship of Casanova. Long before Venice he is
forced to abandon the carriage, because the road is blocked by soldiers, the Spanish and Austrian armies in their winter quarters. The
Cardinal's passport enables him to pass their opposing lines without
difficulty, but he loses his trunk with all his changes of clothing, and
his passport. At Bologna "after I had written to Therese Bellino, I
thought about buying a change of linen, and since the return of my
trunk was at least uncertain, I came to the conclusion it would be
best to have myself made new clothes. While I thought of it, it occurred to me that it was not very probable that I would continue my
ecclesiastic career; but in my uncertainty of what new choice I could
make, the fancy took me to change myself into an officer. This idea
was natural to my age, I had always seen the military uniform respected, and I wished to be respected also. Besides," he concludes, "as
I wanted to return to Venice, it charmed me immensely to show
myself there in an attractive uniform."

Accordingly, dispensing ourselves from any irony, as Casanova, no
fool, sets the example, it is enough to state that he finally settled with
the tailor on a white uniform, with a blue vest, gold epaulettes, and
gold and silver facings. In this guise he showed himself in the principal café and plunges into his new character. On his return to the
hotel he finds a letter from the new Therese (Bellino) asking him to
join her in Naples—a preposterous proposition, which however he
says, "put me for the first time in my life in the necessity of thinking
before I made a decision." But the proximity of Venice, the new

uniform, and the letter in his pocket to Constantinople were too strong for the charms of a girl who a few weeks before might have completed his ruin.

He thus enters on one of the most complicated and shifting periods of his life. By miracles, hazards, profitable confusions and prodigies of bluff he got his new titles recognized and made the journey to Constantinople, passing through Corfu, in the pay of the Venetian army. There he met at last that Bonneval Pacha, a noble French adventurer whose life full of prisons, chances, defeats and successes is almost worthy to be compared to that of Casanova himself. But Bonneval, ex-general in three warring European armies and now Commander-in-Chief of the Turkish artillery, was old, and sedentary. He contented himself with admitting Casanova to his secret wine cellar and passed him on to some of his friends in the city, after an amusing and instructive conversation, lasting two hours.

The adventures of Casanova in Constantinople are written in a far inferior style to the rest of his memoirs; on a thinner, cheaper paper than the rest, it is said. They bristle with chronological difficulties; their matter is almost banal—the seduction of a slave in a harem, arguments on Mahomedanism with epicurean Turks and so forth. All the commentators have felt a difficulty here, as if Casanova had something to conceal, and for the first and last time was consciously romancing to do it. But what that something was, something more than the penal servitude in a galley that one rumor hinted at—for Casanova had no ordinary shame, and cheerfully confessed worse things—the most diligent search of the archives and registries of the time has failed to reveal. We understand by now well enough the character of the man to suspect that if this something did exist, and there is more than a mere failure of memory, it must have been rather some injury to his vanity than any other disgrace or misfortune. In any case the Constantinople quest fizzled out. When he regains our interest, he is at Venice again, out of the army, penniless, hopelessly down and out. He is reduced to playing the violin in the orchestra of the very theatre of San Samuele where his father a score of years before captured the heart of the shoemaker's daughter, Giacomo's mother. Seedy, down at heel, he settled down to the depths of Venetian life, as if all that had passed was a fancy. "Doing myself justice, I no longer set foot in the good society I had frequented before I fell so low. I know they must despise me; I did not care a button. But the position where I found myself after having played such a brilliant rôle humiliated me. I kept my secret to myself. If I was worthless, I was not altogether conquered, not having in the least renounced the cult of Chance. For I was still young, and that fickle goddess does not desert youth."

His friends were of the same condition as himself. After the show, he would join them. Sinister companions who were the terror of the quarters of the lowest debauch and prostitution. Pimps, thugs, or only card sharpers and pickpockets, when nothing better presented itself they would plunder unattended gondolas, or amuse themselves with brutal practical jokes, like the overturning of the venerable marble table placed in the Place of Saint Mark. The infamous culmination of this chapter was the kidnapping and rape of the bride of a poor weaver in full Carnival. The friend of Acquaviva, Malipiero and Bonneval could sink no further.

At the moment when the likely consequences of this affair preoccupied him, the wheel turns for Casanova. It started like a confidence trick. He was leaving the theatre, masked and caped, for it was the third night of Carnival, when he noticed that a man, dressed in the scarlet of a senator, in the act of stepping into his gondola, let a letter fall out of his pocket on the Quai. *Fata viam inveniunt.* Casanova rushed to pick it up and restore it. Evidently it was of importance, for the old man was profuse in his thanks and offered him a place in his boat and to take him to his lodging. On the way Casanova's companion was suddenly taken ill; his left side became paralysed, and he announced that he felt he was dying.

Immediately Casanova took charge of the situation, without the least thought that the safest course of a man of his reputation was to disappear. He orders the gondoliers to draw up at the canal side, fetches a surgeon, makes him bleed the unconscious senator at once, in spite of his protests, rushes both to the senator's palace, takes command of a bewildered and terrified army of servants, then installs himself at the bedside of the patient, choosing and dismissing doctors on his own judgment and authority until the old man is cured.

This was the Senator Zuan Bragadin, head of a very ancient and powerful patrician family. At first in pure gratitude, for the seedy stranger certainly saved his life, he extended his patronage to Casanova. An accident (if the turnings in such a life are accidental) increased Bragadin's esteem to friendship and admiration, which lasted for many years to come. He discovered that Casanova, like himself was a Cabbalist.

Intense curiosity about the future, and belief in supernatural means of discovering it are perhaps equally shared by the very timorous and the very adventurous. In the whole system of fortune-telling, whether by cards or by any of the countless ways of the interpretation of omens that have existed from antiquity to these times there is perhaps a respectably metaphysical doctrine concealed, to be expressed indifferently by saying that Chance is consistent, or disguising the paradox, that Life is instantaneous. However it is certain that this superstition is a constant and not altogether accidental trait of your true adventurer. But while their opposites, life's cowards, who share the mania for fortune-telling, approach their researches submissive and trembling, it is curious to notice that the adventurer saves himself instinctively from logical and ruinous fatalism by a reaction, which is half childish and half cheating. Alexander would never stir a step without taking the omens; he charged in battle with a crowned oracle by his side. But when these omens were unfavorable, he violated them: as when before the battle of the Granicus, he altered the name of the unlucky month, as when the priestess of Delphi would not reply, he dragged her into the shrine by force and took her protest as auspicious. So it is a misunderstanding of his character and his type to say that Casanova disbelieved in his Cabbala, and was a mere charlatan because he often manipulated its replies. Chance, to him and to them all is like Jacob's angel; to be tumbled for her blessing.

This Cabbala of Casanova which now appears in his life as his main way of gaining a living is curious enough to deserve a chapter. Here it must suffice to say that it was a variation, probably of his own invention, of the traditional oracle of the Cabbala, which is an arithmetical operation based on a numbered alphabet, or code. The letters of a question being substituted for their equivalent numbers, and these added, subtracted and divided in an arithmetical pyramid gave a numerical result which, when translated back into letters, was the answer—the legend is, in the form of a poetical verse. Now Casanova's first clients, Bragadin, and his two equally eminent friends, Senators Dandolo and Barbaro, who soon joined the séance, were by no means imbeciles, and perfectly able from their own science to check, at any rate, the results of Casanova's pyramids. His success with them and their innumerable successors was due partly to his own belief in what he was doing, partly to the immense complication of the laws of the operation and the extraordinary genius for mental arithmetic which Casanova undoubtedly possessed, which allowed him to move with dazzling rapidity up and down and across the columns to a result, which, in its main lines he often had in his mind from the beginning. There was no vulgar trickery, more the refinement of a sublime card sharper, seasoned with sincerity and human logarithms.

These two arts, his Cabbala, and a much less expert skill in card sharping, were his principal means of support henceforth. Bragadin and his friends made him a good allowance; the practice of his arts made him affluent. His apprenticeship to life was finished, he was passed journeyman adventurer. Venice was once more open to him, the high and the low, the masked balls and scented boudoirs of great ladies, the dark, sinister alleys, where in pursuit of some perverse beauty of the people he would risk a knife thrust for a night in an attic.

Beside the monumental details of his intrigues, each as dense and full as a national war, his memoirs have many sudden and delightful glimpses of the joys which the mere spectacle of Venetian life had for his enjoyment. Here he walks on the Piazzetta with the delightful feeling of fine linen on his body, and his best clothes "admired by all." Then, leaning back on the cushions of a gondola he mixes in the water traffic of the Grand Canal on a day of holiday, past the glistening palaces, down a shady canaletto, where the roses hang over the mildewed wall into the water. Or over the opalescent lagoon to Murano. Capped and cloaked, with the diabolic white Venetian mask down to his mouth he brushes incognito through the feverish vivacity of the Merceria on his way to a forbidden love in a secret villa. Venice belonged to him from its clandestine card saloons, to its quais where the honest traffic of market gardeners delayed him many a hot morning as he passed on his way from a luxurious orgy to his bed.

So passed nine years, from his twenty-first to his thirtieth year, broken by amusing trips to Milan, Parma, Bologna, even to Geneva and Paris, almost always fortunate, animated by the tireless verve that never allows his long record of the time to drag. His adventures with women become more complicated, even more numerous; in spite of the progressive shortening of the period of each amour, he seems to be more and more entangled in a huge skein of the threads of intrigue, counter-intrigue, from which at the psychological crisis, when it seems inevitable that he has lost himself, the laughing brown giant shakes himself clear. And never once does he sink to a mere lady-killer, or a mere libertine; not one of his loves is a repetition, and hardly one is without a human, almost artistic charm. He is like the vital principle itself, ever spending itself, ever renewing itself in inexhaustible originality, for the many-hearted Casanova had no need of recoining himself. To every sweetheart he gave himself exclusively; he had so many selves. No such vast exploration of the forbidden world has ever been made; and no one gives us the impression like this man in his simple, unboasting narrative of being on the brink of a discovery, an induction, which this age above all others would like to know. What is the essential woman, beneath all those ingrained meannesses, parasitisms, prudences, which ages of a man-made world have set upon her; what is the woman behind the conventions? Only he who approached her there, not merely skin to skin, but heart

to heart in infinite variations of circumstance, untroubled by the
least restraint or the least prejudice, could tell us; if generalizations,
or utilities, or anything but his own bottomless egoism had interested him.

At last the wheel changed its turn. In 1755, at daybreak, the
Venetian chief of police (Capitan Grande) Matteo Varutti, entered
his room and arrested him on the vague but formidable charge of
"irreligion and sedition."

It may or may not be that this referred in some way to his activi-
ties in the new and "occult set of Free-masons." It is more simple and
likely that the coalition of his powerful enemies had at last conquered the influence of the Bragadin circle. More important to him
was the certainty, revealed by the place of his imprisonment—the
dreaded Leads of the Palazzo Ducale—that its term was to be life,
without trial or explanation. He could not hope even for the little
walk across the Bridge of Sighs…

It is in this cell near the roof, heated by its situation and the dog
days of July, in the company of solitude and the rats that Casanova
ended his youth. For more than a year he lived on his hopes of a
message from the outside; another five months in a despair so great
that once when an earthquake (it was the same day that Lisbon was
destroyed) made the cell walls tremble, he shouted, "Another, another, but a bigger one, please God," which terrified his jailer more
than the shock. Then one night he made the famous escape, one of
the most extraordinary, if not the most extraordinary, in history.

There were many difficulties, two apparently insurmountable.
One was that the only entrance to these cells, the "Piombi," which
were a sort of attic in the palace, passed through the inquisitorial
court room, which was guarded night and day by a post of soldiers
on guard. The second was that he had not the least implement to
attack the immensely thick roof, in the circumstances the only remaining possibility. Three archers were always on guard in the narrow corridor outside his cell, incorruptible even if he had money; but
he was penniless. Nevertheless this was the problem Casanova solved.
His prime secret is in his own words. "I have always believed that

when a man gets it into his head to do something, and when he exclusively occupies himself in that design, he must succeed whatever
the difficulties. That man will become Grand Vizier or Pope. He will
upset a dynasty, provided he starts young and has the brain and
perseverance necessary. For when a man has arrived at the age that
Chance despises he can no longer do anything; for without her aid
there is no hope." His tools which he found at long intervals were a
fragment of black marble from a chimney piece and a rusty bolt. In
a fortnight of work, so hard that the skin came off the palm of his
hands and his arm was paralysed through fatigue, he put a point on
the bolt by rubbing it on the marble. After having taken a good
omen from the chance remark of a priest who was admitted to confess him, he set to work to use it. Four chapters of his memoirs are
devoted to that rusty bolt and that piece of marble, to as many
months of inhuman work and superhuman courage, tested to the last
inch by the most fantastic disasters, which even at this distance and
however imperfect the sympathy one may feel for him raise the hair
on the head. Finally he stood on the roof and looked over Venice in
the moonlight—only remained in a supreme burst of energy, physical force and presence of mind, to creep through a window, break
open two or three massive doors, go down the main staircase, brush-
ing guards, spies and clerks, into the Square, and freedom. He is now
thirty-one years old; in everything that follows it is hard to recognize
the same man. He had won by touching the extreme limits of human
possibility. Henceforth he is afraid of risk, though he must pursue it.

Having got clear of the Venetian States at a cost which is an anti-
climax only to his escape from prison, penniless, ragged, hunted he
finally reached Paris. It was his second visit, but most of those who
knew his gayer self were gone or did not recognize him. Nevertheless
he had cards in reserve. The best was the Abbé de Bernis, companion
of Casanova's most scandalous adventure when he was Ambassador
in Venice, and now all powerful Minister of Foreign Affairs. De
Bernis showed a diplomatic pleasure at the re-apparition of this haggard ghost of his past, and immediately set about finding him a
place. Through his recommendation to the Duke of Choiseul,

Casanova was appointed to the board of a State Lottery, where he well understood his real task would be to watch the honesty of its two Italian directors, the brothers Casabilgi. His assurance had returned to him; his ambition was hardened to a fixed idea of becoming rich and powerful, so as to be for ever removed from the return of that fate he had escaped.

Against such an antagonist, the Casabilgi resigned themselves to take second share; in a few months Casanova was rich, and since he had not forgotten the interests of his protectors in the process, well in favor at Court. The reaction and the relief acted on his nerves; an itch to spend came on him. To reassure himself as to the reality of his gains, he set up a sumptuous establishment and began to rival in expenditure the greatest and most authentic lords of the court. Balls succeeded banquets, and orgies closed them. At the same time his appetite for gold increased to a passion he, the libertine philosopher, had never had before. Every trick in his repertory was put to service. His luck at cards became insolent. The Cabbala and with it a thorough-paced cheat on the old motive of the Philosopher's Stone, brought him in thousands from the cranky, learned, perverse old Marchioness D'Urfé. Meanwhile the Government continued to employ him in business which profited them both. In 1757 he was sent for the first time on a secret mission to Holland. He brought this off so happily, that he was sent again, this time as the accredited envoy of the French King to negotiate a vast affair of currency. Again he succeeded. On his return he embarked on a frenzy of spending. Casanova stood at zenith.

It is not easy to follow the events that marked his decline, which he himself could never understand clearly. To him these great days ended abruptly by an expulsion from Paris, caused, he was certain, simply through the jealousy of some powerful rival.

In reality it was a slope, rapid but not brusque, and the cause was in Casanova himself. Excesses that would be amply sufficient to explain the fall of any other man, stories of forged bills of exchange, duped or half-duped creditors, kidnappings, midnight quarrels with men of a class it is scandalous even to quarrel with, mixed histories of abortion, seduction—there was enough to damn anyone but Casanova. But if he had been the Casanova they put in the Piombi all these things might have been passed over; they excused him for worse things in Venice. The truth is that he had ceased subtly to be an adventurer to become a noisy scoundrel, or if that is too harsh, that he had no longer the irresistible charm of being the world's best loser. He was always greedy. Now he was grasping. He was always noticeable. Now he was loud. He had become without knowing it a social man, desperately interested in the stability of his own position which he tried, without knowing how to do it, to link up with the stability of society. He had become a fortune hunter, and shrank from the quest of chance; the supernatural shine had left his eyes. Men saw in him no longer Puck, but a rival.

The degeneration is smooth, but it has its stages which tread henceforth ever closer on each other. In London, where he went from Paris, he notes "I have marked this time September, 1763, as one of the crises of my life. Truly it is from this time that I felt myself aged. But I was only thirty-eight."

And in this word age, Casanova packs worry, timidity, loss of appetite for life, and a growing awkwardness in tight places, the symptoms of Alexander at Babylon. After a few months of unsuccessful and half-hearted (a new default) effort in England he fled again. This time far eastwards, to Prussia.

Here again, failure. He manages to get presented to the terrible Frederick II, who browbeats him, sees through him, contemptuously dismisses him. Then to Russia where he finds a Prince of Courland, all that he could desire, a gambler, debauchee, superstitious, a mad scrambler after the mirages of Alchemy. But Casanova misses the chance; wearies the Prince with his formulated demands of life: a "stable position, a good sinecure, no matter what, provided it is sure and profitable." The blazing trajectory has dipped decisively, the infernal and elusive partner has won again. Casanova has not only ceased to be an adventurer. He knows it. "Now for the first time in my life I reflected on myself regretting my past conduct, no longer nursing any illusion and shocked by the thought that there was nothing before me but the sorrows of old age, without job or fortune, with only a bad reputation and vain regrets to nourish me." He is nearly fifty years old.

Let those who have the heart follow him further in his trudge round Europe. Cast off by the Prince, he goes to Vienna. Expelled from there by the police, he returns to Paris, with the same result. Madrid, Barcelona, everywhere he is undesirable, and growing ludicrous. There is one last flash in Warsaw when the grandee, Count Branicki, learnt in a duel that all but cost him his life what "the sometime hero and imitation grand seigneur Casanova" still had left in him. But after an hour's respect and admiration, which brought the blood back to his cheeks, he is arrested again. "The police contented themselves with scolding our good Knight, and enjoined him with the utmost firmness to continue his voyages elsewhere."

So his graph, haltingly, but ever declining, approaches the deepest drop. Fall, Casanova, who was in his hey-day guilty of every sin, and every crime? Casanova, the cardsharper, quack, thief, adulterer, seducer of nuns and schoolgirls, murderer, jail breaker, and all the rest? Listen, you who hate him; he fell lower still. He returned to Venice. Bragadin was dead, a bankrupt. Dandolo lived in penury, a poor old man, nearly a beggar. Casanova was fifty-two years old. He applied for a post of police spy, to his hated Inquisitors the court who had put him in the leads. By grovelling he got it. His work was to furnish reports on the morality of the city. Some of them are extant; he did not sign them with his own name, but as Antonio Pratolini. In one he brings to his employers' notice "the scandalous scenes he has observed in theatres when the lights are turned down." Another gives a list of forbidden books he has seized from a school-boy; among them the Poems of his first friend, old Baffo. He complains that there are nude models, "young girls" in the art schools and is "practically certain that some persons who are not artists obtain admission under false pretences." For these services he received ten dollars a month. In 1781 the Inquisitors dismissed him. There is a letter from him beginning "Full of confusion, overcome with shame, knowing myself to be absolutely unworthy of addressing my vile writings to Your

Excellencies..." ending "I beseech Your Sovereign Munificence to allow me to keep on the post where I have been serving; I will work harder. So that I can live."

Yet at this moment the prone man had a mistress, one Francesca Buschini, a sempstress who writes of him in a letter, "That great man full of heart, of intelligence and of courage." They lived together in a tiny house in the Barberia delle Iole. I do not know if it still exists or can be identified.

So we avoid the moral. We have two portraits of the man, one painted by his brother François; the other an engraving by a certain Berka, done when he was sixty-three years old. The first evidently belongs to the period of his effulgence, when he had a coat of gray lusterine embroidered with a fine and large point d'espagne silver lace, with a feathered hat of the same ornament, yellow silk vest, breeches of crimson silk; when he affected jewels, "my rings, my watch chain set with brilliants, my diamond and ruby cross which I wore round my neck..." What strikes one most is his eyes, uncommonly long and lit from within, as so seldom brown eyes are. In his age his aspect changed as much as his fortune; he then looked like a bird of prey, if you are romantic, or like a greedy, seedy old blackguard, with that nose, and that absurd survival of the grand air.

From Venice he set out on his search again, and landed at last in the sinecure. Count Waldstein made him his librarian in his castle of Dux, in Bohemia. There were 40,000 volumes; his master seldom asked for one. The old man was a good librarian, and amusing to talk with when Waldstein brought a hunting party to the place. The rest of the time he carried on a war with the other servants, the butler, Feltkirchner, the bailiff Loser, the doctor O'Reilly, Caroline the ward maid. They hated him, and put the villagers against him, so that when he walked outside the grounds the boys threw stones at him, and the little girls ran to hide. After the first reprisals he decided to ignore these people, and spent most of his time in the library.

He kept up an enormous correspondence. Many of his old friends gradually drifted back into communication with him, and the books he set to writing in a constant stream brought him an army of other noble and learned correspondents. This comforted him immensely, for he was become a complete old snob. His "Memoirs," the supreme justification of his life, historically and artistically, were almost his last work. They were not published in his life time, but many knew of their existence, and some, notably the Prince de Ligne, were allowed to read them as they were written and encouraged him. They contain, complete and living, the whole of his times, an age which is amongst the most interesting, certainly the most civilized, if that word is to be given any meaning, that mankind has ever enjoyed. The "Memoirs" is therefore one of the world's great books even in the mangled form that is all we are ever likely to possess. But this superb achievement is only the accidental function, the setting of Casanova's purpose, which was to recall, for his own amusement the course of his own life. As that life was ultimately a sexual adventure, the boldest and largest ever attempted, and as Casanova, though he said he was mortifying himself—he had become pious as well as snob— wrote with gusto, even in his works Casanova is only frequented by a select, or at any rate a limited company. For this reason, which would also have pleased him, he is almost the only great adventurer that has escaped misrepresentation. No Plutarch could do anything with him.

He died at Dux, 1795, of a surfeit.

III.

Christopher Columbus

THESE EXPLORATIONS OF ALEXANDER and Casanova left one enticing corner in the dark. That is, the nature—if not the personality—of their supreme adversary in the game, the unseen dealer of the hand they and Society lost. At times, certainly, even under the thick whitewash Plutarch laid over the world's greatest exploit, I fancy we made out a wavering shadow, the traits of a presence that is neither Greek nor Persian, nor human at all; luring, spoiling, finally strangling with generosity the young demi-god. So, the track of his campaigning that he scribbled in impatience over the map of Asia, Europe, Africa, seems (unknown to him) to be in a planchette writing, the script of destiny. This Destiny, Chance, Fate, Providence, lover and assassin of adventurers, each of whose names is an unproved theory and surmise, whatever its true identity, seems nearer because not so solemn, in the life of the Venetian rake. That midnight catastrophe in the Palace of Cardinal Acquaviva at Rome, that letter dropped by the canal-side by the old Senator, the rusty lock he found in the attics of the Piombi leave the curtain quaking, and a slight pricking of the scalp, even if we have not Casanova's own naïve mysticism.

Then can our profane search hope for a nearer sight of the mystery, of whom all adventure is the religion? This Fate, which all languages have made feminine, perhaps because it is usually impolite to women—can we hope to find out something about it that is more than allegory, more even than the venerable and inspired empiricisms of Casanova's two ancient mottoes? She finds the way. She leads the willing, deserts the laggard. That is already deeper than the gallows comfort of *Kismet*. But not enough.

In short: to give as full a value as possible to the cryptogrammatic that recurs in all these equations: to try a theology of adventure. The only direction is in the attentive study of Fate's own choice; to observe the life of one of her undoubted favorites as a front-row stall watches the left hand of the juggler to surprise the trick. Without hope of spying out more than the subtlest of hints—but if to the elements Alexander and Casanova taught us, we can add a trifle more that is simply probable about her likes and dislikes, and the tactics by which our invisible Third satisfies them in her most unguarded moments, it will advance the interest of our enquiry. For then we shall be able, contentedly, to watch the struggle from the point of view of the adventurer himself, who always sees in front of him not a calculus, but a Personality, or at any rate a calculus more psychological than mathematical.

No one could be better for this slightly sacrilegious enterprise than the admirable Christopher Columbus, Colon, Coullon, Colombo—whatever his real name was—the luckiest and most hallowed adventurer on the whole roster. So lucky that the adventurous nineteenth century proposed to make him a saint. Modern research has robbed him of that honor; it has substituted a thorough-paced adventurer for the plaster dummy we were used to.

He was born somewhere about the date Constantinople fell into the hands of the Turks, that is 1453, the date at which the Middle Ages really end. Like so many other men of fate and history, he was entirely a man of his time. By which is invariably meant, a man with all the prejudices of the time that preceded him. The Middle Ages summed themselves up in this man, as ages do, just as they were out of date. Without any unnecessary trespass on a subject which has been staked and barb-wired by innumerable schools, authors, sects, principalities and powers of thought and propaganda, this mediaevalism which Christopher had was noticeable in two principal respects: in his habit of underestimation, and in his indomitable snobbery. First, like the age that expired in giving him birth, his standard of measurement was the "stature of a man," so that he believed everything in heaven and earth (and especially the Heavens and the Earth), to be smaller, slower, simpler, nearer, than they are. This error of scale is the peculiarity, sometimes the attractively infantile charm, of the Middle Ages, the secret both of its art and its dreary Crusading, both unrivalled in their own style. The stars are only a few cubits away, Asia is round the corner, the world is not old and will die young; Aristotle knew everything.

The Renaissance is in one respect the scrapping of this mediaeval yardstick: the sudden revelation of size; the emigration from Lilliput to Brobdingnag. Christopher, responsible more than any other one man for the change, all his life stuck to the old standard. The concrete results in his career, good and bad, we shall come to in their time. Psychologically, this embedded wrongness worked as a very potent and practical variety of "pragmatic fiction," giving him the calm confidence, the faith of a child, as the books have it, which is necessary to great enterprises, and almost impossible for an imaginative man to get from the cold water of mere truth.

Above all then he was an imaginative man; and a snob—which is an imaginative and poetical form of ambition. Not one of Thackeray's poor snobs, who were after all merely professional men living beyond their means. A mediaeval snob, to whom a pedigree was not only necessary, but inflated with poetry and mystical virtue. For a weaver's son in 1453 would not only find the whole social system hostile to his ambition, but probably would never muster the courage himself to rival his betters, those descendants of the rough-necks of William the Conqueror, or of the lousy soldiery of Charlemagne. There was an inhibitory taboo about these gentlemen with the pretty names, which a Columbus of Genoa could only exercise, as Christopher did, by pretending to be one of them, and believing it himself.

For this, mainly, he has been called a "pathological liar" by those who like medical names for our little weaknesses. If it is pathological to tell lies in the only way they are convincing, that is, after swallowing them oneself, Columbus had the disease, and not only in this matter of his birth and family. So well did he and his innocent accomplice, his son-biographer, humbug the world, that to this day there is a lively controversy; one school firmly holding that he was a Galician Marrano, or converted Jew; another that he was an Italian but from a Spanish family; the third and most respectable (which I propose to follow) that he was the Christopher, son of Domenico Colombo and his wife Suzanna Fontanarossa, baptized in the little church of St. Stephen at Genoa. All these hypotheses must make him turn in his grave, for his own story, held to throughout his life, was that he was the scion of Count Colombo, of the Castle of Cuccaro in Montferrat, descended by legend from the Roman general Colonius, who conquered Mithridates, King of Pontus, and brought him prisoner to Rome. To this fable (which after years of practice he certainly managed to believe) he added the fantastic details that two other noble seigneurs, one a Gascon admiral, named William de Casenove Coullon, and another, George Bissiprat Palæologus, nicknamed Columbus Pyrata, also an admiral, a Greek, and a direct descendant of the Emperor of Constantinople, were his first cousins.

Domenico Colombo was a weaver in a small way, who started a wineshop, added to it a line in cheese and finally went bankrupt—a serious crime in the commercial republic of Genoa—and was imprisoned for some time. Christopher had some advantageous story that he had received a good education, with a specialty of Latin. He must have learned rapidly, for at the age of eleven he was apprenticed to his father, after the custom. As Domenico's affairs, if not his fortune, grew, Christopher and his brother Bartholomew helped him by acting as commercial travellers, or more properly cloth-hawkers, *carminatores*, taking round the products of their evening's work to the farmhouses of the environs. The type has not yet died out. Through the whole of north Italy and as far as Marseilles and Avignon in Provence these young Italians, half pedlar, half counter-hands, are sometimes to be met with, pushing their bicycles desperately over the dusty hill roads, with a mountain of cloth-rolls on their backs. Sweating, serious youths, frantic savers, the men who put the verdigris on the copper coinage.

When Christopher was about eighteen, he seems to have been admitted, or forced, to a part in his father's speculations. There is a bill extant in which he and his father admit a debt of ten dollars for wine sold to them conjointly by Pietro Bellesio of Porto Maurizio. In the same year poor Domenico was jailed for debt; Christopher had to stand security for what he owed to Girolamo del Porto, wholesale cheesemonger, before his father was released.

Three years later, he makes his first voyage. Not as seaman, still less as admiral of King René's fleet, "on a punitive expedition against the Sallee rovers of Algiers," as he claimed (the last such expedition took place when Christopher was nine years old). But quite naturally in the capacity in which he had been brought up: as travelling sales-man, with a cargo of soft goods to the Levant. His employers were the great firm of Di Negro and Spinola, one of the biggest houses of Genoa, and the holders of the wheat monopoly. In 1476, in the same employment, he set sail for England, a great consumer of Genoese stuffs. The convoy was attacked off Cape St. Vincent by twelve war-ships under the leadership of Casenove-Coullon, precisely the same whom Christopher later adopted. Three Genoese ships were burnt, the rest, on board one of which was Christopher, were saved by Portuguese and brought to Lisbon.

Di Negro and Spinola had a branch there. Christopher and the rest of the 120 survivors were looked after, and in the autumn of the same year embarked on a second convoy, which, more fortunate, arrived at its destination. On this trip Christopher wove a daring story about a visit to the Ultima Thule, beyond Iceland, and for cen-turies the commentators tried to reconcile this with the probable economic conditions of the Greenland market for Genoese soft goods. Today the kindhearted suggest that he might have touched at Galway, where there was a small business done in his line.

The next year he is back in Lisbon, first at work in the Di Negro store, afterwards in the Centurione concern, licensed to share in the new trade down the African coast, and in the newly discovered is-lands of Madeira and the Canaries. There is a document dated 25th of April, 1479, relative to a lawsuit about Madeira sugar, in which

Christopher, now twenty-six years old, is cited as a witness. He had apparently been recalled to Genoa in the affair. The notary asks him the curious question "Who do you think ought to win this case?" Christopher answers discreetly "Those who are in their right." He declares that he possesses one hundred florins, and that he must leave next day for Lisbon.

There is a great deal of distortion in the popular idea (mostly due to Columbus himself, and the biographers he inspired) of the contemporary situation of cosmography of which the discovery of America was the result. In place of a world of noodles and cowards bogged in the theory that the world was flat and the Atlantic infested with demons, which Columbus put right at one dazzling stroke, with the genius of Galileo doubled with Copernicus, and something also of the parlor-conjurer, according to the legend of the egg, the truth is more interesting. No one in the world of pilots, scientists, merchant-adventurers, in which Columbus had elected himself a member by his marine stories, believed that the world was flat. In 1481 the Pope himself, Sylvius Piccolomini, Pius II, announced as a truism: *Mundi formam omnes fere consentiunt rotundam esse.* "Virtually everyone is agreed that the world is round." As for the supernatural terrors of travel, there was no greater believer in them than Columbus. His bedside books all his life were the Voyages of Sir John de Mandeville, and the Picture of the World by Pierre d'Ailly, in which fantastic taste in reading he was far behind the times. The mariners of Lisbon and Genoa, and their employers, the great trading houses, which had depots or agents as far as Pekin, had a very fair idea of the Old World, as their maps and portulans show; it was Columbus, not they, who saw sirens, looked for the fiery wall of the Earthly Paradise and annotated with his own hand Mandeville's yarns of dog-faced men, vegetable lambs, and cities tiled with gold. The geographical dogma of Columbus from which to the end of his life and experience he never departed is summed up by himself in his journals: the world consists of Europe, Africa and Asia (therefore about half its real size). It is composed of six parts of dry land and one part water exactly.

The disagreement between his view and that current at the time lay therefore in this: both naturally ignored the existence of the Americas, but whereas Columbus believed that Asia was quite a short westward journey from Portugal, the rest were certain that it was terribly far. Between the two continents in this direction all were agreed there must lie certain islands—peopled with saints and immortals according to Christopher's books—like Madeira, or the Azores in the more current opinion.

In a far more serious degree the Columbian legend misrepresents, underestimates, the contemporary seaman. So far from standing the egg of exploration on its end, except as to success, Columbus was but one of a whole population of explorers. The coast towns of Portugal, Liguria, and Spain were full of hardy seamen lit up with the ambition to explore. Every port was full of stories of what was almost daily being done to enlarge the map, and of plans for new raids on the unknown. It is difficult to estimate, for a curious reason, the true amount of what was known, but it was certainly enough to place Christopher's favorite reading in the class of children's books to a large élite. The Portuguese in particular had been trading far down the Guinea coast; they had discovered Madeira, the Canaries, and organized a profitable trade with them. Four years before the expedition of Columbus, Bartholomew Diaz rounded the Cape of Good Hope and turned back in sight of the passage to India. But besides all the notable discoveries that had been published there were undoubtedly others, the secret of which was the strictly guarded property of the great trading houses and banks, which then as now were not in the habit of blabbing all they knew, that they had gained in the course of the exercise of their business and which was of use to them. It is from scraps of information dropped by the returned captains and agents of such concerns, eagerly shared by the savants of the day, that those wonderful maps were drawn, which amidst a banal and bookish distortion often show details amazing and mysterious in their apparent anachronism. Thus while Columbus was still hawking his father's cloth over the Genoese foothills, Pietro Toscanelli, the learned Florentine, had already inserted the island of Cuba, under the name of Antilia, on his best maps.

The impulsion behind this exploration-fever, which Columbus contracted, was partly the rising power of the Mahomedan Turks, which barred off the Eastward land route which the Italian trading Republics had used for generations; and the European shortage of gold. Economic historians have settled in their own mysterious way that there was no more than twenty million dollars' worth of gold in the whole of Europe at this time, coinage and ornament, and this was rapidly diminishing, by natural usage and by the drain of such eastern trade as remained. The only sources of supply were washings in Saxony and Spain, so miserable that they were abandoned forever after the discovery of America. An irresistible trinity of reasons pushed states and financiers to try the minutest possibilities of finding new supplies of the metal: to pay for a decisive war against the Turk and the Mahomedan, to pay for the Eastern luxury trade (portable goods of European manufacture with a market in the highly civilized East in any case lacking) and for the currencies. The prize of discovery was in short the salvation as well as the mastery of Europe; and in less comprehended form it infected seamen, captains, and, like Columbus, those whose connection with ships was more or less indirect.

Those who—under the influence of Christopher's own lies and bluff, to be sure—have made him out the solitary captain of his age, the great navigator standing in lonely advance of the science, imagination, and daring of his times have missed his real glory. It is that of all adventurers: to have been the tremendous outsider. Until his last voyage it is very doubtful if he could even use a quadrant. He knew no more of navigation than any able-bodied seaman. He was incapable by himself of fixing the latitude and longitude of his discoveries. At the time of his first expedition he had no experience of commanding men, and he never learnt it. By his own policy he had cut himself off from any national advantage; if ever a man played a solo hand against the social universe it was Columbus.

So his was the triumph of the Unqualified, the stigma of the adventurer that ordered Society hates the worst, the man who pushed his way in and did what others with the right were soberly, competently, conscientiously planning to do; the patron example of the crank and the amateur. In her dealings with him Fate snubbed all the worths and competencies.

We have seen his social policy. Its firstfruits were to win him a rich or at any rate a society bride. On the strength of his "family connections" he was introduced in Lisbon to Filepa Moniz Perestrello, whose father was governor of Porto Santo, the companion island of Madeira. Perestrello owed this position to the fact that his two sisters were the mistresses of Cardinal de Noronha, Archbishop of Lisbon, all-powerful at court; the nobility Christopher deceived was therefore highly genuine. His father-in-law had a good library of travel books. Christopher used it; on the margin of Pius II's *Historia rerum ubique gestarum*, the compendium from which the declaration on the roundness of the world is taken, is written in his hand: "India produces many things, aromatic spices, quantities of precious stones, and mountains of gold." The corner boys of Florence knew as much; in their "Song of the merchants who return home rich" the chorus went:

From the far region of Calcutta
With toil and strict attention to business
We have brought here many sorts of spices.
Dagli estremi confin di Gallicutta
Con diligenza e cura
Abbiam più spezierie di qua condutte.

In his copy of the Imago Mundi is the deeper and less true remark written by his own hand: "Between Spain and the beginning of India there is a small sea, navigable in a few days." From this doctrine he never departed.

With his new relations, his situation improved and he left the soft goods business. Naturally he visited Porto Santo, and probably made long stays there and at Madeira. There is no evidence for his story that he went as far as the Guinea coast; his ideas of its position on the map were erroneous; his statements on the matter were not convincing. But in the Islands, he was in the clearing-house of sea-stories. The favorites were about Antilia and Brazil. Antilia was an archipelago due west where seven bishops emigrated in the Moorish invasion of Spain and founded seven cities. Brazil was the land where the rare woods grew that from time to time washed up on the beach of Ireland and Madeira. Charles V of France had his library in the Louvre wainscoted with this jetsam.

Many attempts had already been made to reach Antilia by the Portuguese before their efforts were concentrated on the doubling of Africa. There is a story that one actually reached it; the sole survivor of the expedition, which foundered off Porto Santo, was the one-eyed pilot, Alonzo Sanchez, who died without revealing the find in the house of Christopher's father-in-law. There is a still more mysterious story lost behind the fact that on the map of the Genoese cosmographer Bedaire, made in 1434, Antilia is marked, and ticketed: *Isola novo scoperta.* Newly discovered island. Two years later on in another Italian map by Andrea Bianco, it occurs again with the new detail: *Questo he mar di Spagna.* Here is Spanish sea.*

It is in this period and this ambiance that we should look for the crystallizing process in Christopher's will. It never arrived at the rigid simplicity of Alexander's, nor even of Casanova's. His course forks between India and Antilia; his motor is sometimes gold, sometimes honors. Sometimes—remarkably, at the end—he steers for neither, but the Earthly Paradise; in the same mood he wants all the profits to go to a new crusade. But this latent ambiguity is concealed by the pretentious habit of silence he assumes, like all successful bluffers, in the intervals of his patter.

Through his wife's family, he easily arrived at a private interview with the King of Portugal, João II. We must see him in his dealings with the great as an artist in persuasion. He was tall and blond, with prematurely grey hair, freckled and ruddy, slow and ceremonious in

---

* Compare and put in relation with the "secret pioneering" spoken of before, the fact that Madeira figured on an Italian map dated 1351 under the translated name of Wood Isle, that is, fifty years before the recognized discovery.

his gestures, a profuse talker, but by some special trick of intonation or delivery, quite avoiding any impression of loquacity. The world will never learn to beware of these stately gentlemen with the fixed calm look straight in your eyes, who never joke, and never waver, profuse in cautious hints and allusions, but practised in rightly placed silences—which is why the confidence trick is still running. Strangely enough, his charm seems to have failed completely with the lower classes—sailors particularly disliked him, and—as the only explanation for many incidents of his voyages—despised him. But with kings he was always irresistible. João listened to him with the greatest attention and respect; only the terms of the projected expedition westwards stood between them.

These terms of Columbus are an integral part of the story, the cornerstone of the plot. They were the unvarying crux of his effort, in which all minor indecisions were lost. To João, to the Spanish grandees, to Queen Isabella herself, he addressed one unabated demand: The title of Grand Admiral of the Oceanic Sea (the Atlantic), a life Vice-royalty on all lands discovered, ten per cent of the whole commerce of such lands, the right to nominate governors; all this hereditary and in perpetuity. Christopher's projected voyage was not without precedent, but nothing in the whole history of exploration remotely resembles his price. Set alongside the poverty and unoriginality of his plan, which only the most skilful use of reticences could conceal, the entire lack of qualifications to be entrusted with its performance, his social circumstances in a time when the leadership even of a single ship (and he asked for a fleet), was the monopoly, in fact, and sometimes, as in Venice, by law, of members of the great houses; this demand for a reward which in the case of a success meant the setting up of a power rival to that of the State itself is an audacity that lights up the man like an arc-lamp. If it was a bluff, the first step in some bargain to be beaten out, it would have been sublime; but the King and Fate would have laughed and kicked the presumptuous higgler back to his counter and his yardstick. As it was, Columbus neither here nor at any other moment, even when it was all that stood in the way of his enterprise, even when he was in despair, in spite of the arguments and entreaties of all the noble friends who believed in him, ever abated one comma of it. Yes, greed, too, has its heroism.

The King then, refused; but politely, cautiously. Notice that Columbus simply by his unwavering exorbitance had raised his mediocre proposition to one that had the dignity of being out of reach of the principal sea-power of the age. And Fate's interest in him ceases to have the air of a fantastic joke. She is being pursued by a great man.

In 1484 his wife died, and he took his little son Diego to Spain. The seven years that follow are the most affecting part of the legend. Columbus in his rough robe of serge, holding the darling child by the hand, while stupid kings, ignorant nobles, jealous courtiers, rebuff him, and mock them; many an Academy artist has been tempted by the subject, and many a provincial art gallery has inherited the work. The modern historian must retouch a little. In the first place, we do not know why Columbus left Lisbon. It could not have been the polite refusal of the King, for as the future shows, Columbus is not a man to take a first rebuff. From certain indications there is suspicion that the real reason was an unpaid debt—one of those he asks his heirs to settle so discreetly in his will. Possibly something worse, as the letter of João he received in Spain hints. The King offers him a safe-conduct in these queer terms: "And as you may have a fear of our law courts, because of certain things hanging over you, by this present letter we guarantee you that in your coming, your stay and your return you will not be arrested, imprisoned, accused, subpoenaed, nor prosecuted in any affair, whether civil or criminal or whatsoever nature it may be." Furthermore, contrary to his auto-martyrology, it is certain that he was neither starved nor snubbed in the long period between his arrival in Spain and the start of the expedition. On the contrary, at every turn he finds influential friends, subsidies, hospitality, dukes, great ecclesiastics, financiers like Luis de Santangel, court favorites of the highest quality—an unrivalled record of personal salesmanship. Darling Diego, too, must move out of the picture, for in the first month of arrival, the boy is taken off his hands by the learned, kindly and fashionable Franciscan monastery at Palos.

Like all the exploits of art, Columbus's feat of selling himself in Spain has a graduated construction, a building up of strokes of luck, and the bridging of them by effort and a good technique. I have touched on the latter, its kernel of self-hypnotization, its deft use of taciturnity—the genius of salesmanship. He had three inner fortresses which bastioned each other: he would never reduce his demands, explain his plan, or reveal the circumstances of his birth. The first step in his campaign was to capture the sympathy of the enthusiastic monks of Palos, by his piety, his talk, and his pretensions, in that order. At crises of his life, Columbus put on the robe and girdle of the Third (lay) Order of St. Francis. He arrived in Spain in this rig-out. The Prior had been the confessor of Isabella and still kept her reverence. Through him Columbus walked straight into the sanctuary of the Court, meeting first the Duke of Medina Sidonia, the wealthiest landed proprietor in the kingdom, and an exalted patriot. As such he refused to contribute to any other enterprise as long as the war against the Moors of Granada, then in its last stages, was not completed. But he put the convincing stranger on his pay roll, and sent him on to his friend and cousin, the Duke of Medina Celi. This grandee at once and steadfastly approved of the plan, or rather of Columbus, and would have immediately fitted out a fleet for him. The demands of the adventurer were all that stood in the way. They were insuperable, for no mere subject, even the Duke of Medina Celi, could give him what he required, the title of Admiral, the Viceroyalty and the rest. The meeting is in 1485. Until 1487 Columbus lived at the duke's expense, in the duke's palace. From January, 1487, in addition, his friends obtained for him a grant from the civil list of the queen.

Meanwhile he manoeuvred through all these powerful friends for an interview with the queen. In the interstices of his intriguing, he learnt the *Imago Mundi*, and Sir John Mandeville, by heart; and also seduced a girl of good family—but poor—Beatriz Enriquez de Arana, from whom he had Ferdinand, his future biographer, or canonizer.

Christopher's relations with women bear no comparison with those of the libertine Casanova. Only three women are known to have occurred in his life; the first brought him a small fortune, which he spent, and in none of his numerous documents is there any further mention of her. The second, poor Beatriz, remained in poverty, even when he was rich, the third was that horrifying creature, Isabella, Queen of Spain. Naturally this third affair was strictly platonic, and since chastity is the best policy for company promoters, it brought him most profit. The woman who destroyed Granada, appointed Torquemada to tighten up the Inquisition, and disputed with him for the spoils of heretics, confiscated and banished 1,700,000 families of Jews, made the auto-da-fe a national institution, and in the act of death drew her feet under the coverlet and refused to have them anointed because of her modesty, needs no praise from me of her religion, statesmanship, and virtue. Rasputin or Barnum could never have met such an obstacle as this woman (with perhaps Torquemada standing behind her chair), and her miserly sharp of a husband, Ferdinand; from the first moment Columbus conquered them both. But again his terms stood in the way.

This is the time, the years that followed, in which the hero stood on his price, that he afterwards spoke of "full of cold and hunger, rejected by all the world, with only a poor monk to befriend me." Sometimes he stayed with the duke, sometimes he was at court, asking for new interviews and standing by the Admiralship, the Viceroyalty, and the ten per cent. At one time Cardinal Mendoza, "the third King of Spain," intercedes for him, and counsels acceptance of his price, at another it is the great lady and courtesan, Beatriz de Babadilla, or the duke, or Luis Santangel, the *marrano* financier, whom even Torquemada could not touch; or finally the powerful order of St. Francis, for which both Columbus (and the queen) had a special devotion. At intervals of life at court and palace he returns to Palos to stay at their monastery, and to turn over their library, seeking for citations from the ancients to use in his next interviews.

It was on one of these retreats that he discovered Martin Alonzo Pinzon. There was at Palos a family of ship-owners and navigators of that name, headed by three brothers, of whom Martin was the eldest, as well as the richest and most powerful. Now Martin also had a project of exploration; to document himself he had even made a visit to Rome to consult the most celebrated cosmographers. He had returned with a precious map, with Antilia marked on it. His idea was to reach that island, revictual, and go further on, as far as the Zipangu (Japan) of Marco Polo, where as old "Milione" says: "They have gold in the greatest abundance, its sources being inexhaustible, but the king does not allow of it being exported. To this circumstance we must attribute the extraordinary richness of the sovereign's palace, according to what we are told by those who have access to it. The entire roof is covered with a plating of gold..." Martin seems to have already determined to make the voyage (on his own account: profit or loss), before he met Columbus. The monks arranged a meeting of the influential and mysterious stranger and the hard-bitten local magnate. They arrived at some agreement; the terms and reasons for which we know little beyond the vague accusations made later by Columbus, and the evidence of two witnesses in the lawsuit over the disposition of his property after his death. The first is Arias Pinzon, son of Martin, who deposed that "he knows that the said accord was for the halving of all the advantages the queen might give. The said Martin Alonzo showed Columbus the said document (the Italian map) which was a great encouragement to the Admiral. They came to an agreement and Martin Alonzo gave him money for his next trip to court." The seaman Alonzo Gallego of Huelva confirms this and says: "I declare I heard Columbus say to Pinzon, Mr. Pinzon, let us make this voyage together, if we succeed and by God's will find land, I promise you by the Royal crown to share with you like a brother." If anyone asks if this was the truth, what advantage Christopher could have brought to Pinzon, it is the same mystery as that of all his negotiations; a mystery of salesmanship, one of the many irrationalities which are the commonplaces of experience, and only surprise us when they figure in histories.

In January, 1492, Granada, the last citadel of the Moors in Spain, fell; the dream of Christendom came true; Isabella hastened to wipe out a civilization in advance of her own. It was the moment for the last effort; Columbus simultaneously feigned a visit to the King of France, called in the influence of all his dupes, and so landed the contract. He was granted 1,000,000 maravedis, which Thatcher translates as a little more than 6,000 dollars—the whole expedition cost 1,167,542 maravedis, say 7,200 dollars, the fundamental debt of the Americas to Europe. Let us avoid a too easy humor about the sum; all this seven years' ado was not about this nothing, but the extortionate terms of the new Admiral, which would have meant (but for the sly insertion of a lawyer's cheat in his contract, which entirely escaped him), that until the years of revolution, the whole of Spanish America would have paid the ten per cent levy to his heirs, and have had to put up with a dynasty of Columbian quasi-emperors.

With this magnificent, though double-bottomed document, Christopher returned to Palos. Now that he had the money and a requisition for ships, his first step was naturally to drop Martin Alonzo. The business code is as immutable as the Moral Law itself. But a stupid difficulty arose, one of those insignificant omissions for which the most illustrious organizers have to pay: the seamen of Palos refused to serve Columbus. In all his high diplomacy he had left out these humble fellows, who with unanimity considered him a faker, a landlubber and a bluffer, and conscientiously refused to embark on any ship he captained, even as far as the next port. He was well known in the little town—perhaps he had not been so guarded in his talk and claims as before the Royal Commissions of experts; there was not a single volunteer.

His first impulse in this humiliating impasse was idiosyncratic: he proposed to make up the crews with convicts. But luckily for him this left untouched the grave problem of navigators, and Columbus was as ignorant as an amateur of the science. So he was forced to make terms with the grinning Pinzons, who agreed to bury the past. They immediately fitted out their two best ships, the Santa Maria, and the Niña, and found another, the Pinta. Columbus is rather hard to understand on the subject of these vessels; at the beginning of his journal he praises them highly, but later, especially after he had run one of them ashore, he states that they were old, dilapidated and unfit for the sea. The former view is probably correct, for the three brothers took part in the expedition and were perhaps not likely to risk their own skins for meanness or spite. The largest—the size of a large brig—was the Santa Maria; the Admiral chose this for himself and obtained the friend of the Pinzons, the celebrated Juan de la Cosa, as navigator and captain. Martin went on the Pinta with his brother Francisco, and the smallest, the Niña, was commanded by the youngest of the brothers, Vicente. With them in all 90 sailors, officials of the queen to keep the score, and an interpreter, a learned Jew named Luis de Torrez, who knew Hebrew, Latin, Greek, Arabic, Coptic and Armenian. He was to act as intermediary when they arrived at the country of the Great Khan, that is, the Emperor of China.

The preliminaries therefore are shaped by the ambiguity of the Admiral's aim: where is he steering? To Antilia, the Indies, or the realm of the Grand Khan? Or to Zipangu, as Pinzon urged? If it is to Antilia, what is the use of the interpreter? If to the Indies or the Empire of the Great Khan, how will his privileges of Viceroy advantage him? For no one in that age could imagine that the heritor of Genghis and Kubla could be forced or persuaded (by ninety seamen!) to allow any annexations.

It is probable that the Admiral himself does not know; but although there is this contradiction in his will—it is a trident, if not a spear, Westward Ho, and come what may. Perhaps there is a bias to foresee another Madeira—or the seven years' insistence on the Viceroyalty must be a mental tetanus.

In any case they sailed (3rd August, 1492), at eight in the morning, and instead of setting a course due westward turned south-westward to the Canaries. Wherever his object it was somewhere on the 28th degree, and with a fine air he assures his men that it is exactly seven hundred leagues due west.

The narrative of the voyage, summarized by Las Casas (unfortunately the original has disappeared) is the prettiest document in the literature of discovery. For this Columbus, if you have not yet suspected it, was a poet. Even if his journal had been completely lost, the concourse of all the characteristics is irresistible—his snobbery, his deceptive power, especially over himself, his exorbitancy—very different to that of the hard business man, his essential outsiderism. America was discovered by a poet; Fate would not allow such a prize to go to anyone less, or better. Read how he describes a shooting star on the night of the 11th of September—"At the beginning of this night, we saw falling from heaven, four or five leagues off our ships, a marvellous branch of fire." 18th September—"This day the sea was as calm and quiet as under the bridges of Seville." 20th September—"The air was sweet and very pleasant; only lacked the song of nightingales; and the sea was as smooth as a river." 8th October—"The air this day was so perfumed that it was a delight to breathe." On the night of the 8th of October he writes, "All night we heard birds flying over." Let him who still doubts, discover the whole journal for himself.

Three features of the march of events need to be commented. For the Admiral's yarn that every day he falsified the log book "so that the men might not know how far they had come and be discouraged," which has been uncritically admired by generations of historians as a ruse equal to any of Ulysses', it is perhaps enough to say that it is incredible and could only occur to the imagination of a land-lubber. Christopher did not and could not take the reckoning; if he had he could not have deceived his officers; and the mystification is contradicted by another passage in which he says he gave instructions to the pilots "not to sail at night after seven hundred leagues had been reached." The next matter is the legendary account of the crew's mutiny and his promise to find land if they would give him three days more. The only passage in his journal which can relate to this is as follows: "10 October. This day the seamen complained of the length of the voyage and did not want to go further. But the Admiral (he writes in the third person) comforted them as best he could in giving them a good hope of the profits they would get." It is the last of a series of references to the bad state of *morale* which the Admiral notes. But this grumbling was only aboard the Santa Maria: aboard the other two ships the utmost peace reigned from beginning to end. We have also the evidence of the sailors. Francisco Vallejo, one of them and no lover of the Admiral, in his evidence in the case cited states that the Admiral complained once to Martin Pinzon, who drew his vessel alongside; the ship-owner replied hardily: "All is quiet on my ship and on the Niña. If you have trouble please hang half a dozen of your men, or if you like I and my brothers will come abroad and do it for you."

The third matter is still more curious. On the same day—6th, and not the 10th, according to the same witness—Columbus asked counsel of Martin Alonzo on the course. Can it be that he himself was discouraged? They had come the 700 leagues and no land sighted. Martin replied that they must have missed Antilia, and urged that they should turn south-west to proceed towards Zipangu. "But that was much further." The Admiral hesitated; then agreed, still disputing the distance, which he said could not possibly be much further than a few leagues (as by his theory Antilia was off the Coast of China). The course was changed accordingly. At two in the morning of the 12th October, 1492, a seaman on the look-out, one Rodrigo, perceived in the moonlight a white tongue of sand. He fired the bombard that had been prepared, yelling Land! Land! They immediately furled sails, until daylight. America was discovered.

It was certainly one of the Bahamas, which, the poetry of Columbus makes it for ever impossible to decide, though Watling Island is for some official reason the favorite. Hear the Admiral's description: "I feared at first because I had under my eyes an immense mountainous rock which completely surrounds that Island. It forms however a hollow and a port capable of holding all the fleets of Europe, but the entrance is very narrow. It is certain that there are many depths in this break-water, but the sea has no more motion there than the water at the bottom of a well." In another passage he states that "there are gardens there, the most beautiful I have ever seen in my life, and sweet water in profusion." Let the habitants of the Bahamas, not one of which is surrounded by a reef, let alone an immense mountain, decide which had the honor of exalting the poetic imagination of the Admiral to such heights.

From this unidentifiable *San Salvador*, as he named it, the fleet went on to other islands, finding everywhere charming natives, parrots, cotton loin-cloths and hammocks, but no gold, and no spices. The Admiral relates long and complicated conversations he had with them, one a very touching theological discussion—on sin and redemption—all done by signs. At last they came to Cuba (28th October). Here he is profoundly perplexed: he decides at first that it is certainly Zipangu—"the gold-tiled palace must be the other side." He writes afterwards however: "I believe that all these countries are nothing but lands at war with the Grand Khan of China. It is certain that this place the natives call Cuba, where I am, is opposite Quinsay and Zayto (Hang-kow and Amoy), one hundred leagues from each and both of these two cities. This I know because the sea comes here in a different manner from what it has done until now..."

In this opinion he sent the learned Jew—let those whom the genealogy of colonization amuses remember that a Jew was there but no Englishman or German—Luis de Torrez, with the queen's letter to the Emperor of China, to try to deliver it. After a vain search in the jungle of the island for the monarch, he returned and was scolded. But on second thoughts the Admiral began to imagine that this Cuba must be India and not Japan or China; so he was much less circumspect in looking for gold; India notoriously being governed by less terrible monarchs than the Grand Khan. Every native met with was asked by signs for a gold mine; everyone was understood to reply that there was a big one, but further on. One was successful in communicating, by nods and waves, that a whole island in solid gold was near by, but could not make himself understood as to the exact direction. The peaceful Caribs performed all the ritual explorers expect; they took them for gods, and cried with delight when the invariable beads and mirrors were produced. The Admiral was delighted with them. He consigned that since "they were very docile and easy to persuade," a glorious field of missionary effort was open.

Meanwhile Pinzon took the Pinta and cruised on his own account. On reflection the Admiral liked this independence little, and by the third day of absence became a prey to the gloomiest thoughts, seeing himself betrayed, and fearing that Pinzon had simply returned to Spain to rob him of the glory of the discovery. But shortly afterwards the Pinta sailed back into sight of the Santa Maria. The shipowner apologized for his absence and announced that he had found Antilia. They followed him and landed on the island of Haiti. Here, owing to carelessness, the Santa Maria, the Admiral's ship, ran aground and could not be refloated. After many efforts, they decided to dismantle it and build with the wood-work a fort they named Natividad, alongside a native village. The natives here also were extremely friendly and soft, their women were pleasing, so no difficulty was found in getting forty volunteers to stay, while the Admiral and the rest returned to Spain to fit out a new expedition.

On the way home they ran into a great storm off the Canaries; the Pinta and Martin Pinzon were driven out of sight of the Admiral's ship. His suspicions returned; the last pages of his Journal are an eloquent jeremiad on treachery. But the Niña weathered the storm, put in to Lisbon, and finally arrived at Palos, the 15th March, 1493, after seven months of navigation. Pinzon had not yet arrived. This may have been to the Admiral the crowning joy of his life; he organized a procession from the dock of Palos right across Spain to Barcelona, where the Sovereigns held court. At the head the tall grey Christopher, mum and impassive, with his Franciscan robe, surrounded by bearded and armoured sailors. His followers carried great bamboos, and alligator skins. Next came a platoon of Indians carrying screaming parrots in cages, and smiling, and making the sign of the cross. This circus entered into every Church they met on the way, and stopped to pray at every wayside cross.

And so he arrived at Court; Isabella and Ferdinand allowed him to sit down at their right hand, and great lords asked him for his word for their sons. In the midst of it he showed his careful attention to detail by reminding the queen of the life pension of 60 dollars a year she had offered to the first man to sight land; Rodrigo* the Mariner's claim was brushed aside in the Admiral's favor, and he

---

* Rodrigo is said to have gone to Morocco in disgust, and turned Mahomedan.

bestowed it all upon Beatriz, the mother of his Fernando. It was all she ever had out of him.

Pinzon arrived two or three days after Columbus, in a Gallician port. Unfortunately for his memory he promptly died. The Columbian legend was thus enriched with a villain, with no fear of being confused by any protest or defense from him.

When the Treasury officials had made out the balance sheet of the expedition, however, there was some disappointment. On the credit side were the forty green parrots, a child's handful of thin gold noserings, some rolls of coarse fabric, worse even than they spun in Isabella's Spain, six credulous savages, a mixed taxidermic collection imperfectly prepared, and the bamboos. It was not even certain where the Admiral had been; he mentioned Zipangu, Antilia, China, but finally seems to have settled on India—the Royal scribes wrote down, in the neighborhood of the Indies (*en la parte de las Indias*). However the queen was satisfied. Her woman's sensibility settled on the uses of the large population (possibly a million in reality) of Haiti, to be Christianized, and also as cheap labor. Christopher's own idea of exporting them as slaves, she then and afterwards rejected. A grant of arms was made for the Admiral. The space left for the insertion of his ancestral quarterings was filled in by him with gold and blue. It must have bothered him a little. And a new expedition was set on foot. The queen insisted this time on a skilled cosmographer being shipped; she had written to him before: "And so as to understand your book better, we have need to have the degrees where are situated the islands and the mainland you have discovered, as well as the degrees of the way you passed, please send them to us, and also a map."

This time the Admiral was at the head of a considerable fleet carrying 1500 men, among whom were artisans and agriculturalists and a certain number of sharp-toothed gentlemen adventurers. The funds were advanced partly by the Duke of Medina Sidonia, partly from among the booty of the expelled and expropriated Jews.

He sailed on the 25th September, 1493, pursued the same route, was driven out of his course, lost his way, touched at the Antilles, spent some time there in looking for gold; then arrived at Natividad on the 22nd of November. There was no reply to their salvos. When they landed they discovered that the Fort had been burnt to the ground; the bodies of the garrison were scattered in the scrub, horribly mangled. There was no survivor to explain the catastrophe, but guessing was not hard. The new-comers in fact began to repeat what must have been the story, with, however, no tragic ending for themselves. Large numbers of them as soon as they were ashore threw off "the respect and discipline they owed to the Admiral" and set out to live as freebooters in the island. "They were wont to complain of the hardness of the native's heads, that notched their swords," as the monkish chronicler has set it down. Nor were those "men from heaven" who remained under orders much more lovable. The natives were not accustomed to anything more sanguinary and dangerous than the alligators with which their rivers abounded. Half a century later the aboriginals of this and the majority of the neighbouring islands, some of which were even more densely populated, were extinct.

Columbus spent three years, sometimes in further exploration, and the personal conduct of gold-hunting parties, the rest of the time in government. This was the time of his highest level; his titles were disputed only by his own men; he hoped to compensate for the persistent failure to find gold by organizing the slave trade. In 1495 he sent five hundred Carib women to Seville to be sold, "naked as they were born." *Como andaban en su tierra, como nacieron.* By Royal order this was stopped, but in the islands under his own rule the whole race was gradually brought into captivity. The Admiral was at the height of his trajectory. A law promulgated by him required all the European settlers to sign a statement that Cuba was no island but the continent of India, and anyone going back on his word was to have his tongue torn out. The adventurer was tired of the question; in this simple way he announced that the adventure was over, that India was discovered and all that remained was sober organization.

This organization was not one of the lights of his genius. Terrible quarrels broke out in the bosom of the little community; the despairing natives fled whenever they could into the bush and tried to thin the numbers of their discoverers by arrows, and wild beast traps cunningly hidden. The number of bush-rangers daily increased. One strange and romantic revenge the Earthly Paradise took on its wreckers, the vanguard of Europe, and through them on all future generations of Europeans. The Caribs of Haiti were weak delicate creatures; their lack of robustness was remarked in the Admiral's journal of his first visit, and was often grumbled about by his slave-dealers later. They suffered indeed from a disease which, endemic among them for countless generations, had only debilitating effects on them, but which when contracted by their masters, from their women, and known afterwards by the poetical name of Syphilis,* had far graver effects. A hundred years after the last Carib beauty was dead, Europe was poisoned from end to end.

Having escaped this almost Biblical nemesis by his well known continence, Columbus sailed for home at the end of 1495. He landed at Cadiz, having his reasons for avoiding Palos. His hands were empty; Spain was full of pale men, rotten with disease, who had returned before him to curse his Indies. The King replied to the intimation of his arrival coldly. Nevertheless the Admiral again organized a procession; and at the head of fifteen naked Indians, shivering with cold, but wearing by his command their full headdress of feathers, he set out through Spain to pay his respects to court. He had donned his Franciscan rig-out. It was January. Until he disbanded it, still far from his goal, this procession of dispirited natives and a consciously solemn man tramped along through Andalusia.

It is time to stop and be indignant. Not content with her disgraceful choice of a swollen-headed, lying, incompetent and utterly unsuitable soft-goods salesman for the greatest favor she ever showed to her favorite Europeans, this Fate we are staring after allows herself to be caught outside her cloud playing such an odious joke upon him. There is a school-boy bad taste, a giggling irresponsibility about the way he has been made a fool of, which so far from being funny, fills

---

* From the name in a poetical play by an Italian, Fracastro.

us with deep panic, since we too are mortals and ask of our gods at least to be grown-up. In the last trudge of Columbus the whole of human dignity is involved; we have a right to grumble like Lear:

> Like flies to wanton boys are we to the gods,
> They slay us for their sport…
> hang tails on our heroes; cork the noses of our saints, put
>   orange peel on the polished floor of the shrines we have
>   built to them.

But when you are calmer, is it not interesting to gather up the data that have been accumulating about this Destiny of adventurers, and see how she has given herself away? We know now from this poor devil's experience, that she loves a poet, that with a free choice in front she chooses the unqualified, kills off contemptuously the man with all the claims, Martin Pinzon, and hands all to the outsider Christopher Columbus, the man who cannot read a chart. How she first allows the mild, good Caribs to be exterminated, just because they are mild and happy, and revenges them with unfeeling generosity not only on the wicked Spaniards, but on the good, kind Germans and English and French, who would never have been so cruel. Or at any rate were not there with the first wave to let us see. Then because of some huff—our experience with Alexander and Casanova leads us to think that it must probably have been that attempt of the illegal Christopher to find the Indies and end the adventure by law—she takes an omniscient advantage of the weaknesses of the Admiral, his habit of repetition, his uncultivated idea of pomp, due to his bad education, his very technique of imposture, to send him with his wretched feathered Indians to run the gauntlet of rustic jeers, and civic rowdiness for hundreds of leagues into the heart of Spain—such an end to the greatest human achievement. All through, a coherent injustice.

What if this injustice were the very life of adventure? The man who puts his stake on the roulette board does not want justice, or his stake back unaltered. Justice for Christopher is a small shop in

Genoa, or it may be a foot of wall in a Portuguese jail for fraudulent bankruptcy, or a hole in the ooze at the bottom of the sea, somewhere a few leagues out from the Canaries. Justice for Alexander is another dagger such as killed his father; for Casanova a horsewhipping, or a lifelong judgment of alimony. In this light, adventure is an excited appeal for injustice; the adventurer's prayer is "Give us more than our due." The Martin Pinzons may pray for their Right; an adventurer is more humble—to his god; for to the great mass of his fellowmen, the social pyramid of the qualified, the owners, the entitled, he has the insolence to be an outsider. He is not on the world's staff, he does not even belong to the gang. He is alone, this impious worshipper of an unjust god; who in wisdom has ruled that professors of literature can never be great poets; that the top boy at school rarely gets life's prizes; that the richest woman is never the most beautiful; that the eugenically born does not monopolize the fun and health of the world. The incalculable, malicious power who does not acknowledge any debt; easy to draw a laugh from, never a tear; the spirit of the rain, that falls where it likes, and the wind that blows without prognostication.

Columbus is not ended yet; lives are rarely cut to their plots. In his third trip a rebellion broke out in Haiti. This time the home authorities were tired and sent a commissioner, Francisco de Bobadilla, after him. Bobadilla, jurist-consult, noble, competent, quiet, the man of right and wrong. He arrived at Haiti with full powers. The first thing he saw was a row of hanged men swaying over the harbour. The first thing he did was to arrest the Admiral, hear in half an hour enough of his talk and his deeds to have hanged him as a rebel to the Crown, and he had him put in chains and embarked for Spain. As soon as the ship was out of sight, the captain ordered the venerable old wretch to be given the liberty of the deck. Christopher refused. He had incorporated the chains in his pride. Henceforth he can never forget them; they were the homeopathy of his humiliation.

The queen was very kind; she apologized to him. But did not order or ask for an apology from Bobadilla, nor, though she disguised it with her kindness, take any steps to reinstate the one or punish the other. This is enough to refute all the Columbian version; if Columbus had not been unimpeachably guilty he would have been revenged. And in addition, he was forever forbidden to set foot in Haiti again.

Even after this, the Admiral insisted on another verse. His fourth trip left Cadiz the 11th May, 1502. This time he had promised Isabella the Golden Chersonese, which is the book-mirage of Cochin-China. In his *Book of Prophecies*, which he wrote for her while waiting for ships, and of which a few fragments remain, he mentions that the end of the world is coming in 1650, and that he must find gold soon, so that there can be time for her to conquer the Holy Land with it; in time to get everything ready for the Lord. Vasco de Gama's discovery of the route to India round the Cape of which everyone was talking, he considers a cock and bull story. He has discovered India. But for treachery and Satan he would have already come upon the gold. He has taken a new title: the Ambassador of the Most High. Jesus Christ appeared to him as a vision and promised him gold when seven years were up. Afterwards he will go to the North Pole, which is inhabited by Christians, who will be of service later in the great Crusade. And so on. Madness? Not a bit of it; a little more talkative.

In this journey every hardship and disappointment was accumulated. He touches on the South American continent, discovered and mapped years before by the gold-seeker Amerigo Vespucci and others, and notes it down as "many insignificant islands." He brings his crew to the extremities of hunger and thirst, falls ill in Cuba; is in danger of being massacred by Indians, whom he plots to catch and sell; suffers one of the most terrific storms in literature, confiscates the charts of his navigator so that no one but he can know the situation of the Earthly Paradise, the real one, Sir John de Mandeville's, which is on a mountain between the Ganges, the Euphrates, the Tigris and the Nile and all walled about with fire, to which he came very near.

At last he has had enough. At his journey's end there is nothing more waiting than he brought with him. Isabella died a few days after his home-coming, tucking her chaste feet under the coverlet,

without waiting to hear the last chapter. He troubled the court no
more; two years later he died in complete obscurity. No contemporary chronicler mentions it. He asked for his chains to be buried with
him, which was done.

So ends without music the true only, historical and authentic discoverer of America, the fortunate Christopher Columbus.

Sixty years after his death the last of his descendants died. The
family fortune was claimed by the noble Colombos, Counts of
Cuccaro and by appealing to Christopher's own stories, they almost
secured it.

IV.
Mahomet

G EOGRAPHY, AS COLUMBUS HAS explained, is Adventure's rich
game preserve, where any muff with a gun may hope for sport
in the season. But in her less accessible domains, the deserts and
forests of the spirit, there are the tracks of big game for the boldest
hunters. The religious adventurer does not often fill his bag. But he
has camped out with Mystery. He deserves listeners even if he never
won disciples. The greatest of them have been further than Columbus,
further than Sir John de Mandeville, or Lemuel Gulliver; they have
made the grand Dante circuit of Heaven and Hell. They have lived
on this little earth like an island, and made up their night fires to
scare away the noises of the interstellar dark. There was one of these,
who, throughout his supernatural expedition, kept quite sane, and
even a little stupid, which is the quality of robust sanity, so that his
whole route and what happened to him is clear and dramatic.

This was the celebrated Mahomet, who sealed his letters to the
emperors of the world: "Mahomet, Apostle of God." He was at the
beginning a poor relation of a powerful family, who lived in the decaying caravan town of Mecca, on the highroad through the suburbs
of the Old World, Arabia. The modern literary Arabia is a paradise
of passion, liberty, and dates, but in the year of Mahomet's birth,
A.D. 570, the situation was less enticing. It seemed that after a remarkable historical burst, the destiny of the Semite people who inhabited it was ended, and that the whole race, in its varieties of Jew,
Babylonian, and Ishmaelite, or Arab, was doomed to the vegetative

obscurity of mere Bedawinism, from which only its strategic geography, on the intersection of the great land routes between Europe, Asia and Africa, and remarkable talents for ecstatic poetry had for many brilliant centuries lifted it. All that remained of the magnificence of Babylon was a horde of bandits, the Al Hira, who gave a sort of blackleg service to the power of Persia. In the Syrian north, they served Byzantium and a large variety of Christian trinities. The Jews after their ferocious and horrible resistance to the conquest of Titus had partly trekked to the south, in compact, sullen tribes, or embarked for their vast European adventure. There were small strong kingdoms of them round all the major oases of the desert as far as the Yemen, the Happy Arabia of the ancients, where everything the luxury of Europe desired grew in abundance. They were especially numerous along the great road that flanked the impassable steppe of the interior along between the mountains and the Red Sea. The rest of the inhabitants, the Arabs proper, had in those days no prestige; part of them lived at the depots and halts of the route, and engaged (as we shall see) partly in lodging, feeding and robbing the travellers, who passed; partly in the diminishing transport industry, by convoying the caravans between Damascus and Aden. The rest, when they had the chance, shared in this work or starved in their tents, or when their inveterate inter-tribal wars permitted, formed bands and held up the highroads. Arabia therefore, as a whole, as far as it concerns us—that is, excluding the fertile Yemen—lived on the transcontinental road traffic. But this was steadily degenerating, ever since a cool and thoughtful Ptolemy, Greek Pharaoh of Egypt, tired of the robbery and murder of his merchants, invented a sea-service to Abyssinia and India, which was gradually throttling its expensive rival, the Arab land route. So, in the time of Mahomet the rich caravan cities of the north were fallen into abandonment and ruin; Petra, Jerash, and Philadelphia. Medina and Mecca, the latter the half-way house between Arabia Felix and Arabia Petraea, the "Lucky Arabia" of the south, and the "Stony Arabia" of the north, still struggled for a living. This Mecca was a town of some thousands of citizens, situated in a critical pass of the mountain wall by which Arabia abuts on the Red Sea. The whole region is salt and barren; even the date palm, the only plant that can endure both freezing and scorching, will not grow there. After all these years that the riches of three continents have poured ceaselessly into this wretched place, there are no gardens, and a stunted bush is a civic pride. The component reasons for the existence of Mecca were: first, the trade road—the "incense route"; a well of tepid water—the holy Zem-Zem; a fair for camel-leather and slaves; and the Ka'ba. No one can see which was first. Immemorially, a meteor fell in this valley. It is a reddish-black stone, semi-circular, six inches high, eight broad, today polished with myriads of kisses; but still showing on its surface the molten wrinkles which appeared to its first worshippers a name and a message in the unknown script of the gods of the sky who threw it down. Perhaps before Alexander, or even Rameses, this Black Stone had been found and reverently built into the corner of a cubic temple, the Ka'ba or Cube, and those who came to the fair worshipped it, or its worshippers held a fair—which first no one can say. Such sacred stones were not rare in Arabia, but the Black Stone had a certain preeminence. Connoisseurs in idolatry made long journeys to see it.

This Cube is the centre of Mahomet's adventure. Naturally, since no Arab can make a right angle, it was then and is today in its reconstruction, crooked, on the splay; about forty feet high, long and broad, with a door that has always been a tall man's height above the ground, and only to be reached with a ladder—perhaps because of the floods which are an annual plague of the place. In Mahomet's time this Ka'ba was furnished inside with images; the biggest was the idol Hobal who stood on a pit where the treasures of the cult were stored. Another idol, or more probably another name for this Hobal, was Al-Lat, or Al-Lah.

A few cubits from this Cube was the well Zem-Zem. Its water is brackish and luke-warm. Mahomet's grandfather, Abd al-Muttalib, rediscovered it and found in it two golden gazelles and several complete suits of armour that had been buried there by the antique dynasty of Jurhum, who had walled all up in a defeat hundreds of years before. This Abd al-Muttalib was the head of his clan, and an important personage in the whole Koreish, the tribe who mainly owned and held the town. Eight years before his death the affairs of Mecca went through a catastrophe. The black King of Abyssinia, then as now a Christian, was incited by the Emperor of Byzantium, his co-religionist, to avenge some persecution of missionaries (probably by a Jewish tribe) and sent an expedition, in which was a war-elephant, to destroy Hobal, Al-Lat the Cube, the Black Stone and Mecca. In the passes of the mountains an epidemic of small-pox came on his army, who turned back. This is the War of the Elephant, an essential element of the Mahometan legend, and resulted in an increase of the reputation of the old shrine, with a spurt in the declining fortunes of the tourist industry of the town. Abd al-Muttalib as the discoverer of Zem-Zem shared largely in these, for he and his family enjoyed the revenue of the supply of holy water, and also it appears of some sort of monopoly of the catering to the pilgrims.

In these circumstances Mahomet was born. His father Abdullah died while he was in arms, leaving no fortune; but Abd al-Muttalib spared enough from the budget of his huge family to put the baby out to wet nurse among a friendly tribe of Bedawin in the vicinity. The legends about his boyhood are neither credible nor interesting. He looked after the goats, and from time to time had some sort of epileptic fits. When he was old enough he returned to Mecca. His mother was dead; his grandfather Abd al-Muttalib soon followed, confiding young Mahomet to the care of two uncles, one poor and noble, Abu-Talib; one rich and dull, Al-Abbas. The former took the youngster with him in a caravan to Damascus, which journey no doubt had an educative influence but ended in financial loss.

These men of Mecca had no developed form of government. The richest or most ferocious among them no doubt had some sort of personal precedence in the civic debates, in which all the tribesmen had a right to be present. They were still regulated by that curious and archaic institution of the vendetta, without some insight into which Mahomet's ascendant career will be difficult to understand. In our own days, its survival among the Italians, the Corsicans, and other backward races seems the very definition of civil disorder; but in its youth it is, on the contrary, an embryonic policy, without which, in the absence of any other system of order, life among peoples with the temperaments of Arabs or Anglo-Saxons (for we too seem to have begun with it) would be impossible even for professional bandits. The substitution of the term of "corporate revenge" perhaps makes this easier to see. Mecca was occupied by two tribes, the Khozaa, and the Koreish. Mahomet was a Koreishite. Each of these tribes was in turn made up of families or clans; the most important in Koreish were the Hashimites and the Omeiyads, closely related and impassably separated by blood and history. Mahomet was a Hashimite; his grandfather the holy caterer, Abd al-Muttalib, had been its head. Every native of the town was a member of one of these factious families or owned by one of them as a slave; in every individual's misdeeds or wrongs his family were implicated by tradition, custom, and that strongest of all motives for a fight, self-respect, or vanity. Thus there were two checks on murderous and thievish instincts; one the positive fear of skin-vengeance "to the third and fourth generation," the other the restraint often itself violent of his fellow clansmen against any act that would be revenged on them indiscriminately, as well as on its doer.

Social life in Old Mecca therefore might be likened to that of the boot-legging world of Chicago; characters, tastes, and occupations have a certain impudent resemblance; but the Meccan experience was wider and bitterer, very likely, so that life there stepped cautiously, and even politeness was not unknown. But underneath this pleasing resultant of countless feuds, the old inviolability of vendetta remained; no reason could hold off its assistance to a clan member if he was attacked, and Mahomet in the years of his unpopularity had his clan behind him, unbelievers though most of them were.

On top of this law of disorder hard times had laid the beginnings of another peace. After all, the Meccans lived more and more on pilgrims as the caravan traffic declined, and even an Arab idolator hated to find himself disturbed in his prayers at the Ka'ba by some murderous riot that marked another stage in a local quarrel in which he was not concerned. Donnybrook never attracted a good class of tourists. After centuries of discussion the Meccans under the leadership of the Koreish had agreed and advertised that for four months in the year there should be a sacred peace in the town and its suburbs, during which no weapon might be carried; a moratorium of vendetta. These holy months were at first timed to coincide with the fair, that is, autumn when the date crop was in and food was cheap. But owing to the imperfection of the lunar calendar this coincidence gradually split, until to the baffled dismay of the Meccan people they saw the holy months each year falling later. In the time of Mahomet they fell in high summer, when even water was scarce.

The first public event in Mahomet's life was a breach of this annual truce, known to Koranists as the "Sacrilegious War." It fell in his twentieth year. A creditor of one of the Koreish took a monkey to the fair, seated himself in a prominent place and began shouting: "Who will give me such another ape and I will give him my claim on such a one?" naming his debtor one of the Koreish with his full pedigree and many picturesque and poetical comments. A Koreishite brave came up and lopped off the animal's head; everyone rushed to arms or to safety and the row continued far into the night. That year the holy months were as busy as a Ghetto on a Sunday; there were even pitched battles, in one of which Mahomet took place. He refers to his share without much enthusiasm—he was never a fighting man. "I remember," said the Prophet, "being present with my uncles in the Sacrilegious War. I discharged some arrows at the enemy and I do not regret it." This affair undid most of the good that came from the advertisement of the Victory of the Elephant. Business was bad in Mecca for twenty years after.

Meanwhile young Mahomet went into store as a salesman of agricultural produce. His condition did not satisfy him. When he received an offer of marriage from a rich widow who had employed him in a caravan expedition as driver, he accepted eagerly. This was Khadija, daughter of Khuweilid. She was forty years old and had been twice married. Mahomet was twenty-five years old.

Though there was never any portrait of the Prophet, the minutest peculiarities of his appearance have been piously preserved by the faithful. He was a small man, but he caught the eye. Usually he was taciturn, and more and more subject to fits of abstraction, when he heard or saw nothing. But he could be agreeable, rather boisterous company. When he spoke he turned his whole body and not only his head; when he laughed, which was not seldom, he opened his huge mouth, like a crocodile, so that his gums and all his teeth were visible, and his eyes disappeared. These were piercing but blood-shot; he used to paint his eyelashes with kohl and antimony to make them appear more lustrous. He dyed his beard, some say red, some yellow, and was fond of loudly colored linen clothes, though he abhorred silk, which "was invented so that women could go naked in clothes." He had a great shout; both his anger and his mirth were explosive. He had a curious gait, very important, as "if he was descending a steep and invisible hill."

He now lived in a storied house, in the notable quarter, overlooking the central square, and the Ka'ba and the well Zem-Zem. The sudden change in his circumstances from a counter-hand to the leisured husband of a capitalist, which made his company tolerated in the groups of leaders when they discussed town affairs, first made him compare, and then think. Those who underestimate the almost infallible effects of such a change on a meditative mind, working like an enforced induction, may believe the story that a single curious event occurring at this time changed Mahomet—noun into Mahomet—verb. The old Ka'ba after a severe flood began to fall in ruins; the notables decided to risk the high-tension taboo on its substance and rebuild it. One Ab-Walid had the courage to be the first to touch the holy wall. He seized a pick-ax, gave one stroke, then fled. All retired from the place until next morning to see if anything happened to him. When they found he was still alive, the work proceeded. But at the end, when it came to the question of re-sealing the Black Stone, there was a bad dispute, all the clans claiming the honor for themselves. Finally they agreed to abide by the decision of the first man to appear in the square. This chanced to be Mahomet; he delivered his judgment very nicely. First he took off his mantle and spread it on the ground. On this he placed the stone, and kissed it.

Then he asked a chief to come forward from each of the four chief clans, each to take a corner and lift it to the proper height. Mahomet himself guided it into place.*

However it happened, by the natural mechanism of circumstance or by some such faltering hazard, Mahomet began then to think about the town's affairs; to worry about the decline of the pilgrimage and its causes; to hang on the groups of local leaders who discussed remedies in informal parliament on the stony street corners, or sheltered against the wind under the lee of the Ka'ba itself.

The start of Mahomet's adventure, or in its more usual synonym, the basis of the Mahomedan religion, is this preoccupation of his with the fortunes of his native town. Squeamish pedantry may object to the triviality of the phrase which fits nevertheless with a precision no other can give: Mahomet was a "home-town booster," and this conception will unlock the many obscurities of his life and his doctrine, which the most subtle theological speculations and the most careful minutiae of history are incapable of coping with. The door by which he enters is: "How can we attract the whole world, at least the whole of Arabia, yearly to the Ka'ba?" And the vision of One God, greatest common denominator of religion, is the solution, not the prime inspiration. In fact Mahomedanism is a religion, because Mecca's problem, as a pilgrimage town, was religious. The rhapsodies, the epilepsies of the man while he is still struggling towards his invention, are the symptoms of a process which they sometimes assist and sometimes retard; if they were taken as analogous to the painful mental strainings of a Rotarian enthusiast racking his brain for a world-beating slogan for the town of his heart it might be irreverent (we regretfully forswore reverence at the beginning of these studies) but it would not be a joke; nor a mistake.

So Mahomet embarked on the most dangerous enterprise in the world, the foundation of a religion, with commonsense. A commonsense so rigid and unfanciful that it approached arithmetic. Columbus had at any rate three seaworthy brigs; Mahomet adven-

---

* For this reason his title is El-Amin, the Chosen.

tures into the realm of passion, dream, nightmare, on the rule of three. He began to walk alone, to beat the air with his hands, to sweat over secret thoughts, over a plan, which at nights he would confide to the buxom sympathy of Khadija, by which, at the expense of a certain percentage perhaps of the Bedawin idolators (often so poor that their patronage was not really worth while) he would attract to the Ka'ba rich millions of Jews and whole congregations of the Christians he had seen in Syria, fish from the boundless ocean of Rome and New Rome. For ten years before he ventured to say a word in public he told Khadija about it. First, was not the legend that Mecca was founded by Abraham? That Hagar, his maid servant flying from the wrath of his wife Sarah, with Ishmael his son, drank and discovered this well Zem-Zem? These, said Mahomet, are the true beginnings of Mecca, and Mecca will prosper by them as the forefathers who kept the story never dreamed. For both Christians and Jews reverence Abraham. But they will never visit his temple and the cradle of his son if the absurd, unarithmetical, childish and wicked worship of an indeterminate number of Gods continues in Mecca; all the educated peoples I have seen, Jews and Christians, he would go on, recognize the obvious fact that there is but one God. Hobal and his college of demonic friends must go. There is no God but Allah.

And Mahomet is his Prophet. In the elaboration of his great plan he became more and more absorbed. The noise of the town worried him; he was always afraid of noise, thunder or traffic or war. So he betook himself for long days to the sterile, windy hills round the town, especially to Mount Hira, a sugar-cone eminence three miles from Mecca, where Khadija accompanied him. When he was in town he would frequent Jews, who were numerous there, and talk; and also ask questions from Zaid, his servant and friend, a short dark man with a depressed nose, who had been a slave among Christians, who told him what he remembered of the doctrine. Mahomet understood the Jewish theology better, its dietetic and medical commandments, and he was above all struck with its expectation of the Messiah. The Christians, too, as far as Zaid's confused recollections of the tangled teaching of the heretical Syrian family who had owned him went, were also expecting some prophet, the Paraclete.* Which garbled into Periklutos translated very fairly into Arabic, Ahmed, the "praised," a version of Mahomet's own name.

These promptings, even if nature had omitted to implant ambition in him, would have infallibly brought into Mahomet's simple schematizing the idea of leadership, personal leadership. The idea of religion encloses priest as inevitably as god; put into Mahomet's own style, Mecca needed one Prophet as well as one God. When the embryo was at this stage, his exasperation of hard thinking found its outlet in poetry: the poetry of the earliest Suras of the Koran which are such a striking contrast to the platitudinous prose that too abundantly followed when the intellectual tension was over. Indeed, in the form itself of these curious and magnificent productions, there is a revelation of the man, which dispenses from further detailing; his terrible auto-excitation to thought, which almost burst the veins in his forehead; in the curious elemental oath formula which begins them; and the mediocre restatement of the Hebrew or Christian ethical doctrine beyond which, with all this effort, he rarely arrives. Thus, Sura 100 (the chapters of the Koran are higgledy-piggledy):

> By the roaring panting steeds
> Striking fire flashes with the hoof
> That scour the land at Dawn
> Darken it with their dust
> Split apart the Enemy...
> Verily Man is to his Lord ungrateful
> Verily he is keen after this world's good.

Or Sura 91; to admire the full effect of which it is necessary to know that in the original each verse ends in a panting *ha!* (pronoun third person) as indicated by the italics:

---

* See John xvi. 7.

By the Sun and *his* rising splendour
By the Moon when she followeth *him*
By the Day when it sets out *his* glory
By the night when it covers *him* in darkness
By the Heavens and *him* that made them by the Earth and
   the Soul...
Verily he that purifieth them is blessed
And the contrary is he that corrupteth them.

Then sooner or later, he arrives at the awe-inspiring novelty of the Day of Judgment. The Semites seem to have been slow to bethink themselves of this natural corollary of the concept of divine justice; the mention of life after death itself, of course, is notably rare in the Old Testament, though the Rabbinical schools of Mahomet's time were obsessed with it, and probably the worshippers of Hobal knew no more about it than the contemporaries of Moses, or Homer. There is no reason except sentiment to believe that Mahomet came upon this potent doctrine in any different way from the rest of his borrowed ethics. But once the premonition of the immensity of the notion, which was destined to support the edifice of Mohamedanism, like the green basalt at the base of the Ka'ba, began to work on him, we are enriched with one of the most rare and astonishing of the Suras, a hymn in which we can hear the cracking of the sinews of his thinking. Sura 101:

That which striketh! What is that which striketh?
And what shall certify thee what THE STRIKING is?
The day mankind shall be scattered like moths
And the mountains carded like colored wool
Then as for him whose balances are heavy, he shall enter into Bliss
And as for him whose balances are light
The Pit shall be his dwelling!
And what shall certify thee what is the PIT?
A RAGING FIRE.

In spite of the support of his audience-wife, such efforts began to overwhelm him. The Angel Gabriel began to appear and confide a vast and discoordinated amount of Jewish legend, Christian heresy, proverbial common sense, and philosophical history of the Koreish; the Prophet himself imagined after all it might be a devil. Khadija*
reassured him; the next time the voice in his head spoke to him, they were together in her room, and he gave her as arranged a signal. She pulled off her chemise, and taking him on her knees began to caress him in a very intimate manner. The voice stopped. See, says Khadija, a lewd or wicked spirit would have remained; as it is, it must have been Gabriel.

From this point the religion is ripe to be preached, and henceforth Mahomet prefaces every Sura with the word "Say" or "Speak" to mark its status. Thus in Sura 112, the theological (though certainly not historical) starting point of Mahomedanism:

SAY:—He is God alone! God the Eternal!
He begetteth not! nor he is begotten!
And there is not any like Him.

Nothing remained but the practical: to present his religion to Mecca, clear out the idols from the Ka'ba, announce the changed management to the Christians and Jews and amass the results. Mecca would again know palmy days; and under the beneficent rule of *its benefactor itself* proceed to enjoy its prosperity in peace and order. As for that positive hindrance to this prosperity of the vendetta brawling, that would be settled by the teaching of the new system that all believers were brethren and forbidden to injure one another.

This offer of Mahomet to Mecca is the great offer of all adventurers to Society: to exchange all that is loved, owned, established, for a dream; with the leadership of the candid outsider thrown in. Brass

---

* According to the story of Al-Tabari, Gabriel used to grip the prophet by the throat until he thought his death was near.

lamps for gold; the kingdom of the world if you will fall down and worship me, all the folk-lore trade of sorcerers and devils. To the people he proposed: burn the gods of your fathers and your children. To the privileged: give up your offices and be one of the crowd again. To the clan that was just getting the score right with their hereditary enemies after fifty years' loss: throw in your winning hand. To the potentates of the town: obey, as you never have obeyed any man, this little bloodshot fellow, the exploiter of a fond widow's fortune. The offer is invariable! So is Society's answer; first laughter and then curses.

Mahomet is now forty-four years old. His first converts are remembered by name in the prayers of hundreds of millions today; they are Khadija, who tested the Angel; Zaid, who had been a Christian slave; Ali, the Prophet's cousin, son of good down-at-the-heels Abu Talib; Waraka, poor, toothless cousin; and Abu Bekr (who afterwards became the first Caliph of Islam), a thin weedy man, with a bulging forehead. He was a business friend of Khadija and had a moderate fortune which he spent in the cause. This Abu Bekr brought in the first outside converts. They have become saints, but to the unbeliever seem of poor quality, slaves, boys, women; except one Bilal, an Abyssinian negro with a mighty baritone voice. We will see what a curious destiny awaited this gift. In the first four years there were about forty converts, mostly slaves, few among the Koreish or among Mahomet's own clan at all; so that already Islam jumped over the tribal divisions of Mecca, and tended to throw some confusion into the politics of the town.

At first his opponents contented themselves with laughter. Mahomet for years was a good joke to the loungers in the hot evenings round the Ka'ba. But gradually irritation grew at the attitude of his slave-followers to their master's gods, and there were many beatings, and when these were not enough, condemnation to the stocks which in Mecca were placed in the sun, and included the pain of thirst from sunrise to sundown. The only one who did not recant under this treatment was Bilal, the negro, who shouted all day Akhad, Akhad. One, one. A neat and practical summary of the simplicity of the new religion for such circumstances. Abu Bekr bought him from his idolatrous master and set him free.

In these circumstances Mahomet began to have a rapid series of revelations, very encouraging to the dispirited sect. Sura 15, a unique possession of this religion of common sense, came to the rescue of the demi-martyrs:

Whoever denieth Allah after that he has believed (*excepting him who is forcibly compelled thereto, his heart remaining steadfast in the faith*) on such resteth the wrath of Allah.

The gloss of the traditionalists on this passage leaves no room for doubt. Mahomet one day passed a certain slave named Ammar, who was sobbing and groaning, and inquired the reason. "They would not let me go, O Prophet, until I had abused thee and spoken well of their gods," says Ammar. Mahomet: "But how is thy heart?" "Steadfast in the faith." "Then," said the sagest of prophets, "if they repeat their beatings, repeat thou also their recantation."

In addition to this valuable dispensation, the faithful were cheered with a new motive for perseverance. Hitherto they had been drilled by the fear of hell, now they heard news of Paradise. Gabriel brought the good news of Sura 78.

Verily for the pious is a blissful abode
Gardens and vineyards
Damsels with swelling breasts of suitable age
And a brimming cup.

This wine, forbidden in this world, is later described as "sealed with musk and spiced with ginger." And then there is luscious Sura 5.

Besides these there shall be two gardens
Which then of the signs of the Lord will ye deny?
Of a dark green,
Which then of the signs of the Lord will ye deny?
In each two fountains of welling water,
Which then of the signs of the Lord will ye deny?

In each fruit: dates and pomegranates,
Which then of the signs of the Lord will ye deny?
In them women, smooth, lovely,
Which then of the signs of the Lord will ye deny?
Black-eyed damsels kept in pavilions,
Which then of the signs of the Lord will ye deny?
Whom no man has yet enjoyed, nor even a Djin
Which then of the signs of the Lord will ye deny?
The Believers shall lie with them on green rugs
Which then of the signs of the Lord will ye deny?
And lovely soft carpets,
Which then of the signs of the Lord will ye deny?

It is not recorded that there were any more recantations after the revelation of Sura 5. With it and the daily prayer (Sura 1) made famous by thousands of European novelists and dramatists as the distinctive local color of the warm East, the elements of Islam are complete.

Praise be to Allah, the Lord of creation,
The merciful, the compassionate
Ruler of the Day of Judgment
Help us,
Lead us in the path,
The Path of those to whom thou hast made promises
Not of those you are angry with, who walk in error.

Mahomet himself, Abu Bekr, and all the free citizens of Mecca who joined him were subject to nothing but the most guarded abuse, being protected by the very institution of vendetta they desired to abolish. The words of one Hisham, prominent gangsman and inveterate idolator, are recorded when it was proposed in his presence to suppress Islam by force. "Beware if you kill one of my tribe," he answered, "for I shall be obliged to slay in his stead the chiefest among you." The opposition in this deadlock took the form of muttered abuse, and a rather easy accusation of plagiarism against the Prophet. "He gets all his stuff from the Jews, and Zaid the ex-Christian," was the commonest taunt, to which Mahomet only made the weak reply, "How could a foreigner, Jew or Christian, tell me these things, since they are in pure Arabic?" Unnecessarily weak, for while Mahomet's borrowings from Christianity are many, they are so distorted that they must have passed through at least three misunderstandings: Mahomet's miscomprehension of what some mistaken informant told him of the confused ideas of some Monophysite heretic, who had not quite grasped the teachings of his own sect—surely in the circumstances this may count as an original revelation. As for his much wider borrowings from Judaism, even reckoning that his source was late Talmudic legend and not the originals, he has given them such a fanciful, ingeniously imaginative twist, that here, too, the harsh word plagiarism is unjust. Thus there are pages, volumes almost, in the Koran of such tales as these: that Mount Sinai was suddenly raised in the air and held threateningly over the heads of the Israelites to make them accept the Law; that the mountains where David was walking joined with a sublime bass in his songs; that Jews who broke the Sabbath were suddenly changed into red apes; that Ezra was raised from the dead after a hundred years, still sitting on his ass. But the problem of the slave-converts, and of those strangers who were also unprotected by the vendetta system, remained unsettled, since both Khadija's and Abu Bekr's funds began to diminish by the exorbitant price asked for them by their persecuting masters. A certain emigration of these began towards the Christian negro Kingdom of Abyssinia. This is called the first Flight; it was encouraged by Mahomet, who was now nearing the age of fifty, and growing tired, as the increased prosiness and platitude of his revelations show. These first fugitives included the fanatics, who felt the burden of living near an idolatrous shrine intolerable, and Mahomet saw them go with relief. The adventure weighed on him; he had reasons to believe he could bring it to a happy end, in which all or most of the advantages that had lured him to undertake it could be obtained. The chiefs of the town had allowed him to see

that an arrangement was possible; on a certain day after the refugees
had gone he came to the Ka'ba, found there as if by accident all the
chiefs assembled, and squatting beside him he began to recite in his
loud sing-song:

I saw Gabriel another time
By the tree at the furthest boundary
Near which is the restful Paradise
I did not look aside
And I saw some of the finest wonders of the Lord...
Then he went on:
(I asked) What think you of Al-Lat and Al-Ozzo
And Manat also?

(These last two were the females in the Ka'ba college of gods.)
Gabriel answered:

These are exalted females
Whose intercession is certainly to be sought after.

All Koreish stood up and cheered him; and bowed down and
worshipped.

The automobile trajectory of Mahomet then brought him safely
to that great bourn of all common sense: compromise. This happy
reasonable scene under the Ka'ba wall, out of the wind, is as far as
Mahomet may be projected by his own power. The town-booster, the
ingenious planner of a nationwide Come to Mecca slogan has decided to liquidate, and distribute himself the bonus years of the effort
of thinking and unpopularity had won for him; he signals the gods
of adventure to stop and let him get down.

This is in fact the fatal turning-point to which in turn we have
watched with anxiety his predecessors arrive; when the retreat from
adventure begins. In every case we have yet examined, the wreck that
follows has been caused from within their own characters, a rupture
of the motor, a shift of balance between *want* and *have*, that has

toppled them to ignominy, misery, derision. Had he been travelling in mere geography, or mere history, no doubt his story would slide here into the monotonous "and he lived unhappily ever after" of the rest. A few months' popularity, a few years' influence, then this obscure municipal theorizer would have been bustled off the stage, perhaps by some ironical back-working of the vendetta principle—his bodily safety till now—which he had done his best in the ascending days to destroy. But however dumpy his personality, this merchant of the supernatural has dealt with the Night, he has dabbled in the immense and chartless seas in the depth of the human heart, and in this hour there is no mere tumble before him, but a terrible and resistless rebound, as if the powers he had pawkily invoked took him by the scruff of his neck and threw him shouting out of sight of common humanity through the air. Not his Allah indeed, nor any of the bearded and irascible sub-deities of his theogony, Gabriel, Azrael, Eblis, but that boundless, tentacular, blind omnipotence, whom no one has ever worshipped, on which none has ever dared to see a human face; who has never had the smallest idol made in his image—the collective weight of the Past, the sum of all that has happened since the ether first trembled, the vast arithmetic of causality, which has its tides and currents like the ocean, and on whose crest this little gesticulating prophet was now carried in a resistless surge to the conquest of the world. For mark, as we say more soberly, the time is ripe for Mahomet and his religion.

Judaism is lost in an impalpable powder of angry, haughty exiles, shut up in ghettoes of their own devising, preparing in universal misanthropy for universal martyrdom. Christianity is involved in the West in the endless task of getting the Frank, Aleman, Saxon, Celt to renounce murder and theft and fornication. In the East it has lost itself completely in the paradox of power and riches; it is racked with a hundred organic diseases of theology; the unaccountable but real impulse of its devotees to hate easier than to love is splitting every unity in the Empire, even military and economic. But Christianity and Judaism have poisoned the natural religions of the vast area they have touched, from Gibraltar to Bombay; they have not converted the idolator but they have made him sceptical and apologetic; the old gods are sick and sorry for themselves.

At the other pole of the situation, Arabia is starving; so slowly however that its people are at the stage of hunger-anger, and not hunger-weakness. We have noticed the trade factor; in addition the climate has been drying for centuries. Already the fat plains of Babylon are deserted, the aqueducts choked with blown sand, the cities buried in mounds. The swarm instinct is among the Semites, as it came to central Asia centuries before; it is struggling desperately with the myriad tribal jealousies, incompetencies, fears, like a new river trying to find its bed through a rock-littered ravine. History is piling up behind the loud little man; and he digs his heels in in vain.

Recapitulate what Mahomet has invented: a super-tribal unity; an arithmetical theology to replace the complicated and discredited tribal gods; a motive, Paradise; a driving fear. Hell; prayers; an ethic which has all the elements men demand, even to a few of the food restrictions no religion can do without; he has removed the fear of death that hitherto balked the Arabian warrior, and he will soon sharpen their instinct for plunder tenfold by appointing it a duty.

The lever of his position is now his own converts, his own past, the picked fanatics, who returned in haste from Abyssinia at the news of the compromise. It is too much to expect a religion to have kept count of what they said to the prophet; we must be content with the unusually candid chronicle of the bare events. The emigration; then Mahomet's compromise; three months afterwards the return; and then cancellation of the "Satanic Verses" by a new revelation; and the beginning of a new fiercer stage of the struggle. Mahomet's peace was gone. Indignant Koreish made a firm attempt to detach Abu Talib from his nephew, "to uncover Mahomet from his clan"; the old man, though still hostile to Islam, refused, and went further. With chosen young bloods from his family he went to the Ka'ba, listened to the assembly, and then answered, turning to his following: "Uncover what you hold under your coats." They drew out their weapons and held them up. Then to Koreish: "By Hobal and Al-Lat and Manat, if you kill him, there will not remain one alive among you." Following on this success, Mahomet made two notable converts. Hamsa, son of Abd al-Muttalib's old age, and a gigantic bully of the town, Omar. Koreish, scared off bloodshed, declared a solemn boycott of the Islamites, and also of the whole clan of Hashim, unbelievers and believers, from Abu Talib to Mahomet. The ban was written: "that they would not marry their women, nor give their own in marriage to them; nor sell anything to them, nor buy aught from them." An invisible wall henceforward separated their quarter from the life of the city. Mahomet himself, willy-nilly, urged on by a logical working outside himself, whose momentum increased with every development of events, now began on a new phase. Hitherto his message was for Mecca; now he began to preach to the pilgrims, at the fairs; especially to the Jewish traders. Wherever he stumped on this gospelling, he was followed by hostile Koreishites, jeering and threatening; one especially, "a squint-eyed man, fat, having flowing locks on both sides, and clothed in fine Aden stuff," dogged his steps, shouting out: "Believe him not, he is a lying renegade." This was his own uncle, shut up with him in the boycott, Abd Al-Ozzo Abu Lahab.*

The faithful were thus treated for the next two or three years, during which the doting Khadija died (A.D. 619), and also the good uncle Abu Talib, faithful both to Mahomet and his idols to the end.

In this new stage the Prophet showed great energy. He even journeyed as far as the next town, Al-Taif, to preach; the inhabitants threw dust on him and ignominiously expelled him. He had more success with the men from Medina, that rival of Mecca eleven days' camel-journey to the north. The Medina pilgrims were won over in considerable numbers; the Jews were very powerful and numerous in their city and at this period extremely sympathetic to the man they regarded as a sort of unofficial convert. Twelve of these Medina men at the pilgrimage of A.D. 621 actually took the oath of blood alliance with the

---

* Mahomet's reply is in his best style:
  Blasted be the hands of Abu Lahab! and let him be blasted!
  He shall be cast into the frying Flame,
  His wife also, the beast, laden with fire-wood
  With a rope of palm-coir round her neck...*Sura III.*

Prophet (in great secrecy) which is called the Pledge of the Akaba.

This Pledge is the next turning point of history. From here Mahomet psychologically abandons Mecca, and turns to every point of the Arabian horizon with the words: "Ye people, Say, THERE IS NO GOD BUT GOD. Ye will be benefited thereby. Ye will gain the rule of all Arabia, and of Al-Ajam (foreign lands) and when ye die ye will live like kings in Paradise." Koreish, seeing a part of his new policy, though ignorant until the end of its full amplitude and success, increased their petty persecution. The faithful began to drift to Medina, each family departing by night and locking up the door of its house. But the extent of this persecution had been exaggerated; the worst thing recorded, which perhaps even has a certain humor (to my taste) is a deed of the indefatigable Abu Lahab, who climbed on the Prophet's roof with a goat's entrails in a bucket, which he threw down the chimney as the Prophet was preparing his meal. Mahomet rushed out carrying the offense on a pointed stick and shouting, "What sort of a refined neighborhood is this?"

But as the clandestine emigration proceeded, and quarter after quarter, street after street, emptied, his enemies advanced by degress from curiosity, mystification, to an alarm all the more dangerous because none knew exactly what was afoot. The operation was carried on with all the rather sinister secrecy of an Eastern mutiny; the growing number of locked doors seemed like a creeping disease. The moment arrived when only Mahomet and Abu Bekr remained of the faithful in the hostile town, steadfastly going about their business and pretending that all was normal. Koreish held a secret assembly. This time there was a plan and no dissentients: a delegation from every clan were to call on the two and carefully and simultaneously plunge a knife into their chests—a round robin of revenge. A bazaar murmur warned Mahomet and Abu Bekr, and made them speed up what they had planned long before, their own escape.

A few lines must sum up the vast mythology that has grown up about this escape: which is the great Hedjira. The outline indeed is quite simple. Since the road to Medina was certain to be blocked, or on the direct line of pursuit, the two agreed to hide in the vicinity until the scent was cold. In his old excursions with Khadija Mahomet had found a cave, on the peak of Mount Thor, or Thaur, about an hour and a half from the town, and they settled on this for their retreat. In the evening they crept through a back window of Mahomet's house in a boycotted and now deserted quarter of the southern suburb and made their way there unobserved. Modern pilgrims assure us that the road they followed (which is now a very meritorious pilgrimage) is still excessively steep and disagreeable.

In the early morning the vigilance committee of Koreish cautiously attacked the empty house and found the birds flown. Pickets mounted on fast camels were immediately sent out on to the Medina road, and armed bands beat all the country for miles around. Naturally the fugitives were helped by angelic intervention, a spider made his web across the mouth of the cave; two wild pigeons made their nest in the entrance, etc.; in any case Koreish never found them, and after five days the two came out, found camels that had been supplied by various complicities in the town, and set out by forced marches for Medina. The day of their flight, the Hedjira, was the 20th June, A.D. 622, and the beginning of the Islamic era. Mahomet was then fifty-three years old.

Medina, the new epicentre of the adventure, was both larger and incomparably more habitable than the abandoned Mecca. It was in a fertile valley, and surrounded by a belt of date palms and groves and gardens, to which even more than the caravan trade that passed through it equally with Mecca, it owed its fame and wealth. As Mahomet and Abu Bekr approached they were met by hordes of rejoicing converts. The question of their lodging immediately arose, and needed some tact to settle. Mahomet with his unsleeping common sense realized that there was a great danger of arousing jealousies at this critical moment; so the inspiration came to him to ask his camel, the celebrated Al-Kaswa, to decide for him. The mob of excited and wrangling faithful (it is remarkable that Mahomet never inspired fear) opened their midst to allow the beast to pass, and all in the silence which such an operation, half theological and half gaming, requires, followed. Al-Kaswa was leisurely. She ambled through the centre of the crowded market place, and down the principal streets, occasionally, as if teasing, hesitating to snuffle in some open gateway but never stopping until she had clean gone through the town and come to a deserted part of the suburbs. There, with great premeditation, watched by the awestruck and baffled congregation, she nosed into the dusty and neglected courtyard of a derelict villa, and squatted down. Arrangements were at once made for buying the place (which had long served as a yard for tying up camels) and on the spot thus divinely chosen was soon afterwards begun the first and most famous Mosque of Islam. In whose purlieus Mahomet lived the rest of his life with his harem, and where he lies buried alongside the tombs of his first two successors, Caliph Abu Bekr, and Caliph Omar.

The history of Mahomet in this Medina phase has been obscured and ornamented with a unique mass of traditional detail, the least item in which is an immutable part of the Islamic code of morals, customs and law. But though much of this hagiology is psychologically amusing, yet the unity of his character observable until the time of the Satanic Verses and possibly even to the Hedjira is, though not changed, transposed into another key. In short this Medina prophet now behaves like an institution rather than a man; his adventure has become the majestic, inevitable unfolding of an historical logic in which, in everything but one, he is a mere instrument or proposition. That one thing is his taste for women, which he now indulged generously. Instead of Khadija he now possessed, as the nucleus of a gracious party, the little Aisha, twelve-year-old daughter of Abu Bekr, whose own testimony in her old age was that "the prophet liked three things most, women, scent, and eating, but mostly women." With quickening progression he added new faces to his collection as the occasion offered: one of his principal sources of supply was the death of a follower, and the acquisition of his widow.

The soberer part of his history falls easily into two parts: his relations to the Jews, his combat with the Meccans. Something like a goose-flesh comes on the explorer in the curious labyrinth of early Mahomedan history when he realizes that the Jews, if they had wished, if (as Mahomet would have put it) they had had the sense, could have appropriated Islam. Mahomet, we have seen even in so condensed a sketch, was their pupil, their imitator, and in the beginning of his stay at Medina, almost their creature. It was the Bene-Nadir, the Bene-Amar and the rest of the rich, warlike and politic Hebrews of Medina who opened the doors of his refuge to him, when his followers were too small in numbers and poor to have influenced the councils of the clan-leaders. It was to Jerusalem, their holy city, that the prophet and his faithful turned in prayer in these early days; and there still exists a document which is a definite overture of Mahomet to them for at least perpetual alliance. This venerable monument of a missed (or doubtless, rejected) opportunity provides for "war and peace to be made in common," sets out that "the Jewish clans are one people with the Believers," assures "whosoever of the Jews follows us in our expeditions shall have aid and succour."

Underlying all this is the definite candidacy of Mahomet to the Messiahship. It is probable that a certain part of the Jews supported him in this; and remonstrated with their co-religionists for waiting for any fulfillment of Isaiah better than this fervent monotheist, Talmudist and testifier to the integrality of the Torah, much more likely than any Bar-Cochbar to give them that military world power the realists required. The dispute, characteristically and astonishingly, between Mahomet and his supporters and the recalcitrant Jews of Medina turns, not on any lack of what we may call supernatural theatricality in his person, absence of any unusual atmospheric phenomena to support his claim, but whether or not the prophecies both appealed to, applied to a son of David (as the Jews insisted), or to a mere son of Abraham, through Ishmael the first Arab, which none disputed Mahomet to be. The Davidists won, and the world was spared or deprived what would have been the greatest of those reunions of the Semitic race which have illustrated some of the most brilliant pages of the history of civilization. Mahomet entered into a rage, then cooled to a vindictiveness that cost his rejectors dear. The symbol of this break is the sudden changes of the Kibla, or orientation of the Mosque. The prophet was leading the prayers of the faithful in what has received the name of the Mosque of Two Kiblas, near

Medina, about two years after his arrival. He had already performed two prostrations with his face towards Jerusalem, when his anger mounted to his throat and he suddenly swung round in the direction of Mecca and the Ka'ba. All the worshippers imitated him at once, and ever since Judaism and Islam have parted their ways. At the same time, being at a loss as to a distinctive signal to call his followers to their prayers, bells being Christian, and the ramshorn roarer of the Jews which he had hitherto used, being also out of the question now, Mahomet bethought him of the far-reaching baritone of Bilal, the African, and commissioned him to mount in the minaret at dawn and chant the office of the first muezzin: "Prayer is better than sleep. I bear witness that there is no God but Allah"—and so forth.

Now Mahomet by the use of every possible form of persuasion, perfidy, manœuvre and political sagacity, ended by establishing himself the undisputed master of Medina. With this power he set about revenging himself on the Meccans. He attacked their caravans, even in the holy months of the truce, as they passed his stronghold, and divided the booty with his followers in the sacred proportion of eighty-twenty. The incidents of this robbery under arms are surprisingly varied and dramatic. The story-tellers of Arabia replenished their stock with them for a thousand years. Hamsa, Abu Bekr, Abu Sufyan, the idolatrous chief of Koreish, Bilal the big-voiced, the painted prophet always in the rear, inventing such battles cries as *Ya Mansur Amit!* Ye conquerors strike! the timely interventions of Gabriel and his angelic host, "as numerous as a nest of ants," these are some of the ingredients of the story that men still discuss round every camp fire of Africa and West Asia. Mahomet showed an increasing greed for spoils, and cruelty to his prisoners; only the prettiest girls could be certain of mercy after the battle. The two principal affairs were those of Bedr and Ohod; the last being drawn. It led to an accusation of treachery against the Jews, and their piecemeal massacre and exile from Medina occupied spasmodically the years that followed. Not content with his revenge against those resident in the city now completely in his hands, Mahomet began his roll of conquest by the invasion of neighbouring Jewish settlements in the deserts. In one of these (Kheibar on the Syrian road) the faithful fought under the great Black Flag, the "Eagle," which was none other than the chemise of Aisha. After the victory, Mahomet sent Bilal to secure Safiya, the young Jewess, whose beauty was famous even to Medina, for his own prize. Bilal on purpose brought her back through the battlefield past the corpse of her father, "in order that I might see her fright." In spite of this brutality, she willingly agreed to a place in his harem. But another Jewess, Zeinab, was not so accommodating. "She dressed a kid with dainty garnishing and having steeped it in poison placed the dish with fair words, before Mahomet on his nuptial feast." Mahomet took a few mouthfuls and spat one out; his commentators vaguely feel that he should have known better. One of his guests ate more and died; Zeinab was made over to his relatives to be tortured to death by them. The prophet, according to his own complaint, never quite recovered from the effects of this poisoning, and is supposed to have died from it in the end: this is the meaning of the common charge against the Jews of having martyred him.

Seven years after the Hedjira Mahomet made a truce with Koreish and led his followers to the pilgrimage which had been his far-off starting post. The unbelievers abandoned the town to them and camped out on the hills to watch. At the head of two thousand mounted pilgrims, shouting the ancient cry of this pilgrimage: *Labbeik, Labbeik!* the prophet reached the Ka'ba, touched the Black Stone reverentially with his staff. Although Hobal and his graven company were still standing in the Cube, Bilal mounted the wall and sent up his call to prayer. After three days the faithful locked up their houses again and went back to Mecca.

The conquest of Mecca two years later was on the whole a tame affair. The forces of the prophet had grown overwhelmingly greater than those of Koreish; the home faction was sapped with sedition, and when Mahomet at last appeared the place fell with hardly a blow. Abu Sufyan himself accepted the new faith. After making the seven tours of the Ka'ba, Mahomet pointed with his staff at each of the idols which had been taken out and stood along the wall for execution, Hobal towering above them. "Truth is come" he shouted, and a negro with an axe hacked these ancient confidants of the secret prayers of Old Arabia until they were utterly destroyed, "screaming and sobbing," says the legend.

The force that was driving him did not falter an instant at this triumph, once hardly dreamed of. It is carefully recorded that he reestablished one of his uncles in the family privilege of selling water to pilgrims from Zem-Zem; but much more inward in his mood is the notion of announcing himself to the kings and princes of the earth. One of his followers suggested that such potentates accepted no communication that was not sealed, so Mahomet had a seal made for himself of silver, inscribed in the old Arabic character, "Mahomet, the Apostle of God." With this he sealed despatches to the Emperor of Byzantium, the Emperor of Persia, the Governor of Egypt, the Satrap of Syria, announcing to them (the exact terms are lost) that God had again intervened in the affairs of men.

These missives were carried by special emissaries from among his body-guard. They probably arrived; that to Constantinople they say was lost in the labyrinthine intricacies of the government offices; that to Persia torn in pieces ("Even thus, O Lord," said Mahomet, "rend his kingdom from him."), that to Egypt brought a strange reply: two beautiful Coptic girl slaves as a present from the Roman Governor. One, Miriam, gave Mahomet the joy and sorrow of his old age; a little fat son, Ibrihim, who had a whole flock of white goats set apart for his nourishment, and who died in infancy.

But Mahomet the adventurer has been swallowed by his adventure, which is now openly independent of his personality. Out of a pilgrimage stunt it is growing into an avalanche of destiny in which kings, peoples, whole civilizations and religions, will be carried away into irreparable oblivion. Out of the mass of incoherent writings, cursings, distichs, that he is still pouring out in his old age,* half

---

* Abd-ar-Rahman says that near Mecca he saw the pilgrims urging on their camels. They were shouting: "Inspiration has come on to the Prophet." He came near and saw that Mahomet was mounted on a she-camel, which was behaving in a queer way as if affected with wild excitement, sitting down and rising up, planting her legs rigidly and throwing them apart. The prophet was shouting a Sura.

buried under the minutiae of new laws obviously inspired by the domestic bickerings of his harem, there is vaguely visible the plan to which the old man is arrived: the species of vast plunder gang, the Bandit State, in which he will brigade all the faithful, the gigantic enterprise or organized looting of the whole world to which he calls his race. And they came. The new religion poured through the desert like smoke from a damped fire in a gale of wind. The men of the desert, and the men of the ruined cities, hungry and lean, rushed to the Black Standard, or joined forces with the irresistible hordes he sent against them. "Light of ear, bloody of hand, hogs in sloth, fox in stealth, wolf in greediness, dog in madness, lion in prey," the Arab was at last on the move. Every man shares in the plunder, said Mahomet, those who were not there draw from the prophet's fifth. Christians and Jews may not share, it is their punishment; they shall stay out of our expeditions and pay tribute.

So when he died (June, 632) Mahomet is no longer the motor, but the curiously carved and tinted figure-head of the adventure. He died in Aisha's arms, manfully insisting that everyone in the room should share his medicine, except his old uncle Al-Abbas. "Let no one remain without being physicked, as ye have physicked me..." He was succeeded by Abu Bekr, and he by Omar. Three years after Mahomet's death, his followers had conquered Damascus; in another year the Emperor of Byzantium withdrew from Syria, in another five, Egypt and Persia were in their power. In the life-time of a man who could have seen Mahomet as a boy, the borders of Islam were the Pyrenees on the one side, China on the other. Exactly one hundred years after his death the Moslem wave reached its furthest point at Tours in France, and but for the cavalry of Charles the Hammer would have been the next year in England.

V.

Lola Montez

THE CASE OF THE woman adventurer grows only more imperative the more it is postponed. That is the urgent reason why the first of them, Lola Montez, figures here, after Mahomet; and it is the delay, not the incongruity, which is more serious. From its first step, indeed, the enquiry has achingly missed a datum which until now I have hesitated, perhaps too long, to try to find: we have been driving with only one head-light, in the inadequate assumption that humanity was one-sexed and not irremediably hermaphroditic. Our forces have been all male, woman only a direction, a motive, a prize, a disaster. So even if modesty might have been better pleased with a wider space between the revered prophet who invented the Houri, and a minx who could have put Becky Sharp out of countenance, the turn was overdue.

But now they are seated side by side, at the same table or in the same dock, they are not such bad company, this seer who "liked women most," this loud-speaker who asked God in the name of humanity for "smooth, black-eyed damsels with swelling breasts…of suitable age…on lovely soft carpets…" and therewith implicitly guaranteed that this would be enough to make compensation for all the woes His inscrutable schemes have laid upon us all—and Lola. She possessed twenty-six of the twenty-seven canons the voluptuous Moresco lays down for beauty. Three of these points are white: the skin, the teeth, the hands. Three black: the eyes (hers were blue), the eyelashes, and eyebrows. Three red: lips, cheeks, nails. Three long:

body, hair, hands. Three short: ears, teeth, chin. Three wide: the breast, the forehead, the space between the eyes. Three narrow: the waist, the hands, the feet. Three thin: the fingers, the ankles, the nostrils. Three plump: the lips, the arms, the hips.

But although the contact would conceivably not have displeased the Prophet, we must count on a quite opposite reaction from the Courtesan: one too which is a determinant and essential part of the rôle of woman-adventurer she played out. Most commonly the relation of the adventurer to woman is that of the majority of men; to them she is one of the great quests of desire, shaping according to temperament, as a hunt for quarry to be devoured, or for a rarity, an orchid or a jewel to be ravished and adored. But this sexual direction, as we have already seen, is no part of the definition of the man-adventurer. Two out of four, Alexander and Columbus, not the least typical of the breed, moved exempt from the quasi-gravitational pull of sex on the trajectory of their lives, without their adventures being thereby chilled or enfeebled. In the Law of Adventure, male adventure, love is no more than gold or fame—all three, glitterings on the horizon, beckoning constellations.

But with the woman-adventurer all is love or hate, the sole poles of her field. Her adventure is man; her type is not the prospector, but the courtesan. That is, her adventure is an escape, developing inevitably into a running fight with the institution of marriage. In which inevitably join against her the strongest and most mobile unity of society, the whole pack mounted on morals, laws, interests, jealousies, vanities and fears. She must learn the defence of the hare, and the counterattack of the solitary tigress. Every adventure is out of law: the very adventurers themselves are *her* enemies. Risk herself hates women. So that even beside the most heart-stopping gambles of the greatest of them all, hers can stand by virtue of its predetermined failure, like a forlorn hope beside the noblest of cavalry charges, lost before it started, with a magnificence that is not to be obscured by its lack of size. The adventure of Lola Montez is out of scale with those of the rest of our studies only materially; I leave it to you to make another comparison.

She was born (in 1818) in that ambiguous level of society, where, to survive, the first need is a concentrated imagination and a firm uncritical talent. Her father was an officer in a line regiment, and further, a ranker-lieutenant. That is, an aristocrat by courtesy, which was seldom shown him, without birth or fortune; required to live and think like a squire turned knight-errant in the space comprised by the married quarters and parade ground of a mean garrison town, on the pay and more than the limitations of a curate. Like his shirt under his uniform, his life, inside the official poetry of his situation, was threadbare and embarrassed; his daughter, Dolores-Eliza, was brought up with the curious mental adjustments produced by the situation. In spite of the contradiction that he had a fine uniform and was not quite a gentleman, such a life was a form of shabby-gentility, which is one of the usual recruiting grounds of adventurers as well as of poets, actresses, clerks and congenital suicides. This Lieutenant (Ensign) Gilbert had married a Miss Oliver, "of Castle Oliver," as Lola used to confide, who was probably one of that attractive class of native Irish gentry where recklessness, poverty and beauty are endemic. In those days Spain was the magnetic pole of the reveries of her likes; it predominated in the Byronic spectrum; so Mrs. Gilbert adopted a row of Spanish ancestors, all complete in fancy dress and history.

From her side Dolores-Eliza—Lola henceforward for short—received her name and the theoretical variation of Novalis,* that life is not a dream but should become one, and perhaps will. Also as many of those twenty-six points as Mendelists allot to the influence of a mother who was herself ravishingly lovely.

When this family had lasted four years, they obtained a transfer from Limerick to India, then, as it was until the Montagu Renunciation, the paradise of the English middle class. There all budgets shall be straightened out, all Sahibs pukka, all servants cheap and polite; and once a year comes Simla. The voyage took four months; it was 1822. They touched at swarming Madeira; steaming

---

* "Unser Leben ist kein Traum, aber es soll und wird vielleicht einer werden."

St. Helena; Cape Town, cracking with heat and wind. From Calcutta they went up the immemorial Ganges to the garrison of Dinapore.

We have already remarked the supercharging effect of an early transplantation on the vital growth, observable almost as infallibly on human minds as on the seedlings which the gardener knowingly shifts. There may be some biological general law in this phenomenon, for the rise of nations and races, and the growth of civilization itself as well as individuals, regularly contain analogous incidents in their early history. Without being inevitable—too many delicate factors of moment and personality enter into it for that—the result on the imaginative individuality of a small girl, subjected to such a formidable contrast as this bodily and spiritual removal from the special peculiarity of lodgings in Limerick to the *officina gentium* of the East, where "man is a weed" more luxuriant and strange than the vegetation of jungles, swarming in vast empires immeasurably older than those jungles themselves, almost than the rocks out of which he has built huge and mysterious cities, where the ceaseless commerce of riches and squalor in the streets is fiercest and most full of color because it is inextricably rooted in memories of myriads of lives and deaths that have passed there, like the deep, rich fermenting stratum of decaying vegetation under tropical forests: this might be watched for. Anyway, the earliest impressions of a mind are exactly the incommunicable element which is the hinterground of personality, the mystical secret of likes and dislikes, motives and desires, the part which even love can never possess nor give (except perhaps with artists): the only mystery we must leave alone in Lola is the world of her subconscious dreams furnished with the scents, longings, sights and sounds implanted in her by this first transmutation. The rest is logically dramatic and simple.

Gilbert died in the first chapter. He caught the cholera at Dinapore and was dead in two days. His friend, Captain Craigie, piously and gladly took over his widow and married her; Lola's changes accelerated their rhythm. For Craigie was a man of some means, influential in the way of promotion. In a year or two he was a Colonel; Mrs.

Gilbert was an Anglo-Indian station queen, Lola the exquisite little idol of a regiment, a depot, and a principality.

But the English holders of India have always had a custom, allegorical and premonitory,—though like all spiritual ceremonies from circumcision to fasting provided with an unimpeachable medical reason to hide its real nature—of sending their children back to England from a land which is their empire but never can be their colony. Lola was sent to Craigie's people, merchants in Montrose, Scotland. These home Craigies were strict Calvinists. That must by no means be assumed to mean that Lola was depressed or embittered by them. Calvinism, like all the logical sects, attracts rather the unimaginative type of mind, but its audacious conceptions, the reeling heights and abysses it sets between heaven and hell, good and bad, the sense of the intimate danger of all reality which is the least accidental Ingredient of its atmosphere by no means repels the quite different types of R. L. Stevenson and Lola. In fact she never quite ceased in her whole life, in the midst of her most outrageous adventures, to be a back-sliding Calvinist. On the one hand it sharpened her courage: with the smell of hell-fire in her nostrils how could she worry over lesser perils? And this was the special perfume that enthralled her admirers, though they ignored its origin in Scotland instead of Spain. Lola was as spoilt in Montrose as Dinapore; her soul grew in the rain as interestingly as in the sun, and no doubt in addition her complexion gained by the change.

As if the chemistry of fate was trying out all its reactives on her, after a few years she was transferred to the care of Sir Jasper Nicholls, a retired General of wealth and temperament, who placed her with his own daughters in a smart pension in Paris. Here she heard receptively the foreign doctrine that marriage was a custom, but love an aim; and a technique quite impracticable for her own career.

This career was of course marriage, in that abstruse form which the modifications of sex-jealousy, contract law, early taboos, and the Syro-Christian metaphysics of the sense of touch have made of a natural partnership. In short her mother had destined her for a rich marriage; the husband to be chosen among the nabobs of her frequentation. For this practice, the only one by which a woman can make a respectable fortune, there is needed a delicate training quite different from that which the dowried girls of her Paris school received. The prime requisite (given the natural postulate of looks and youth, without which the enterprise is almost impossible) is a commercial sense, an inner acceptance of the most rigid principles of business, such as only an old huckster possesses after years of experience in the gutter market. She must dream prices, abhor cheapness, renounce even the taint of generosity, value herself to her faintest smile with avarice. All this is undeniably difficult at eighteen; Lola failed hopelessly; with a sort of glorious stupidity. Half-way through a shopping expedition in Paris with her mother to buy her trousseau, she ran away with a penniless subaltern named James, and with a last indiscretion, married him.

Her trajectory therefore has described a loop, one of those vicious circles of force with which economists and astronomers are ruefully familiar. In as exact a way as lives can ever duplicate each other (which is nothing more, after all, than the similarity of finger-prints), Lola recommenced the life of her mother; Mrs. James instead of Mrs. Gilbert. Even to the passage to India, which came after she had retasted the mean distresses of an Irish garrison town. Lieutenant James resembled her father, as any two dull fellows resemble; he drank more, was just as handsome in the sulky English way, had the same collection of imprecise ambitions, summed up in "a good time": more money, more rank, more women, servants and horses. Karnal, between Delhi and Simla on the Jumna Canal, instead of Dinapore.

With the timely help of providence, or cholera, perhaps she would have come out of all this near enough to her mother's success to be greeted by her once more, and forgiven, and so after all have been able to escape the tragedy of a history. But Lieutenant James, instead of dying and releasing her, one morning before breakfast ran away with a brother-officer's wife; Lola retreated into life and Europe. This was in 1841. There was some proposition of returning her to Montrose, there to live the rest of her days in the cataleptic situation of a judicial separation. But on the voyage, the forces behind her, her vital charge and her beauty, which had been heaping themselves behind her as a chess doctor accumulates power of position behind a forward pawn, moved her into a new circuit, dangerous, impossible but inevitable, that almost instantaneously sent her out of sight of her old life. Instead of Mrs. Dolores Eliza James, we are henceforward occupied with Lola Montez. The instrument was some anonymous male, some vague attaché or officer met and used in love as the ship crossed the Equator, with no more personal importance than the tiny wandering spider the portentous female of the species beckons to her embraces to serve for an hour and then be eaten.

The beginning of a woman-adventure is always "going to the bad," just as that of the man is "running away from home." The difference is that between giving and taking; humanity with its sturdy Yahoo instincts can forgive a thief, but not an indiscreet generosity, which is the base of the mystery of more implacable hatreds than the whole code of torts. You need more tact in the dangerous art of giving presents than in any other social action. So with the supreme natural object of men's desire; there is a graduation descending from the highest respect, attaching to the married woman, who has accepted nothing lower than the legal contract of life-long support, with a swift drop, yet still calculable, to that of the mistress (but she must choose a rich man and show clearly that she has made him pay handsomely) who has made easier terms. There are thirty-six pages of bad names in the English slang dictionary for the prostitute, that is the bargain-retailer. But in this graph, the ordinate line cuts the base, in its steep depression, far down beyond zero in an endless minus when it registers the contempt, in contempt's most extreme form mixed with broad jeers, when men look on the woman who gives herself for *nothing*, without even a promise. Few can forgive that even for the space of time they are taking advantage of it. It is true the case is rare. So in the act that irremediably cut away from her the remotest vestige of the affections of her family, and her friends, all claim to anything in social life but the barest protection of her life by the law, by surrendering without conditions to this fellow on the boat, Lola had

done worse than irremediably commit herself to adventure. She had
"done a deed," they said, "which the crocodile and ibis tremble at."

Her mother, when she heard, put on crape. Lola never in her life
heard from her, nor communicated with her or any one of her relatives again. The lover himself hastily decamped. She was stranded in
London.

The London of those days—this is 1842—was in full gestation of
modernity, a brutal black-guard life, fertilized with a fierce and tri-
umphing Puritanism. The ingenuous nursery legends of Victorianism
as retailed to us by those who cannot remember any time when
London went to bed after half past ten, must not be allowed to obscure the reality of Lola's position. Today the control of the law is so
complete and painstaking that lucky youth is able to get an inspiring
sensation of wickedness and daring from the minutest liberties taken
or precariously allowed. The English palate has grown immeasurably
finer; it can taste the percentage of alcohol in ginger-beer. In 1842,
lawlessness was a principle, imposed with fanaticism by the compact
oligarchy of Manchester, mad to stave off ruin and grip on to prosperity by Ricardo's theory of *laissez faire*.

This liberty the Berserking, desperate English temperament fell
upon with greed; unbalanced, and fed with a violent prosperity it
might have ended in some catastrophic orgy—the English are the
only truly original people—some vast collective horseplay beside
which the Neronic feats would have been creditable. But with an
opportune growth that can only be considered as a manifestation of
a life-instinct of the swarm—the English are the only truly instinctive people—there came into the field, arising from the very mercan-
tile classes who, by their sociological credulity had loosened the
beast—one of those terrible drives towards asceticism, analogous no
doubt to the frenzy for self-mutilation that seized the orgiastic dancers at the extreme height of their passion, which have destroyed the
readability of whole pages of world history: Albigensism, Anabaptism,
Iconoclasticism, etc., essentially pessimist and therefore destructive.
It is the greatest mistake to imagine this Victorian piety as prim or
in any degree timid; almost as bad to call it mystical. The Puritan of

1840 abstained with bitterness; his art was bad with savage intention; he forbade the slightest reference to sex not because it shocked, but because it disgusted and enraged him: exactly the attitude of the American public to Germany in 1918, or any other exasperated nationalism. The misguided solecist who risked a reference to trousers or drawers had the same, and no more lightly to be dared, reception as any joker who defended the sinking of the Lusitania, in 1917: a risk not of upheld hands but of bludgeons. Nor were those embroidered texts over the marriage bed sighings, but civil war banners. The fight between Morality and License was exterminatory—and Lola found herself caught between the lines.

On one hand her position was exposed to the Indefatigable social persecution of the good and pure, which did not stop at mere excommunication, but dogged her in the most trivial details of her daily life, from the most unexpected public snubs to the fomenting of the insolence of servants and furnishers. Her lodging cost her more, and was supplied grudgingly: whole regions of the town were barred to her either as a tenant or a hotel-guest. Her very charwoman had the support of public opinion in cheating her and cheeking her. So much from the side of the angels. The attentions of the ungodly were certainly no more pleasant. The new beauty in the town could not walk abroad in any public place without being saluted with that sort of laughter and those nudges amongst the company which must be one of the most severe penalties of hell; the fat smiles of men about town, fops and fools and lady-killers, self-satisfied to damnation. When they discovered the truth: that Lola was two degrees worse than they thought—loving for love, and loving not them—their beastliness took an edge. She had found an engagement at His Majesty's Theatre as a Spanish dancer—the adjective is as significant as the noun—and a cabal organized by Lord Ranelagh and his club-friends hissed her off on her first night. Next morning she left for Brussels; she said she had not enough money for Paris.

So her young adventure changes horses at its first stage. She had faced her first mob; she chose her profession: the Stage, and what is more, dancing. And she fled in the direction of Paris. Features so recurrent in the route of woman-adventure, that they might figure on a chart. As for the baiting by the town set, it is a compact example of the administration of that stimulant, acting by despair and exhilaration, which is necessary and apparently usual, like a ritual stirrup-cup, to the woman-adventurer before she can decide to launch herself whole-heartedly into risk. On the one hand, it was the brutal materialization of the impossibility of retreat and the intractable danger she must face: the corner that puts fight into the rat. On the other, contrary to male sentimentality and psychology, the confrontation of a hostile crowd, to a woman, is like a tonic, bitter but stimulating. Sarah Bernhardt's dictum "Let them talk ill of me if they wish, but at any rate talk" is as deep in the psychology of the sex as it is in that of advertisement. That night Lola for the first time was the emotional centre of a crowd; that it was negative and not positive is comparatively negligible. It did not crush her. It frightened her in the exciting, not the deadening, way. Indifference could have destroyed her; a few lazy hand-claps instead of that deafening, unjust, fiercely *interested* roar would have sent her back to Montrose, instead of the Continent.

This Latin-Hedjira must also be a constant in woman-adventure. It is truly instinctive in all adventurers indeed to get away from home; to a woman stepping aboard the brig that plies between earth and the unknown an initial call at Paris, city of women, is as indispensable as a honeymoon. Paris, Stage, Dancing: these are not products of acute calculation; yet they are not only the right but the sole means by which her trajectory of adventure may be prolonged. For Paris, or failing Paris one of its substitutes such as the Brussels she chose, is the field where her forces are at a maximum of advantage; the stage is the fort of beauty; dancing, the deployment where its striking force loses least power and immediacy. For in the dance beauty is free from scrutiny; no dresses can rival the disguise of motion and rhythm.

In Brussels, she says in her memoirs, she was reduced "to singing in the streets." Poor Lola sang even worse than she danced, which was "passionately but unlearnedly." Whether this "singing" was a romantic euphemism or not—all heroines have to sing in the streets, as all heroes have to be unjustly accused—history does not know. In any case she was saved by a German, "a poor man, but he knew many languages" and this amiable scholar took her to Warsaw. On the fragment of description is the stamp of truth. For in Lola Montez, as distinguished from Dolores-Eliza Gilbert or James and from the towering majority of all other women of record back to a remote time, there was this noble peculiarity: she loved learning and genius. Not by calculation but by taste, a preference as irresistible and exclusive as that which other women have for nonentities and simpletons, a treason, aggravating that, hardly greater, of her black-legging generosity, since it may well be against the sane interests of the race.

In Warsaw begins her period of successful self-expression where for the first time a glance into her mind may discover lines and directions that are not ephemeral and tentative. Success is uniform with itself, which no failure, except the most pig-headed, can be, since it is merely an inorganic series of false starts. Her hour has at last come; it finds her straining towards an object which neither her instincts, nor her intellect can define.

Now her only originality is to pursue that object with a singleness of mind equal to Alexander's, or any of the other heroes we have discussed, for that object is romantic love. Where is the woman who under the manifold wrappings of prudence and cowardice, providence and avarice, sex-rivalries and their primeval meannesses, æsthetic hungers degraded into simple vanity, does not harbour the same life-wish as Lola? But they are inextricably interwoven into the fabric of society, the warp of it as law is the woof. She is a wandering thread, delivered to the wind, cursed with the tragic liberty of the Adventuress. The ancient sidetracks, position, security, children, are barred to her beyond even the possibility of temptation; she, the light-of-love, a unit among untold millions alone can keep straight, and show the hidden course.

The German quitted her, then; their paths diverged. In a last exchange, he found her an entry to an engagement at the Opera. This was the year 1844, seven years after the mutiny of the Polish Army.

An ignoble persecution had succeeded to a not altogether glorious revolt; stupidity was at grips with incompetence, and the Prince Paskievitch was viceroy and despot of Poland. This grim fellow, like most Warsaw, saw Lola dance. She was at the height of her loveliness, which when helped out by whatever she knew of dancing made men gasp, rather than dare to admire; she was one of those curious and rare cases, like Helen of Troy or the other Ladies Villon celebrates, which end the discussions on taste by an inimitable and indescribable reality, acting like an hallucinatory shock on all alike. I remember two or three such women; one in particular, a factory hand in the old quarter of Cape Town, who used to take the five o'clock train every afternoon to a near suburb. I cannot say with certainty whether she was blond like Helen, or dark as Lola, but as soon as she got out on the platform the whole train from the hard business men in the first-class smokers to the poor Hottentots in the end-coach crowded the windows; just to look, for I never saw anyone dare to accost her. I heard long after from a great gossip that she was very "silly," and ended by running away with a married carpenter to Australia—that may well be, for in history Lola is almost the only one of these exquisite phenomena of nature to have both a brain and a heart. Paskievitch wanted her, and sent for her. He was sixty years old, a dwarf, vain and cruel, and in consequence a bore; but he offered this penniless, outlawed waif a fortune, a title, and his awestruck, not wholly repugnant devotion. Lola answered him at first softly; then when his desperate illusion about life's possibilities led him to threats, she laughed at him.

The director of the Opera, and the Chief of Police were sent to add their persuasions. Lola, as she always did in the great moments of her life, lost her temper and ordered them out with a whip. That night she was hissed by the claque; her second meeting with the mob. This time the monster did not get off lightly. She rushed at it as far as the footlights, and managed to get enough details of the offer and the revenge to turn the Polish majority in the house wildly in her favor. The claquards were maltreated, and thrown out and a huge crowd of

Poles shouting for beauty and rebellion escorted her home, holding off police charges, like the Trojans defending Helen.

Her own story, in the "Memoirs" under the banal distortions of the newspaper men who wrote it for her, sometimes contains gleams of identifiable truth. This carries the matter further:

"So she found herself a heroine without expecting it, and without intending it. In a moment of rage she told the whole truth, thereby unintentionally setting all Warsaw by the ears. The hatred which these Poles intensely felt towards the government found a convenient opportunity of demonstrating itself and in less than twenty-four hours Warsaw was bubbling and boiling with the signs of an incipient revolution. When Lola Montez was apprised of the fact that her arrest was ordered, she barricaded her door; and when the police arrived she sat behind it with a pistol in her hand declaring loudly she would shoot certainly the first man dead who broke in. The police were frightened or they could not agree among themselves who should be the martyr, and they went off to inform their masters what a tigress they had to confront; and to consult. Meantime the French Consul gallantly came forward and claimed Lola Montez as a French subject, which saved her from arrest; but there was a peremptory order to quit Warsaw."

This physical courage and violence, in whose beginnings here, at the juncture of her first success we must probably believe, afterwards became her most celebrated idiosyncrasy. From Warsaw, it is said without evidence that she went to St. Petersburg and had a familiar interview with the Czar. What is more serious is that she certainly was mixed in a brawl in Berlin with a mounted gendarme while the review given by King Frederick William in the Czar's honor was in progress. Lola's horse bolted into the royal enclosure; the gendarme caught hold of his bridle to turn her out, and she slashed him with her whip. Joined with vague rumors of her exploit in Warsaw it made the beginnings of a reputation for her throughout the capitals of Europe. Through some side-effect of this she was borne within range of the great Franz Liszt.

Liszt, like herself, was then at the height of his beauty; he had the looks of Byron without his pose, more sense, more heart, and some say more genius. Even today his portrait as a young man makes women thoughtful. If Lola's adventure had any possible issue, that was Liszt; and the pianist, entangled in long intrigues that were steering him remorselessly to some final domesticity, caught at her, like a rope or a rainbow. They met, loved and were together—no one knows how long. Not more than a few months, in any case. In the winter of 1844 they were at Dresden, where Liszt had an enormous, mad success. Then in spring of 1844 they arrived at Paris. Because of Lola Liszt broke with the mother of his children, the Comtesse d'Agoult. Soon after their Paris visit they parted forever. Neither has told the world what happened, not even the beginnings, not even the end; they chattered willingly about every secret but this. Nor did anyone have their confidence about it. It is a strange thing.

Our moonseeker, after this excursion into reality, is soon off again at full speed, and fallen into an interminable Boulevard adventure, whose details seem quoted from one of those witty, dreary novels of the period. Paris of Louis-Philippe was in its legendary prime, the biggest village in civilization, before Napoleon III wickedly made it a world city. All its life hung about the main street, that is, the Boulevards, where all the lads knew each other, and were clever, and all the girls were celebrated and beautiful, so they say.

Food and wine were cheap, lodging practically given away, cooking still an art: so poets were happy and productive. Every café chair three times a day occupied by the most brilliant second-raters of the history of literature and the stage. And behind them, tinting all, was the light of authentic greatness, though usually too busy to appear: Balzac, Hugo, De Musset. In this world she chose a certain Dujarier, a spiteful and tactless young journalist, who got himself killed in a duel for her. To succeed Liszt? That also was Lola's secret. Dujarier left her some money and she set out for a tour of Germany. The natural end of her adventure was treading on her heels; women cannot wait like Columbus for seven years for a fleet. She was now twenty-seven years old, and getting frightened. Whatever had passed between her and Liszt, her plunge into the incident of Dujarier shows that she was losing momentum, flying nearer the ground. If luck, the adventurers' fuel, without a trace of which she had proceeded hitherto, held off much longer, she would be forced down into that condition of professional courtesan, less interesting except to callow boys than the quietest spinsterhood. In her worry she scribbled long zigzags over Germany, as Alexander did to the map of Asia Minor, but she was defeated everywhere, and sometimes disgraced. She had an episode with poor Henry LXXII, Prince of Reuss—complicated with stories of walking over flowerbeds, unpaid bills—in which she appears only ill-bred and bad-tempered. The danger to anyone who seeks only the happiness of humanity, prophet or woman-adventurer, is that of becoming a common pest: she had started out to give herself to genius and was turning into a vulgar whore. Her first wrinkles round the eyes, her failure, the nature of it above all, interworked to increase her worry, and themselves.

Now it is queer that this is the first instance we have had of such a turn—the premature death of an adventure by sheer lack of luck; and that this is the first woman on our list. So far as she has come in the storm alone, she has had nothing without deserving it, and only a fraction of what she deserved. But at last there is a sign of life in the dark. A hand comes out to meet her, to save her, not from tragedy, but from banality.

This was Louis I, King of Bavaria. He was now sixty-one years old, a fine grizzled man, saddened but not soured, with as many of his dreams, illusions, left as Lola started with. He had all the romanticisms, for he had survived Napoleon, patriotism, chivalry, democracy, yet on the whole he was the most civilized man in Europe, one of the few who have ever been its Kings. In his way he had come the same way as Lola, fighting for an unaccountably impossible beauty of life. Like hers his ideal was eminently real and Quixotic. He wanted only a kingdom to be happy and prosperous under a good rule, a time for the flourishing of arts, streets full of music, a ham hanging in the chimney of every peasant's shack. At the moment when Lola was realizing that she must soon reconcile herself to become coarse and melancholy, a mere Cora Pearl, Louis had decided to take a heavenly second-best; to surrender his bankrupt mirage to be liquidated by that eternal legatee of lost hopes, the Church; to put up with priests instead of troubadours, bells instead of fairs, clericalism instead of universal goodwill. In fact the Ultramontane party, which was in battle with the new Europe everywhere from the Tagus to the Volga, had scored a victory in Bavaria. The eager troops of Christ, the Jesuits, poured in. Louis locked away Zeus and Odin who had had forty years of his worship with his old love-letters for the rats to eat.

At this moment the two tangents meet in intersection. Lola applied for an engagement at the Munich Court Theatre. The Director, a creature of the Congregations, refused: this vestigial remnant of Louis's Florentine plans had become a *patronage* with a mission to edify; which neither Lola nor her dancing could claim. She refused to take the refusal. As I have said, she had become rather vulgar and pushing. So she used the offices of a certain Count Rechberg, an aide-de-camp of the King, to get an audience with Louis himself. As so often happens in fateful meetings, it was granted unwillingly. "Am I obliged to see every strolling dancer?" he asked. "This one is well worth seeing," was the true answer.

While the King was grumpily hesitating, Lola pushed open the door of the antechamber; and with surprise and silence they saw each other for the first time. In such a glance between two who are fated to mix inextricably their lives there is, without being a Platonist, some sort of recognition, which enforces a sort of familiarity, and dispenses with the preliminary manœuvres. They began talking as if they were resuming a conversation; seeing how it was, the introducer effaced himself and left them alone. Lola had not to say anything; the King, who was nevertheless no ladies' man, entered at once into a long, half-puzzled praise of her beauty. She remained looking at him; when he half to himself expressed some complimentary doubt about her figure she uncoquettishly and quite simply unbuttoned her bodice and showed him her breast.

So began a queer and touching relationship that embellished the dull times. In Council, the King communicated to the astonished and scandalized ministers: "I know not how, I am bewitched." There does not seem any stage when they fenced; or played. Almost from the first day the King was Lear to her, Lola his Cordelia in prison, and they entered into an extraordinary partnership of ideas and mutual encouragements.

The King had refound his enthusiasms, now at last he had an ally; Lola threw off her vulgarity and fear, like a muddy travelling wrap and became a great lady. It is absurd to suppose as some obsessed English idealists have, that she was a mere Beatrice or Laura to him, a fanciful peg for sonnets, an excuse for an ecstatic and slightly vicious asceticism. She was his mistress. But she was also his daughter, most of all his ally and his saviour. There was no period of courtship. So there were no ticklish quarrels, makings-up and all the enervating ritual of lesser love-relationships. The time to kiss and clasp and they went into battle together. His battle, for his hopes and rights, which before this reinforcement of life he thought he had renounced.

So begins the "Lola Regime," one of the most curious and sympathetic experiments in government of the nineteenth century. One by one the pious works of reaction were demolished; the general censorship first, then the several leading strings of clerical tutorship which good Louis in his discouragement had permitted. Where had Lola learned her Liberalism? Probably nowhere; and the multitudinous stories of her Free-masonry (?), her mission from Palmerston, etc., are the usual continental slyness that theorizes all politics as a plot, like the old grandmother, whose unvarying comment on every catastrophe in the newspaper from earthquakes to aboriginal protection acts, was: "It is a gang." Or "Wheels within wheels." Her politics were nothing but Louis's dream, which she prepared to fight for with an energy, intelligence, and courage never before or since given to the impossibility. The very daring of this astonishing intrusion, suddenly sprung from nowhere, disconcerted the opponents; they were startled into the stupidity of offering her money. Metternich himself made the coarse blunder of offering her ten thousand dollars a year if she would quit Bavaria. She refused with uncommon calm.

But the enemy soon rallied. Bavaria was for the time a key-position of high-politics. Next door in Switzerland the war of the Sonderbund was in progress, a question in which political Catholicism was intensely interested, and as far as it can ever compromise itself on an earthly event, engaged to the hilt. The anti-reactionary forces of Europe, through their brawling, fierce leader Palmerston, had turned back all the interference of Metternich and the Ultramontanists on behalf of the insurgent Catholic cantons: except Bavaria, too far to see the truculent fist of England. No situation in a Hentzau romance equalled this of Lola alone and by her beauty alone (if you can disassociate it from her personality) standing with her little whip across the path of parties, Empires, the Church itself: recreating the old poetic Louis, in the most inconvenient corner of History. This and a thousand other spiteful allegories of the situation filled the clerico-monarchic press of Europe: Louis a crowned satyr, with a naked nymph and a flute, a "pup-dog, an ass with a crown tied to his tail," and a thousand other inflammatory burlesques... It was what we call propaganda; the propaganda against Lola and Louis fills large illustrated tomes for learned Germans, and under cover of their own policy of No Censorship appealed for their destruction to the people of Munich itself. Under the ink-storm Louis would have quailed; but Lola was beside him, inured to the hisses of mobs. She even taught him to enjoy it.

On the 15th December, 1846, a few weeks after their meeting, the King issued a Royal decree returning his schools to the non-religious, modern regime from which his discouragement had transferred it to the Christian Brothers. The blow was painful, in the most sensitive member. The enemy retorted by the Abel memorandum. This Abel was the chief tool of his party, and Minister of the Interior. He drew up a document such as few kings have had to read, except immediately before their abdication, protesting with the minimum of official politeness against the influence of "Señora Lola Montez" by name, setting forth that "Men like the Bishop of Augsburg daily shed bitter tears at what is passing under their eyes," enclosing copies of the most villainous of the attacks in the "good press" to prove the case propounded, setting forth that these feelings are "felt throughout Europe in the cabins of the poor and the palaces of the rich." Lola "compromises the very existence of royalty itself." His friendship is a "state of things that threatens to destroy the fair fame, power, respect, and future happiness of a beloved King."

And they took care to send a copy to their newspapers.

The Louis who was alone might have swallowed this. He had sunk very far. But if Marie Antoinette had been an eighth of a Queen as Lola played it, the Third Estate would have been strung up together the night of their Tennis Court oath and we should have been spared much history. Lola's retort was swift and sure, like an aimed bullet. Abel was given twenty-four hours to reconsider his attitude, then summarily dismissed from office and a Liberal, von Schenk, put in his stead. The whole cabinet, while debating nervously the next move, found it taken from them by a collective resignation issued by Lola in their name. Lola was raised to the peerage with the title of Countess of Landsfeld, and Baroness Rosenthal, and granted an annuity of twenty thousand crowns. The éclat of the action was not lost on liberal Europe. The London *Times* wrote a grave and approbatory leader on the victory; Bismarck and Bernsdorff and thousands of lesser voices approved her with enthusiasm. She was near becoming a world target for the largest hates and loves.

The principal fort of her enemies, after the loss of the Government entrenchment, was the University. Both students and professors were bitterly hostile to her and to the King's dream of a neo-Florentine principality which she superintended. Students can always be reckoned to take up, and with violence, the unpopular cause of the past generation; whether it is left or right, socialist or Tory, depends on contemporary history and not themselves. Here in Munich they were in full reaction from the pagan democracy of Louis's youth; Lola was the *symbolum antichristi*, and they persecuted her with boyish cruelty and slyness. When she appeared in public with her English bull-dog, some young corps-student would set out to provoke her to one of those sudden outbursts of temper which were her habit, and the most serious detriment to her popularity. In most of these encounters, the ragger came off worst. Baron Pechman had his ears boxed with such a swing that he stumbled to the ground; another had his cheek opened with a cut of her whip.

More serious was the grave perfidy of Professor Lassaulx, who organized an address, filled with the most discreet venom, to Councillor von Abel, the dismissed Minister, full of double-edged sympathy and congratulations. Lola struck back in her manner, instantaneous and painful, by dismissing Lassaulx. His students massed under his windows to cheer him. His house was in the same street as Lola's "fairy Palace," and they moved on to complete the demonstration with shouts of *"Pereats Lola."* At once the servants disappeared from sight, the curtain of the bay-window was drawn and the mistress of Munich showed herself to the mob, with a glass of champagne in her hand, which she drank in little sips, toasting them contemptuously. Stones were thrown. The leaders attempted to organize the infuriated youngsters sufficiently to rush the front door. Lola watched the fierce and awkward evolutions of the crowd, munching chocolates from a box on the window-table at her side. The King himself mixed incognito in the outskirts of the crowd to admire his lion-tamer in her new act; finally he tired of it and ordered out the mounted police, who cleared the street. Later on in the evening another outbreak occurred, which ended only after a cavalry charge with drawn sabres.

Lola described the incident summarily in a letter to the London *Times:*

"I may mention as one instance that last week a Jesuit professor of Philosophy at the University here, by the name of Lassaulx, was removed from his professorship, upon which the clericals paid and brought a mob to break the windows of my palace and also to attack the palace; but thanks to the better feeling of the other party, and the devotedness of the soldiers to his Majesty, and his authority, all this failed."

She followed this up by reorganizing the University, by removing the censorship on the books allowed to be sold to students, by pressing on the King's architectural plans for the recreation of Munich. This was the hey-day of the couple's power and imagination; Munich began to be a world centre.

Politically it had so changed sides that when the Sonderbund was crushed in Switzerland (November, 1847), the refugee Jesuits were turned back at the frontier of Bavaria. The English *Punch* published a cartoon, as this suggestion for a statue of Bavaria: Lola holding a banner inscribed "Freedom and the Cachuca."

Now '48 is in sight, the glorious year in which Europe martyred itself for the gospel of the ballot. The poets manned the barricades for the politicians; in the taste of the war to end war, this was the revolution for the New Jerusalem. Everything was simple in those days; all Kings were bad, all republicans noble. The two-seated canoe of state of Lola and the King approached these rapids unsteadily. Her war with the students had taken a new turn. At one of her dances some students of the Pfalz Corps, or Fraternity, appeared wearing their distinctive caps. At two o'clock in the morning Lola snatched one of these and put it on; next morning the Fraternity expelled the owner and his friends. These formed a new corps, endowed at once by the King with all the privileges of antiquity, and named Alemannia. It became from the first the loyal bodyguard of Lola, standing guard on her house, invited to all her parties. On the 31st January, 1848, the other corps, Franconia, Bavaria, Isar, Suabia, turned out in force, reinforced by thousands of revolutionaries, and hundreds of seminarists. By some process of digestion all these mutually hostile elements fused on the slogan of "Death to Lola," and proceeded to her quarters. The Alemannen, hopelessly outnumbered, were manhandled and cleared out of the way. All except four, Counts Hirschberg, Peisner and Laibinger, and a Lieutenant Nussbaum, afterwards dismissed from the Army because of his share in the affair. These and Lola sallied into the street to meet the ugly mob. By some prodigy, the youngsters beat a way far into the crowd for her; while she (no doubt a little shrilly—every exploit has its imperfections) shouted insults and threats and made play with her whip. At last there were no footlights between her and her enemy, and for a beginning it was not she who was defeated.

When she was tired of lifting the whip, and when her guard had disappeared, torn half to pieces, she retreated, head high, keeping them at a distance, as far as the door of the Church of the Theatines, where the forgiving priest took the magnificent little Calvinist inside and no doubt saved her life. It is one of the few instances in history of anyone, man or woman, attacking an angry crowd and keeping her life and limb.

The old King began to waver. First he decreed that the University should be shut, then suspended, then reopened in the space of a week. The enemy poured into this breach in his will, which even Lola could not close in time. Another demonstration, this time carefully avoiding Lola's palace, cut her off, and Louis, this new Lear, gave a new turn to the tragedy by abandoning his Cordelia. He had had enough; dreams, love, beauty, romance, he packed them all up with a trembling hand to pay for all that he now desired, Peace. The evening of this surrender he sent police to arrest Lola. A huge mob collected to see the end, which was worth a good deal. First she locked the door on young Nussbaum and his friends, who had gathered for the last desperate fight for her, so that they should not get hurt again. Then without allowing the overawed police to touch her, she made her way alone through the crowd, who parted in silence to let her pass. At the railway station she was joined by the three panting Alemannen, who had jumped out of the window. That night the crowd sacked and looted her palace. The King, for some strange self-torture, came to watch what he dared not prohibit. As he was surveying the wreckage, he was recognized, and a lout stunned him with his stick.

The end of this episode is wonderful. Apparently she asked for a last interview with the King. On the advice of his confessor she was told first to confide herself to a certain exorcist, one Justin Kerner, in a suburb of Munich, who says in his published correspondence: "Lola Montez arrived here the day before yesterday, accompanied by three Alemannen. It is vexatious that the King should have sent her to me, but they have told him she is possessed. Before treating her with magic and magnetism, I am trying the hunger cure. I allow her only thirteen drops of raspberry water and the quarter of a wafer."

In another letter: "Lola has grown astonishingly thin. My son Theodore has mesmerized her and I let her drink ass's milk."

A few days after this she is in Switzerland, where in gratitude they allowed her to stay. The three followers stayed some time with her; then dropped off, on their own business, never, whatever it was, to compare with the days when they stood by Lola.

As for the King, he had committed the blasphemy which cannot be pardoned, either in Heaven or on earth. I do not mean the mere treachery towards the woman he loved, towards loyalty and friendship. Thank Heaven, a man may do that and yet not be lost. But he had traded his life-purpose, his own meaning, against peace and safety, an illicit transaction which offends against the laws of existence themselves. In six weeks, the average time that lies between sentence and execution, he was hustled into an ignominious abdication and expelled from the capital.

Lola has now finished. The remainder of her action has only the vile interest of a study in vivisection; her movements are those of a flayed animal in a cage. One by one she shakes at every locked opening; travel, hermitage, religion, even marriage. In 1849 she got a poor booby of a Guardsman to take her to the registry office. Immediately afterwards the man's family had her arrested for bigamy, Lieutenant James being still alive, but the action was dropped. In 1851 she went to New York and danced there, with some success, more of curiosity than esteem. From there to New Orleans, where she caught a gold fever and went overland to California. That pretentious fellow, Russell, the English war-correspondent, saw her en route and relates: "Occasionally some distinguished passengers passed on the upward and downward tides of ruffianism and rascality that swept periodically through Cruces. Came one day Lola Montez in the full zenith of her evil fame, bound for California with a strange suite. A good-looking bold woman, with fine bad eyes and a determined bearing dressed in perfect male attire, with shirt collar turned down over a velvet lapelled coat, richly worked shirt front, black hat, French unmentionables, and natty polished boots with spurs. She carried in her hand a handsome riding whip... I was glad when the wretched woman rode off on the following morning."

Then there are stories of other marriages, other affairs, uncertain, unfastidious, ephemeral. There was an editor named Hull; a German hunter, Adler. Hands clutched for a moment through the bars, tugged despairingly and released. In 1854 she is living alone in a cabin in Grass Valley, at the foot of the Sierra Nevada, with a half-farm, half-menagerie of animals. A newspaper despatch describes: "On Tuesday last Lola Montez paid us a visit in a sleigh and a span of horses decorated with impromptu cow-bells. She flashed like a meteor through the snowflakes and wanton snowballs, and disappeared in the direction of Grass Valley."

Next she is in Australia, in Ballarat, again looking for gold, but finding the Australian. A series of lamentable rows, put on her by the indiscreet and unrivalled vulgarity of British colonies, where the subtle social civilization of the mother country has gone sour, finally chased her out like a mangled hare, back to her starting point, Ireland, and the Calvinist religion. It is a curious secret in "repentance" that those who have been conquered by the matter of fact flee to the suave romanticism, the ennobling melancholy of Catholicism; but those like Lola, who are sick of love, adventure, life, turn Puritan. Where, with her own remark written in her spiritual journal, alongside details of pious lecturing, growing poverty, chapel going and prayers, we leave her.

"But now all is wonderfully changed in my heart. What I loved before, now I hate." In 1861, she died, forty-three years old.

VI.

Cagliostro (and Seraphina)

THE CASE OF A double adventure—Lola with Casanova, or Alexander with some honey-colored chieftainess, instead of that little Persian gazelle Roxana—is an inevitable conjecture, now we have come so far. Would not the natural duad, man and wife, survive in the life of risk longer and healthier than any mere monad of adventure, if male, doomed to fail of a surfeit of his luck, if woman, to peter out from inanition of hers? In any case, one would look for important and amusing modifications of the laws (or rather dynamical habits) that seem to govern adventure. These are likely to be harmonic rather than logical, for life abominates logic; and this complication is heightened by the rareness of the case, almost necessarily confined to a particular class of adventure. For indeed what could Alexander have done with a partner, or Columbus; or Casanova for that matter, or Lola? Their isolation was not a flaw, but the very order of the architecture of what they did, and suffered; the destruction of which would have turned all into that most insipid of fairy-tales, the novelette. For our duad chord, we must look among adventurers whose activity was a business. That is, we must steer between the opposing dullnesses of swindling and trade—I can hardly think of anyone but Cagliostro and his Seraphina, the last colors in the sunset of Old Europe.

The man's real name was Giuseppe Balsamo. We are used to the habit of change of name, almost as regular in adventurers as in the three other professions that regularly use it, the monastery, the stage,

and the streets. We know its almost ceremonial reason: the symbol-
ical abjuration of ties, tasks, duties, those of family preparatory to
those of society; its most general motive: ambition in its plainest
symptoms, even to the poetry of snobbery. His father was a small
store-keeper in Palermo; the date 1743. This Giuseppe, for short
Beppo, grew into a stout, blunt-faced gutter-hero, thievish, daring,
calm, the bug-bear of all the house-wives and milk-sops of the neigh-
bourhood. He cut washing lines, incited dog-fights, bullied the timid
urchins and led the bold ones to expeditions against street vendors'
carts, and added as much confusion as he could to the labyrinthine
noise of the hot old city, where at any moment of the day or night
there is a quarrel or a bargain being made. At the age of twelve he
was sent to the seminary of St. Roch to learn his letters, was beaten
industriously by the teachers and the porter, and ran away. His father
was dead. His mother's brother got him admitted to the Monastery
of the Benfratelli—the entrance to the only career for a cleverish boy
of his class. Here, after a time, he was sent to work for the apothecary
of the establishment; to clean phials, weigh herbs, tend the alembics
and sweep the floor, as well as learn the elements of the most sensual
and exciting of sciences, Chemistry. Even in its modern austerity, a
chemical laboratory is the most fascinating place in the world to
those lucky enough to possess strong curiosity and sense of smell. In
the eighteenth-century Sicilian monastery, where every bottle looked
like a toy and contained a secret, where the materia medica was the
Arabian Nights, and every piece of apparatus uncanny folk-lore,
Beppo's faculties caught alight. He conceived the idea of magic. He
learned so easily and well that his master took a fancy to him, and
the queue of beggarly out-patients often had to wait for their potions
while the two were lost together in speculatory discussion and operations, in the dark, aromatic crypt. As a spiritual antidote to this
exaggeration, the brothers gave Beppo the task of reading to them at
mealtime. The book preferred was some interminable martyrology—
another potent irritant to his imagination, already alert with desire
to commerce with the supernatural. But one day in Lent these stories
of devil-worsting bishops, lion-taming virgins, fire-proof fakirs and

invulnerable confessors palled on him. Or his nature, which pushed him to practical jokes, suddenly saw the humor of the unkempt solemnity with which the brethren ate their soup; and he began to substitute as he read the names of the most notorious whores of Palermo for the holy ones in his book. For this he was beaten with thongs and then chased from the community.

He must have known more than he should to play this jackanapes trick; no doubt there must be a lost story of un-monastic escapades and encounters before the definite expulsion. It was not then as a lamb that he plunged into the "loose life" which his only official biographer, the Grand Inquisitor of Rome, now sets down. His next calling was that of a painter; which to him, to his city, and to his country included a shabby, dabbling admixture of marble-counterfeiter, distemperer, sign-writer with the making of those canvas storms at sea, in the distance Vesuvius in eruption, whose manufacture (along with that of plaster casts of sentimental statuary) is the largest artistic product of Italy to this day.

But art was overcrowded, even then. Beppo was forced, or chose, to eke out commissions with another local industry, inseparable as chaperonage from all societies where there is strict seclusion of women, that is, pandering. One of his clients was his pretty cousin's Romeo, whose letters he passed, and whose presents he intercepted. With admirable vitality, he added again to this sort of thing some amount of bespoke forgery; that is, he put his services and his pen at the command of persons in difficulties about a signature. It has been dug up that on one occasion he forged a whole will for the benefit of a religious community, and a pass out for a monk in the name of his Superior in Rome.

With these mean and clever resources he earned enough to eat well. All his life he had an enormous appetite for food, as common an accompaniment of great nervous force as its opposite. The superfluity he worked off in a violent bullying life; he became very muscular, and picked quarrels with sailors, beat the night-watchmen, established his reputation as a ward-terror. All these essays are comically out of proportion, and superficially out of relation to the particular splendour of the destiny before him. Half a hooligan, half a crook: the two commonest and least interesting of human qualities, this is all his peevish biographers, Carlyle and the Inquisitor, make of him who was to become Cagliostro. Deduce that there must have been something that escaped their survey from his last scene in Palermo. This "obnoxious lout" appears abruptly to have captured the confidence of a goldsmith called Marano, and engaged him on a treasure hunt, in a coast cave, at midnight. In his nagging, prosecuting style, Carlyle presents this as an absurd swindle, an affair (like most events in history to him) of knave and dupe, with an easy laugh in it for Scotch canniness. But we, the jury, must notice that there are facts that do not fit into this view, any more than the Inquisition's Beppo fits into the Cagliostro who has less one-sided chronicles to attest him. There is magic in this affair, not only talk of dowsing, forked hazel rods and the rest, but circles in the moonlight, and burning earth, and the invocation of devils, quite out of character with the loutish Beppo we are told to see. Only in the bare fact that, following a quarrel with the goldsmith, Beppo fled from Palermo, are we satisfied to acquiesce.

His own story of the years that followed must be left to its proper context, the personality Seraphina helped or goaded him to compose. Actually he must have gone East, to that old right wing of the Roman Empire to which all adventurous Italians (as distinguished from honest) still are drawn, to Minor and Hither Asia. Cairo, Bagdad, Smyrna, Aleppo, even Constantinople, may have received him, and fed him in return for his yarns, his daubing, his pandering or his cheating. Like his innumerable compatriots who still drift through all the cities within a week of Suez, he would find himself at home anywhere but out of a crowd. He emerges for certain in Rome, lodging at the Sign of the Sun, poor, and engaged in a messy little business (but which few consider immoral, especially not Carlyle), of selling bad art to the middle class, in species—touched up pen-and-ink drawings of the usual monuments. A precursor of the picture postcard trade.

In this shapeless state, he met his Seraphina, whose real or socially imposed name was Lorenza Feliciani. She was the daughter of a small tradesman, a girdle-maker or glover, and a handsome girl, with, like most others, romantic ideas. Unlike most others, she was prepared to put them into action. In fact she was a born adventuress, and, if there were more recorded about her and her share in the enormous life of her husband, very likely entitled to be called one of the greatest there have ever been. Nevertheless it is true that her own will is so invisible for a long interval or rather separately inaudible in the chord of adventure in which they were both merged, her share so apparently passive, that she is usually forgotten by the writers whom the theme tempts, or, still worse, exhibited as a brave poor thing. The advantage of sentimentality is its short cut through psychology. Nothing in the facts of the case can give us another version of the Griselda legend. Instead, it is probable (though there is not much more than the significant chronology to support me) that the metamorphosis of this obese caterpillar, Beppo Balsamo, into the gorgeous moth, Count Alexander of Cagliostro, Pupil Adored of the sage Althotas, Foster Child of the Scherif of Mecca, putative son of the last King of Trebizond, named Ilso Acharat, and the Unfortunate Child of Nature, Grandmaster Supreme of the Egyptian Free-Masonry of High Science, Grand Cophta of Europe and Asia, was due, effectively, to little Lorenza, his mystical Seraphina. That is, the impetus, the welding of the dual will came, as it came in that other coupling of Lola and Louis, from the female side. Before the joint adventure existed that, single and successful, of Lorenza: the turning of a needy lying lout into—what his nature was capable of becoming.

This, for short, was a charlatan. The greatest charlatan the world has ever possessed. Or suffered. Which does not matter to this enquiry.

The tonic note of her adventure was thus his personality, the education of his will, if the respectable term may be borrowed for a moment. In this she conformed to the tendency which we made out from the case of Lola Montez, that the type adventure of woman is Man. In his ungainliness she perceived dignity, in his loutishness, an undeveloped quality of weight. In his untiring, eager torrent of lies, boasts, about himself and his travels, she detected, not only an un-commonplace imagination, but that rare glint of auto-suggestion, self-belief, which is the radium of imaginative life. Dividing this stage of her adventure into the exploration of Beppo and the invention of Cagliostro, in the first she penetrated the mud-flats and mean deserts of what he was, far into the tropical hinterland of what he might become. This talker might become convincing, because he was half-convinced himself. Even for a little Roman stay-maker this insight into the man she loved was not specially remarkable, though audacious. Probably some sort of subconscious quasi-economic appraisement is inherent in the falling in love of all women. But what was extremely rare, in fact original, was the constructive effort with which she gave this intuitive exploration practical value. The education of a personality (as distinguished from that merely mental and physical), though it has had many illustrious exponents—the majority, it is true, no less illustrious bunglers—is still as strictly empirical as dowsing, or mediumship, or political economy.

Learning, which she certainly did not possess, would not have helped her out. In her walks with him through the luminous squares and endless streets of her Rome, sitting on the steps of the Piazza de Spagna where the swallows fly, or on the lip of Baroque fountains, in the vortex of the pilgrim tides of half the world, she must have studied her material and invented her practice. Which for months while they were betrothed, she must have used in an audacious campaign on the citadels and palisades of his essentially barbarous spirit.

Balsamo was evil-tempered, touchy; he must have resisted like a bull-dog the ablation of those vices, those virtues which she decided to drag away out of him; traits like weeds choking the consistent outline of Cagliostro. She had to cure him of his low Sicilian penny-fever; his mongrel habit in time of danger to snap and yelp; his cringe and his strut, both out of place in good society; both his fear and his hatred of the police—and to substitute in their place an unchallengeable indifference. To do all these things was delicate, for the balance of his confidence in himself must not be touched with a feather, or all was lost, both lover and venture. Higher and easier was the twin operation of fortifying what she left; out of his lying to make a visionary; to select a coherent story from his luxuriant brag, and confine him to it; to deflect his bent for pandering, and make him specialize in the trade of commodities, more spiritual and also more costly than Eve's flesh; to extract a latent talent for stage management, such as he showed with the Sicilian goldsmith; to collate the colored scraps of legend and superstition his rag-bag mind was stuffed with; to deepen his fear of devils, and his hopes of supernatural powers and finally to believe in them all herself, and even in him.

In short, she had luck and judgment, but no morals. So she made a personality out of a nonentity, and unravelled the darkest problem in human dynamics, constructing out of a tangle of greedy contradictions a single, sharp will, that could discharge itself upon the world like a bullet, instead of a cartridge of small shot. Whatever her share of the adventure, she was the maker of the adventurer: an operation rarer and more dangerous than any magic Cagliostro ever knew.

The direction of this new force, liberated by the love, vanity, and inspiration of a sharp little shop-assistant, was through the spirit of the times to a personal power that both were content to wish as large as possible, without any limitation or detailed idea. This spirit, since it was the Age of Reason, was love of Mystery. For it cannot be disguised that the prime effect of knowledge of the universe in which we are shipwrecked is a feeling of despair and disgust, often developing into an energetic desire to escape out of reality altogether. The age of Voltaire is also the age of fairy tales; the vast *Cabinet des Fées*, some volumes of which Marie Antoinette took into her cell to console her, it is said, stood alongside the Encyclopédie. Alice's Adventures in Wonderland belongs to the same age and within seven years of the same date as the Origin of Species. Indeed the beginning of all folk-lore, should be postdated to the time when primitive man had lost his brightest illusions. This impression of disgust, and this impulse to escape were naturally very strong in the eighteenth century, which had come to a singularly lucid view of the truth of the laws that govern our existence, the nature of mankind, its passions and instincts, its societies, customs, and possibilities, its scope and cosmical setting and the probable length and breadth of its destinies. This escape, since from Truth, can only be into Illusion, the sublime comfort and refuge of that pragmatic fiction we have already praised. There is the usual human poverty of its possible varieties. The shortest way out of Manchester is notoriously a bottle of Gordon's gin; out of any business man's life there is the mirage of Paris; out of Paris, or mediocrity of talent and imagination, there are all the drugs, from subtle, all-conquering opium to cheating, cozening cocaine. There is religion, of course, and music, and gambling: these are the major euphorias. But the queerest and oldest is the side-path of Magic, where this couple chose to establish themselves, priests, touts, at your choice; a sort of emigration agency for Prospero's Island for those wearied of any too solid Dukedom of Milan. At its deepest, this Magic is concerned with the creative powers of the will; at lowest it is but a barbarous rationalism, the first of all our attempts to force the heavens to be reasonable. Whether there is any truth in this desperate sortie from truth is no matter; it is important in this story to remember that the operations of Cagliostro were entirely dependent on that focussing of the will, that is called belief, not only in the followers, but most of all in the leader himself. There is a smart ignorance that explains men like Cagliostro with the one word "hypocrite," or "cheat," a thesis which neither history nor even rudimentary psychology will swallow. The requirements of this adventure, of will and belief, they had chosen, were an absolutely single will and at any rate a workable and temporary conviction; without a measure of both they could not have sold a gold-brick to an agricultural laborer. Their public was educated, often subtle, fantastic, but as critical as the paying audience at the first night of an opera. Even in the political branch, or spellbinding, the magician must believe in himself, if it is only as long as he is spouting.

But will and belief before they are marketable demand a vehicle; that is, a personality. The substance of a personality is its past. Lorenza—not yet Seraphina—set herself to adapt out of the rich but incoherent yarns of her lover a *ne varietur* edition of his beginnings. As finally adopted this made a remarkable story. Palermo events were cut out, as she had cut out his Palermo character. He was, they agreed to believe, the unlucky son of the last monarch of Trebizond, disinherited and exiled by the ruin of that distant kingdom. In his flight he fell in with bandits, who sold him in the slave market of Mecca. Whose noble Scherif bought him, and reared him in Cabalistic wisdom. But when he grew, neither the magnanimity nor the favor of the Scherif could keep his ambitions and mission sedentary, so that at last the Mage let him go, bestowing on him the romantic and pitying title of Unfortunate Child of Nature. In his travels he met a sect of whirling Dervishes, also an Osirian fraternity, and a Domdaniel of Alchemists, all of whom received him with honor, initiated him into their mysteries and were reluctantly forced to let him go on his insatiable wandering. At Damascus he found the mahatma of all arcanic wisdoms, the sage Althotas, with whom he embarked for Malta, where the secret remnant of the Gnostic Knights possessed a subterranean laboratory. Here Althotas and he did great works in spiritual chemistry, in every work of the transforming and transmuting irreducibles which is proper to the imagination. They hinted he was obliged to kill Althotas.

As for Lorenza, she contented herself with the name of Seraphina, mystery, and suggestion. She was left to the imagination, which she helped only with such hints as a foreign cut in her dressing, and a foreign accent in every language.

With this complete equipment of personality, will, and belief, the adventure might begin. But first there was an accident. The couple had taken up their lodging in her parents' house. Cagliostro had never been so comfortable. He knew more of the world than Seraphina and assured her that it was folly to go further. With a basis of three good meals daily, and a feather bed, he felt that his talents had their best chance of development, here in Rome. All that they had planned might well be executed without stirring from the base.

Seraphina was at a loss. Fate was obliged to lend her hand; or her foot. For when all seemed spoiled, and the pair seemingly bound to waste their impetus in some hugger-muggery of fortune-telling, palm-reading, horoscoping in this back street, they were kicked out by the father, who came to a decision that he liked neither the face, the stories, nor the pretensions of his son-in-law. So with a sulkiness that unintentionally put the last touch to his make-up, Count Alexander Cagliostro put on his Prussian Colonel's uniform, to buy which, practically new, his mysterious Seraphina had spent a twelfth of her savings, and accompanied by a hooded velvet figure, took the coach for Milan.

We have no precise knowledge of their adventures for the next years. Even a bald account would have been better reading than all the poems of the time. Only the statement of the Inquisition-biographer who sets down instead a descriptive catalogue of their dupes—official synonym for the converts of a heretic. This contains a full set of personages for an historical drama: Italian Counts, French Envoys, Spanish Marquises, Dukes and masked ladies of fashion. The couple appear at Venice, Milan, Marseilles, Madrid, Cadiz, Lisbon, and Brussels. They travelled in a japanned black coach, with sober heraldry in gold on the doors, with six armed attendants in dark livery, and a great deal of luggage.

Everywhere they stopped they had the same introductory technique, which was probably that of their poor and doubtful beginning. The romantic coach would draw up at the best Inn of the city. They ordered their meal in a private room, asking for strange dishes in a grave voice and a strong yet indefinable foreign accent. At first they must then have staged some little comedy of appearances at the window by Seraphina, looking unutterably sad and sweet, or chance collisions on the stairs and long, impressive, old-fashioned apologies by the Count, to attract the right curiosity. But as soon as they had servants, to be bribed and pumped, the introductions must have been much easier.

The profession of magician, in which our wandering couple were thus rising to inaccessible heights, is one of the most perilous and arduous specializations of the imagination. On the one hand there is the hostility of God and the police to be guarded against; on the other it is as difficult as music, as deep as poetry, as ingenious as stage-craft, as nervous as the manufacture of high explosives, and as delicate as the trade in narcotics. Technically in its upper atmospheres where Cagliostro and Seraphina flew, it is social. For it aims to satisfy the deepest wishes of the human heart, which are rarely individual; and its tools are secret societies. The fear of death, crypto-sexual longings for supernatural terrors and beauties and all the rest of the complex motive that sends men to Mahomet, Beethoven, or Cagliostro, cannot be satisfied adequately except by a church, an orchestra, or a freemasonry. In occultism this apparatus must be secret, for it is not a salvation, but an escape; an escape from the prison of reality, into another world, without birth or death, outside the organic flux, with another rhythm than the eternal Out and In, conception and corruption, eating and excretion. The inscription over the little side door, where Cagliostro dangled the key is

OSER
VOULOIR
SE TAIRE.*

So a better idea of the skeleton of their doings, while the couple were posting over Europe, is not at all a plotless succession of coups, like Gil Blas, or Eulenspiegel, but in the venerable records of missionaries, propagating a faith and building a church. Their work was not the making of a black-list, but a cult. Their captures were converts, to be preserved, not dupes to be fled from, disciples to be put on the registers of the initiated members of the Egyptian Freemasonry of High Science. President: a great Unknown, living in the unknown recesses of the mountains of the moon. Grand Cophta for Europe and Asia: Count Alexander Cagliostro; Grand Mistress: the disincarcerated Seraphina.

This reticulated organism that spread its threads before it was done over a thousand miles of Europe did not itself, in the magical way, spring full grown out of the night. The first contacts between

* DARE, WILL, KEEP SILENCE.

the couple and their adepts, those meetings in close-shuttered sitting rooms in the inns of the route, must have been rather masterpieces of suggestion and allusion than definite propaganda for the huge machine of which not a cogwheel yet existed. The curious inquirer who paid for the first dinner of the adventure must have been the beneficiary of a performance, of unusual artistic value; some virtuosic confidence trick worked with only the talk of the man, and the silence of Seraphina, as distinct from the elaborate later exercise of the Egyptian Rite as lyric from dramatic. Still, even without apparatus, the couple must have traded substantially the same commodity: mystery, and the invisible. That is, spiritual romance.

From this artistically penurious embryo, their adventure developed and branched rapidly. In their second town they were able to offer a materialization of the devil. In their third a range of those transformations which are the first object of necromancy, hemp into silk, pearls out of pebbles, roses out of powder. They had a crystal ball, and could produce in it the little iridescent scenes, bed-room interiors, inexplicable nostalgic landscapes, concentrated perspectives where figures of the past and future walk out and in that are the recompense of long staring. Cagliostro could for a consideration show you a mandragore, those little earthly creatures who cry at night out of the earth at the foot of trees, and are born of the "voluptuous and ambiguous tears" of a hanged man. He had like Descartes in the legend a satin lined chest with him that contained a sylph six inches high, of the most perfect beauty and life. He reproduced the secret of Count Kueffstein, who knew how to fabricate homunculi by rare distillation and fermentations, who answered questions, and lived in bottles, carefully sealed because they were quarrelsome.

But all these curiosities were represented as preliminaries, instalments of incommensurably greater mysteries he had in store. He showed them as a travelling circus puts a juggler and a clown on the platform in front of the ticket office, to advertise the main show inside. Those who wished to go further were set on the first initiations of his Egyptian Freemasonry, and as it grew in his mind and in numbers, promoted through successive grades. The only details that remain of this organization are unfortunately mutilated and de-formed. They give no fuller idea of the reality than a hostile detective could of the secret performance of a new opera, if he had only heard the chatter of scene-shifters. The music is not there, in these malig-nant accounts in the Inquisition records which is all we possess, nor the plot, nor even the glitter.

"The men elevated to the rank of Master take the names of early prophets; the women those of Sibyls.

"The Grand Mistress Seraphina blows on the faces of the female initiates, all along from brow to chin, and says: 'I give you this breath to germinate and become alive in your heart the spirit of truth, which we possess by the names of Helios, Mene, Tetragrammaton.'

"The recipient is led by a dark path into an immense hall, the ceiling, the walls, the floor of which are covered by a black cloth, embroidered with serpents. Three sepulchre lights glimmer there showing from time to time certain wrecks of humanity suspended by funereal cloths. A heap of skeletons makes an altar. On both sides of it are piled books. Some of these contain threats against the per-jured. Others contain accounts of the working of the invisible re-venging spirit. Eight hours pass. Then phantoms slowly cross the hall and sink, without noise of trapdoors.

"The novice spends twenty-four hours here in the midst of silence. A strict fast has already weakened his thinking faculties. Liquors with which he is provided wear out his resolution and make him sleepy.

"Three cups are at his feet. At last three men appear. These put a pale-colored ribbon round his forehead dipped in blood and covered with silvery characters, some of them Christian. Copper amulets, among them a crucifix of copper, are tied round his neck. He is stripped naked; signs are traced on his body with blood. In this state of humiliation five phantoms stride towards him, armed with swords and dripping with blood. They spread a carpet on the floor to kneel on. The pyre is lit. In the smoke is seen a gigantic transparent figure who repeats the terms of the oath, etc."

The stuff, as it is, is probably no worse than the current hocus-pocus of any secret society in the world. But in these vestigial, mangled remains of what was, quite likely, part pasteboard when new, it is vain to look for the most faded fragment of the high excitement it once stirred in souls that were neither simple nor trivial. It is a charred leaf of a score written in a mode and for instruments that are irremediably lost.

However there is something else to be found in rummaging this junk: a clue to the hidden progress of their adventure. For this rigmarole is a religious, not a magical rite. Its purpose, that is to say, is obviously the same as that of all Mysteries, an initiation into a method of gaining immortality for the soul. The couple have been turned clean off their first course, by the gulf tide of the human mind, that rises in the depths of its profound constitution—the fear of death. Instead of their first offer, an escape from the cosmos, they have come down to offer merely escape from the grave. Their magic peep-show has turned into a religious circus. Instead of sylphs, they trade in ghosts. Instead of an anodyne against disgust of human life, an elixir for prolonging it *in saecula saeculorum*.

Following the glistening japanned coach of their destiny to and fro on the trunk roads of Europe there are other similar changes of horses to be observed. The Unfortunate Child of Nature progresses if not in the science of the supernatural, in the science of men. He has discovered that drugs against life are infinitely more desired even than drugs against death, and he supplies them. He is as flexible as Casanova to the hints of his destiny. When he finds that Seraphina's body pleases even more than her aura, he was willing, says the Inquisitor, to supply even that. Seraphina too. And with impetus he descends (since the road leads downwards) to the vulgar branches of the black art, quite deserting its subtilties. He makes love-philtres, he has the secret of turning copper into gold. He asks his Ariel no longer for aerial music, but for cures for the gout. The noble and refined despairs that came to him turned out in the end to be only desires, and common desires, for health, for women, for survival, and above all for money. And it is curious to see how the pharmacopoeia of tricks of Cagliostro shrinks, as he grows in wisdom, to the single chapter of alchemy, the single nostrum for the single elemental desire of man, Gold. The difficult therapeutics of *Weltschmerz* can be resolved, in his experience, into prescriptions for unrequited love, unsatisfactory health, unappeased fear of death: all these, with scientific economy, in turn superfluous if he can only teach the secret of quick and easy riches. So following the well-beaten road, he turned from magic to doctoring, from doctoring to psychology.

Seraphina his companion pursued her private parallel to knowledge, by his side. She learnt with irritation that all men want mystery in woman; but more than mystery, poetry; more than poetry, love; more than love, the urgent satisfaction of desire. After desire, comes satiety; then use, the use to which Cagliostro put her—to get him money, which brought her out after an uncomfortable excursion to the summit of his own discovery.

Come together to this much more venerable than Egypt's science of the human heart, their joint course leaves the mists and proceeds for a time in strict prose. They became a business partnership; in the immortality, love-philtering and alchemist trade, that had its regular booms and depressions. Very likely it is true that Cagliostro was willing to oblige the widespread demand for a dependable and quick poison, often needed in the tangled affairs of great families such as formed the most esteemed part of his clientèle: to simplify a succession, or solve a domestic estrangement. It was not for this, in the age of La Voisin and the Marquise de Brinvilliers, that his troubles with the high police of the whole continent progressively increased, nor because of the complaints of those dissatisfied with his expensive recipes for making gold cheaply. Alchemy like Astrology breeds no sceptics. It was the religious and political penumbra of his doings that fascinated Society's bull-dogs and foxes; the infringement of the Christian monopoly in his Egyptian Lodges, the odd twigs of democratic doctrine this eclectic jack-daw had built into his ritual.

Cagliostro himself clearly saw how things stood, and desired to excise the cause by abandoning, or at any rate reducing what displeased his persecutors, the Egyptian Scientific branch, and confining himself to the more paying pursuit of practical sorcery. But

Seraphina had not come out for mere gain. With true womanly idealism, she loved the things that money can buy; especially the meals
(she shared Cagliostro's enthusiastic appetite), the dresses, the com-
forts, but despised and misunderstood the materialism of earning it.
She assisted him in his imaginative chemistry against her will; except
perhaps in the matter of love potions; and never ceased to nag him
for his neglect of the pure though less profitable supernatural.

So their unitary will showed signs of disintegration. Cagliostro
turned his head irritably towards his national and hereditary ambition; the status of a retired millionaire. Seraphina gazed constantly
towards power and rank; some joint Papacy of a vast underground
religion, where in the becoming majesty of the robes he had invented
for her, she would share in an Empire over the minds of all the romantics in Europe, shake governments, shape lives, receive homages,
in the combined principles of hope and a little blackmail.

Restated constructively, the end of the adventure already drags the
course of the man; he is in love with satiety. But she is in love with
adventure. Her pitch is higher.

This is the moment of the Palermo catastrophe. Every day
Cagliostro grew more sullen. Frequent quarrels were heard; questions
of money to those that listened; underneath, the profound discord of
their projects. The heavier prevailed. They travelled to Palermo,
where Cagliostro wished to round off his fortune and retire. We have
seen what happened to Mahomet, when he too tried to step off his
adventure in full motion, the merciless recoil of the past that shot
him forward with accelerated velocity and higher trajectory than
ever. So now with Cagliostro. His invented past had obliterated the
real in himself, but not in his enemies, who were waiting for him
with a vengeance matured to over-proof by the long wait. He was
recognized and clapped into jail for forgery (in the matter of the
monastery will) and fraud, or sorcery (in that of the goldsmith).

Seraphina saved him with the greatest devotion and difficulty.
There was a Lodge of Egyptian High Science in Palermo. Its president, or Cophta, was the son of a great Sicilian noble.

Seraphina knew how to settle the doubts that had come to this personage, from the revelation of Cagliostro's real name and history; and not only aroused his interest in the prisoner (who stood in some danger of a capital sentence) but his fanatical zeal. To such an extent that failing in peaceful manœuvrings to get the case stopped, the adept came into the court with his followers, seized hold of the prosecuting advocate and beat half the life out of him, until he agreed to abandon his brief. The judges themselves, never eager about the case after they learned what powerful friends now stood behind Cagliostro, consented readily to have seen nothing and forgotten everything, and our Count was set free.

For a long way from this, the duad is again perfect; its interior forces composed. Consequently this is the period of their magnificence. The ritual gateway of the Invisible Kingdom is enriched by the full resources of their joint imagination. The Egyptian Lodge creeps into every reserved part of the society of Europe. Its adepts grow to thousands, with a fine proportion of princes, millionaires and court ladies among them. Everyone capable of curiosity has heard Cagliostro's name, even if they do not hope anything from him. He and Seraphina and their coach became a sign of the times. Sometimes in honestly untidy antiquarian shops you can still come across one of the busts that were made and sold of him, in plaster or biscuit or porcelain, "a most portentous face of scoundrelism, dew-lapped, flat-nosed, greasy, full of greediness, sensuality, ox-like obstinacy, a forehead impudent, refusing to be ashamed, and then two eyes turned up seraphically languishing, a touch of quiz too, the most perfect quack face..." Of Seraphina there remains, as far as I know, nothing material on which to base even such a manifestly prejudiced portrait as this of Carlyle; but intuitively we know that her eyes must have been more intense than his, her pose less rhetorical, less explanatory.

The besetting disfigurement of his personality, thrift, has for now quite vanished. They spend money splendidly, are never caught making it, so that mere speculation on their fortune is a pleasure to all imaginations. In conscious or unconscious mimicry of their only serious rival in history, Apollonius of Tyana, Cagliostro gave a bonus to his personality, by giving the hospitals and the poor the preferential benefit of his science. The rich often failed in their first or second attempts to consult him; and he would visit in pageant the local infirmary as soon as he arrived in a city, dispensing to all the patients his Extract of Saturn, the most famous and genuine panacea of those times.

In 1780 he was in St. Petersburg, and had more persecution there, notably from the Court Physician who was a Scotsman, and reported to the Emperor that Cagliostro's "Spagiric Food," intended to increase the life span of its eaters to two centuries was "unfit for a dog." The German Ambassador entering into the cabal with a complaint against the Count about the unauthorized use of a Prussian uniform, he was expelled.

He lost more than he could afford on this spoilt voyage, and in Warsaw he botched an experiment in gold-making, was denounced by a rationalist courtier and again forwarded out of the country. But at Berlin, Frankfurt, Vienna, he recovered his balance. So that when they arrived in Strassburg in 1783, the couple had arrived at the very altitude of their adventure.

In that rich city, where the roofs are superstitious, and the pavements cobbled like the contradictory character of the Alsacians, the great man was that most distinguished ass of history, The Prince Cardinal de Rohan, of the blood royal of Brittany. This de Rohan was immense in every way, in his person, his wealth, his importance, his vanity, his good nature, and in the unexampled mess into which these magnitudes were destined to lead him, the court of France, the institution of monarchy, and derivatively the general history of Europe itself.

Into the centre of this mess, the affair of the Diamond Necklace, the first epicentre of the universal upheaval, the French Revolution, whose time was now near, the line of the duad adventure led as straight as the pull of gravitation. Rohan wrote to Cagliostro as soon as he arrived to say he wished to meet him. The Count replied, with his unvarying technique, "If Monseigneur the Cardinal is sick, let him come to me and I will cure him; if he is well, he has no need of me, I none of him." The Abbé Georgel, the Prince-Cardinal's memorialist, describes the further course of their relations:

"Admitted at length to Cagliostro's sanctuary, the Prince saw, according his own account to me, in the incommunicative man's physiognomy, something so dignified, so imposing, that he felt a religious awe, and spoke to him reverently. Their interview, which was brief, excited more keenly than ever his desire of further acquaintance. This he finally attained, and the empiric gained the Prince's entire confidence without appearing to court it, and mastery over his will. 'Your soul,' he said one day to the Prince, 'is worthy of mine; you deserve to be made participator of all my secrets.' This captivated the whole faculties of a man who always hunted after secrets of alchemy and botany. Their interviews became long and frequent. I remember once having learnt, by a sure way, that there were frequent, most expensive orgies in the Archiepiscopal Palace at Strassburg, where Tokay wine ran like water to regale Cagliostro and Seraphina…"

From another testimony of the same period, by one Meiners, professor at Göttingen, we have a fact of importance. "The darkness which this Cagliostro has spread over the sources of his necessarily immense income and outlay contributes even more than his munificence and miraculous cures to the notion that he is a divine extraordinary man, who has watched Nature in her deepest operations, and stolen the secret of Gold-Making from her…" Gold-making again… He had also fallen into what was, for him, bad company. This was one Jeanne de St. Remy de Valois, a poor relation of the royal house of France, a sharp, bird-voiced creature who lived just over the border that divides adventure from resolute swindling. She was as attached to de Rohan as Cagliostro himself, but without any other apparatus than her wits, her tiny body, and her knowledge of court scandals. One of the juiciest of these was the long standing bitterness between de Rohan, who had suffered quasi-exile in Strassburg through it, and Marie Antoinette, the Queen. Jeanne also knew about the Diamond Necklace, the treasure and the ruin of the court goldsmiths, Boehmer and Bassenge, who had locked up the value of a warship in it, hoping and hitherto failing to find a purchaser. It was known at court and to de Rohan that the Queen had been dreadfully tempted to acquire it. But the chronic bankruptcy of the royal exchequer, the King, or her own reasonableness, had dissuaded her from this. Jeanne had interrupted Cagliostro's mystical tête-à-tête with de Rohan with her plan, which the Grand Cophta, after much resentment and hesitation agreed to share in and assist. Cagliostro was anxious to get to his dessert; to make in one coup enough to transmute his supernatural adventure into the solid, material castle in Sicily we have spoken of before—the natural breaking-point of his single fate, from which hitherto the underpinning of Seraphina's has saved him.

There was to be a great deal to share: exactly, the value of the Diamond Necklace. The Queen wanted it. De Rohan, the only man in France who could afford it. But Jeanne had something better than this bare coincidence, for the bare truth is no bait for fools. She knew de Rohan, and she told him the Queen had fallen in love with him; deeply; to the extent that she longed for *him* to give her the Necklace.

There is a library of conjecture on the quality of Jeanne's authority for this request, the sum and point of her obvious lies. We know that she was a liar, but also that Marie Antoinette loved to exercise the rights of a pretty woman to be treacherous and imprudent; also that the Queen hated de Rohan very much. Our part of the story is that de Rohan fell into whoever's trap it was, and that Cagliostro brought up all his ghosts, sciences, predictions, and supernatural counsels to help him into it. The magnificent ass bought the Necklace, and sent it through Jeanne to the Queen; since when it has never authentically been heard of.

But human stupidity, the source these two experts were tapping, is as ultimately treacherous and incalculable as any other elemental force, wind, water, fire. Here, it betrayed them disastrously. If de Rohan had had a grain of sense, the plot would have succeeded. Instead the booby must needs go to the jewelers, Boehmer and Bassenge, enjoy their thanks, and indulge himself in the nobility of telling them to thank, not him, but the Queen, for the transaction. Which they did.

There are moments in history, when the mind with surprise, and excitement rather than consternation, becomes suddenly aware that the general train of events it has been watching is only a prelude. So at the Bridge of Sarajevo in 1914, so with the visit of Boehmer and Bassenge to Versailles to Marie Antoinette. It is as if we were startled by the rap of a conductor's baton, and the following crash of the drums of the major orchestra of Fate, whose invisible existence we had clean forgotten.

The curtain rattles up on the first scene of the Revolution. As if they had been carefully coached in foolery, without making a single error of sense, all these personages we have collected together played out their parts. The Queen with perfect naturalness had de Rohan arrested at the one moment when it would cause most noise and damage to her reputation: when the whole Court was present to hear him say the Mass of the Assumption, the 15th August, 1785. Her police, to make certain that the affair should do its maximum of damage by remaining a mystery, allowed de Rohan to destroy his papers. Cagliostro's arrest that followed made triply certain that the remotest curiosity of the whole of Europe should follow this public examination of the virtue of the Queen and the prestige of a whole regime by her enemies, the Parlement de Paris. Folly built on folly, in the true farcical style in which all the tragic chapters of human history are written.

The steeple of this edifice was the verdict; ambiguous, mysterious, exonerating the condemned Jeanne de Valois by the acquittal of Cagliostro, whose complicity was a necessary part of the case against her; branding de Rohan as a fool by denying he was a knave; leaving on the Queen's reputation the fatal marks of an officious discretion.

So Cagliostro totters out of History, his glamour torn, his mysteries in rags, and worst of all, hopelessly unfashionable. He took refuge in England, the sanctuary of the out-of-date. If he had been alone, there he would have ended, in some seedy City debt-jail, or in some legend of begging or guzzling hung round one of the unauthentic taverns in the tourist trade, that are the fortune of the purlieus of Fleet Street.

But in the imaginative silence that conceals him in London for months, there is at last a commotion, the track of his lost and heroic

duad, Seraphina, to the rescue. And following on the reconstitution
of the atom which his will had disastrously split in Strassburg, there
follows a sudden, painful emergence of the old Cagliostro, starting
into our view again as a drowned man bobs up to the surface out of
the mud. "One de Morande, Editor of a Courier de l'Europe published in London, had for some time made it his distinction to be the
foremost of Cagliostro's enemies. Cagliostro enduring much in silence, happens once, in some public audience to mention a practice
he had witnessed in Arabia the Stony: the people there, it seems, are
in the habit of fattening a few pigs annually, on provender mixed with
arsenic, whereby the whole pig carcase by and by becomes, so to
speak, arsenical; the arsenical pigs are then let loose into the woods,
eaten by lions, leopards and other ferocious creatures; which latter
naturally all die in consequence, and so the woods are cleared of
them. This adroit practice the Sieur Morande thought a proper subject for banter; and accordingly in his seventeenth and two following
numbers, made merry enough with it. Whereupon Count Front-of-
Brass writes an advertisement in the Public Advertizer (under date
September 3rd, 1786) challenging the witty Sieur to breakfast with
him for the 9th of November next, in the face of the world, on an
actual sucking pig, fattened by Cagliostro, but cooked and carved by
the Sieur Morande—under bet of Five Thousand Guineas sterling
that, next morning after, he, the Sieur Morande shall be dead, and
Count Cagliostro be alive. The poor Sieur durst not cry, Done; and
backed out of the transaction making wry faces. Thus does a king of
red coppery splendor encircle our Arch-Quack's decline; thus with
brow of brass, grim smiling, does he meet his destiny."

Or rather, so, feebly, but inimitably, the reconstructed adventure
lifts itself from the mud into which its fragments had fallen and essays to drive the old course. The inflexible, unadaptable course of
Seraphina, which passed across all practical materiality, like the base
line of an astronomer through space. Her adventure could be broken
off short, as it was when he gadded with Jeanne in Strassburg. But it
could not be bent. Now that she had triumphantly regained her man,
she had and could have no new plan; nothing but to begin all over

again the parabolic graph of her fate.

The two set out therefore from London, on the same course they had laid, twenty years before, from Rome, to make a fresh start. There was nothing left of her but her eyes; Cagliostro had grown into a piece of unwieldy luggage. It was 1789; the grand days of terror and excitement. The two rolled like dismasted caravels in strange seas, through Basel, Aix in Savoy, Turin, at every stopping place presented by the police with an order of instant expulsion. Nowhere was any trace of Egyptian adepts, the temples of unreality were all vanished; they were hopelessly lost. The only thing Seraphina could think of to pick up her bearings was to go back to Rome. Cagliostro no longer counted; so from frontier to frontier they drifted heavily along to their starting point.

Destination, rather, for there on the 29th December, 1789, "the Holy Inquisition detects them founding some feeble moneyless ghost of an Egyptian Lodge, picks them off, and locks them hard and fast in the Castle of St. Angelo."

No; Adventure does not end her stories in that style, with slick cues for pity or yawns. You must wait a moment for the end; until the inevitable has revenged itself, in its obscenest manner on the dowdy, battered couple who had so long complotted against it. Both the Unfortunate Child of Nature, and the Grand Mistress of the Fixed Idea are now finished by any human dramatic rules. The zagging course and the soaring have both come to term, and the audience wait only to be released by a solemn curtain. Even some sort of a happy ending was possible, in matter of fact, for the Inquisition hesitated about letting them go. After a while Cagliostro might have become Old Beppo, one of the curiosities of back-alley commerce in Rome, with a dignified, slightly cracked old wife, whose eyes were fascinating as long as she lived. Instead of that we have the meaningless, unprofitable wickedness of the truth. When the accusation of impiety and "liberalism" was on the point of dropping for lack of evidence, Seraphina began to talk. Venomously, treacherously, disastrously, blurting out the whole truth, and much more than the truth against her life's companion and meaning, supplying much more than the judges hoped for. She even told them the final secret, the one which Cagliostro cherished most—the details of his real name and unromantic birth. The sort of frenzy that makes women round on their lovers in the dock beside them, to their common doom? Some specific weakness of the sex under the torture of justice, court rooms, police, cells, which they can no more resist than tickling on the soles of their feet? But Cagliostro talked too. Between them they made a horrible duet across the prison of betrayal. They spent nights of concentration, when they had emptied their stock of memories before the police, devising cunning charges to down each other still deeper.

Even the inquisitors at last tired of listening to them. Long before they died in the old prison, nobody paid any more attention to the two queer old dodderers.

VII.
Charles XII of Sweden

I F, AS I HOPE I have shown, Adventure has some sort of resemblance to a religion, then I am justified to sum up Charles as one of its saints. For unless you are going to grant patent rights in such a useful term exclusively to the cosmogony you personally fancy, there is some thing, and that an essential, common to St. Simeon Stylites; the present holder of the title for dirt and deformity in the great congregation of fakirs in Benares; Lenin and others in that Essenian, crucigerous sect, the Communists; and this Charles. The merest glance will, in fact, reveal that their resemblance in a super-quality sincerity is just as obvious as the grotesque incongruity of their spiritual shapes.

Examining, then, a little more closely this remarkable psychological substance that enters into such incompatible results you are likely to be struck with surprise: not that saints appear from time to time, but that, given a religion that is believed in, why every one of its adherents is not a saint himself. The saint is not a curiosity, the sinner is. For if, as millions of girls besides that ravishing genius, Therese Martin (of Lisieux), firmly believe, the heir of the Kingdom and the glory of the universe passionately offers them a supernatural romance, why should indeed a single one of them hesitate to make her renunciation of the inconceivably lesser life that is the alternative? It is not calculation—for that would imply disbelief—and it can hardly be taste that prefers to everlasting rapture the petty comfort which is all the World can mean to most such girls. The five or six yearly visits to a provincial theatre, the trifling occasions of exercising her own judgment and will that the social laws and mere mundane usage allow her. The gawky caresses of some young lawyer or tradesman, his poor company for the few minutes that by hypothesis she believes is the duration of the earthly span. And mark that the ghostly promise is surrounded by such guarantees in any pious family in Christendom, philosophical, historical, institutional, such as not another part of her knowledge possesses.

If there is a puzzle in the believer, whatever his religion, it is the irritating mystery of the lukewarm and the sinner. Granted that a man can bring himself to believe with Lenin that some scientific law (I believe they say it is scientific) commands that the unskilled workman should rule in the degree that he is ragged, then the massacre of those who in this doctrine are usurpers is merely the natural enforcement of a law against brigandage. But the soft, temporizing Communist they export is an inexplicable monster, who boggles the imagination.

And so, useless to elaborate, with all believers. It is the inconsistency that torments the mind, not the natural flow of consequence, reasonable, obvious, restful, of saints. It is this intellectual irritation, I fancy, that is the emotional impetus of all the preachers and prophets: who from Isaiah to Trotzky, through Robespierre and Calvin, all seem to hiss some such phrase as "maddening idiot" to the backslider and the Laodicean, who does not know the road to his own mouth.

The saints, whose lives are straight deductions from their beliefs, are no more crazy than the tot of a column of figures is a joke. It is an insensible impertinence of historians so to treat them, which they often do, and never more persistently than this Charles, our latest specimen, the saint of adventure; "the only man," as Voltaire, no star gazer, said, "who lived entirely without any weakness." That is, without any illogicality.

But before we can begin to follow him in the incidents and consequences of his sanity, there are still a few preliminary generalities to endure, of course as brief and non-controversial as ever. This stupidity, this unreasonableness of the normal man, who knowing the better follows the worse, who refuses what he wants, and takes what disgusts him, who sails his life against his compass, and yet stares and gasps at the lunacy of such rare persons who keep the course, is, as a plain matter of fact, when taken as a general law, of the most notable and perhaps supernatural use to the race. Humanity, in the horrible situation of consciousness, like a sane man confined in an asylum, or like a child marooned while wide awake in the centre of a nightmare, has, like all other, luckier animals, a certain store of protections and guides, which as we surely did not invent them ourselves, possess a certain comfort, if not sufficient foundations for a hope. Some of them are of an unaccidental kindness, like the feel of a nurse's hand to a baby who is making his first steps. Checks much more often than pushes, which is the contrary of how insects are treated by their instincts. Often, it seems to me and always with a sort of resentful fear, there is an unpleasant flavor of a joke in these cosmical interventions or mechanisms, as if the all-powerfuls were fooling with us, in horseplay. I have noticed this already in the destiny of poor Christopher Columbus; and at times the philosopher in his cabinet, the scientist in his laboratory, and simple humans in the course of their own lives, indeed, must from time to time hear through their meditations a cackle of laughter. Like flies to wanton boys are we to the gods. Or not to be bitter, humanity is playing blindman's buff with a handkerchief round its eyes, and is steered by trippings. The unseen is in high spirits. So with this stupidity we are pondering. Without it, we would be lost. Imagine what would have happened to the race if all or any of the great, beautiful doctrines we have believed in had been practised as faithfully as they were held, and you will come to the undignified conclusion that mankind's incurable stupidity is its principal safeguard. It has, as they used to say, survival value. We are saved by being ridiculous, lazy, weak. It is as undignified, if you like, as being hooked from the water by the seat of the trousers.

Of these doctrines of what to do, by far the greatest majority have at the centre of their power an imitable personality. That is, practical ethics is based on biography, which is enough to show where the danger, from which our innate crassness saves us, is situated. For no true biography has the power of exciting imitation; only myth has ethical magnetism.

Life, that winged swift thing, has to be shot down and re-posed by art, like a stuffed bird, before we can use it as a model. There is, therefore, in religion and ethics always art; personality has to be simplified, wired; both its incidents and its results theorized and co-ordinated before it can awake that only instinct working to our own advantage with which we are endowed: imitation. And this art, the active principle of mythology, can only be called poetry: the poetry of the epic.

It may seem, then, that the epic, for short, has a great, though usually unsuspected, importance in most human lives. And this is even probable. How many huge and subtle investigations philosophy and psychological therapeutics devote to the riddle of a character, which could most often be solved by the search for some book, and the hero of that book, read in youth or even childhood. Or in the case of a woman, it will be most likely some actress seen playing in a rôle that polarized the whole subsequent life of her who saw and admired her. Most men, in the most inward explanation of the apparent diversity of their characteristics, in the terms of their own secret, are the hero of an unwritten book, a sequel to one they once read. It may be a book they have forgotten even to the name; it may be a life of Alexander the Great, or Buffalo Bill, the Light of Asia, or Huckleberry Finn, or Frank Merriwell, or a gospel, or Jesse James, or John Inglesant, or Jack the Giant Killer; find that book and you will know that which is most intimate and revealing about their actions, their moods; that technique of attack on life which Jung exalts as an elemental, under the divisions of extrovert and introvert. Even to why he chooses that color in ties, or does not trouble to choose at all. And for the lady, why she speaks loud and frank or soft, why that peculiar grace of the hands, why that smile: do not search for their origin in the mysterious difference of her unique soul: they are her version of the way her favorite actress smiled, spoke, beckoned, when she saw her in that last term at school.

This self-realization by imitation of heroes and heroines, found in books, legends, dramas, this self-direction by the help of fiction, very widespread or unprovably universal, we will call, if you like, Imitatio Herois, saving the name Quixotism for the special case, when the model is most obviously ridiculous, and when the devotion is extreme, logical, or saintlike.

This was the secret situation of the extraordinary Charles, and the hypothesis of madness, which usually prefaces an account of his life, character and adventures, is superfluous as well as false. He had a book and he had a hero: the Alexander the Great of Quintus Curtius; and all his irrationality was that he followed his faith without any irrational dilution.

In short, the adventure of Charles, which looked as long as he lived dangerous for the whole of humanity, was the strange one of a boy who took adventure utterly seriously. What would happen if the dream of being a pirate, or a Buffalo Bill, lasted on into practice, untempered by the sloth, the stupidity, with which we are protected by kindly and contemptuous providence? You will see.

But first to try for an explanation of this singularity, or accident. The racial and hereditary factor presents itself with its usual confidence. Gustavus Adolphus, the "Northern Hurricane," was, in his genealogy, one with numerous other dynamics, explosives and ascetics. His people, the Swedes, may have kept in their blood-stream some part of the pessimistic Titanism of the Vikings—the only men who ever dared to believe in the religion that everything, Gods and men and matter, would end badly. These Scandinavians and their English cousins occupy in the early history of Europe something like the position of the greater Carnivora in the zoological schedule. Pirates, destroyers, killers, they were subject to mysterious checks of nature, oddities and maladies, psychological as well as biological, seemingly designed to prevent their unlimited increase from depopulating the rest of the world. So lions are subject to mange; antelopes, not. Anyway, without dispute, there is a Northern neurosis, with manifold and obscure forms ranging from wanderlust to spleen, from that peculiar phenomenon of Berserkism to the strange schizophrenic genius that produced Alice in Wonderland, which all by devious ways lead out, up and sideways and down from the healthy life of humanity. There is something unearthly in this race, if you are content to take it in a strictly neutral sense and not as flattery.

Therefore the ambiance, the environment of this will's growth, was favorable to eccentricity. The songs and stories of the people, the tradition of his house, would stamp on a simple mind the Northern ideal of getting your pleasure in life crookedly. He was a mute boy, with a ferocious cold obstinacy, that could only be manoeuvred by appealing to his rather implacable vanity. Thus he consented to learn Latin only after his tutor had proved to him that all the Northern Kings knew it. The same inducement brought him to a good knowledge of German.

He inherited the throne, under the regency of his grandmother, when he was only fifteen. There was general agreement at court that he would turn out a mediocre personality.

Darkness and silence are often mistaken for nothingness. He spoke seldom, confided himself to none, attended the sessions of the Privy Council regularly, but seemed to sleep at them, his head on his arms.

Inside this unexpressive chrysalid, the strange creative work of imitation was ceaseless, night and day. I remind you again that his model was not Alexander; none can imitate life without the intermediary of art. Not that moody, jealous, inspirational, human Alexander, but the Alexander myth, what the humbug Quintus Curtius had made of it. The book never left his side or his thoughts.

The will is predisposed to asceticism. It finds there its convenient exercise, and therefore all religions that appeal to the will, and especially this hero worship, must, to be attractive, prescribe mortifications, and build the system on them. The priest of Alexanderism, this Curtius, having operated Charles's conversion, obviously by appeal to his vanity (for this was his only gate in a mist-colored vision of Fame), that is, everlasting publicity, set him the task of being mythically chaste, mythically obstinate. In reality, or rather, in reason, not a practical path to world mastery; but more likely to be the lonely war trail of a Red Indian.

But with the single-minded and cock-sure faith of the saints, Charles hunted out every fanciful detail of the legend for ruthless imitation. Alexander's preference for sleeping on the floor. His fondness for water—especially at the beginning of a battle. His economy of wardrobe. His contempt for competitive sports and races: the whole range of gallery tricks, which might indeed have had some basis in Alexander's earliest self-expression, when he was desperately trying, as you remember, to differentiate himself from his father Philip; taken seriously, distilled, painted and painstakingly stuck together in the epic.

Charles taught himself further to talk as Curtius said Alexander talked, in monosyllabic words and single-membered phrases. He invented himself a way of sitting, walking, and standing, that expressed his own view of how Alexander carried himself, as a quasi-automaton. Even his smile was artificial, composed to fit an inner picture. It was a slanting grin, that would appear as often as he thought of it, very perplexingly to anyone who did not know what he was at, for he had no sense of humor, and his eyes remained pale and unspeculative, though bright, whatever the circumstances. Charles was a tall fellow; for those days, a giant. Before he was out of his teens, he began to lose all his hair. He was clean-shaven (like Alexander), and very white.

Such was this representative of all the boys who have ever played at Indians and pirates when the story begins. In 1699, the grave matter was brought up, in his council of ministers, of the hostile coalition of the three kings.

These three were all Charles's neighbors. Frederick of Denmark-Norway, an indistinct person, ordinarily mean, virtuous and pious. And a marvelous couple worthy to figure on the same stage as our hero: personalities, forces, with a faint taste of allegory in their composition, which Fate, like a common dramatist, likes to put in her best pieces.

One was Augustus the Strong, ruler of Saxony-Poland, Fortinbras-Falstaff, the uninhibited man, if you please; a huge, wide creature of the lusts of health, with no malice, great ability, inexhaustible cheerfulness. He could bend pokers and snap horseshoes in his two hands, and, says the story, had three hundred bastards.

The second was Peter Romanoff, still called the Great, the magnificent hooligan who first joined Russia to the continent of Europe. Brought up in the midst of murder, trained first by a court jester and then by an international crook, he is history's own Gargantua that outdid his model. Every appetite and passion man suffers had grown to perfection in him, without crowding its neighbors. He loved a book as much as an orgy, work as much as drink and women; and his life is a parade of the most far-fetched contrasts, in which he showed every quality but invention and good taste.

This Czar, who left his throne to become a ship's carpenter at Deptford, found time in the midst of a very sincere application to his work to have himself wheeled every morning in a barrow to and fro along the top of Evelyn the diarist's five-feet-thick holly hedges, the pride of England; until he had irremediably ruined them. This was he who later built his people a new capital, in a marsh, in whose making more workmen were killed by hardship than for a hundred years it had population.

If there is any salient to hold on to in this elemental being, Peter, it might be that—very curious in one of that race, which summed itself up in the anthem of the workshy, the Volga Boat Song—it is his incarnation of inexhaustible energy. The true energy of the elements that is always spilling over in the roaring horseplay of thunder storms. This man, master of a hundred handicrafts, including that of cannoneer in his army, his own sail-maker, anatomist, mortar-mixer, and public hangman, was picked to fight Charles.

The Coalition had been combined by a personage who deserves a mention, for he has had many poems written about him. This was Patkoul, a Livonian or Esthonian nobleman, whose country was subject by anterior conquest to the Swedes. Patkoul belongs to that type which Byron and Napoleon put in fashion up to the Treaty of Versailles—the patriot liberator, only imperceptibly different from hundreds of his sympathetic likes who now have their statues in all the small capitals of Europe. Like them all, he began with adoring the folk tales of his country nurse, grew up to years of lobbying in the courts of states whose laws were in their own language, with a portfolio of little tinted ethnic maps under his arm. He plotted and cross-plotted with spies, bankers, cranks and soldiers of fortune, had a strictly political assassination or two on his conscience, and then, like some, died a martyr. He was also brave, handsome and noble as well as a little treacherous, and a bore.

This Patkoul had been repulsed by Charles's father, in whose time he had not dared to risk a revolt. With a boy and a dull boy (as they all said) on the throne of Sweden the time was more promising. This coalition was Patkoul's work; the means were intricate, the idea simple: that the three kings should pay themselves for establishing the independence of old Esthonia out of the spoils of the whole Swedish Empire, which bordered each of them.

Many great European powers arrived on the sill of the eighteenth century noticeably fatigued. Such was the case with the Swedes; they had retired with their gains, and a much less formidable challenge would have made them very anxious. The counsellors were old. While still religious, they were not so certain as their fathers had been that God would be with them in any war. Life was very likely not so much fun then as it had been in the century before, and people who are not enjoying themselves very much always most dislike risking their lives.

So at that council meeting, where Charles presided lolling in his seat, there was first of all some sort of glum unanimity for exploring the possibility of terms, and one or two had already almost committed themselves to a policy of tractation and delay. This was the first, and nearly the last time they heard Charles speak. He took his head from his arm, rose up as stiffly as possible, and said in his even, undramatic guttural: "Gentlemen, I have resolved never to make an unjust war, but to end a just one only with the utter ruin of my enemies. I will attack the first to take the field, conquer him, and then deal with the others."

The historic moment is always simple and brief; it belongs to one man and one will alone, without possibility (if it be truly ripe) of any confusion of rights. The council's surprise was their consent. They bowed themselves out of the room and also out of the story.

So, with only his book to guide him, without any experience of the science of war, our imaginary Alexander embarked, in the silence rather than with the support of his country, on the strangest and loneliest military feat in history. The King of Denmark, our typical realist, was the first victim of this irruption of the power of fiction, which can think away mountains. Frederick's action was prudent, reasonable, expert: it was to seize on the ill-defended lands of Charles's Holstein protectorate behind the cover of the impregnable defence of the sea. Wherever the passage was navigable, it was covered by land fortresses and by the positions of a superior fleet.

You will so often meet the concepts of "impossible," "impregnable" and all the family in any account of Charles's adventure, that it is better to give them a brief effort of the attention at the beginning. In one sense, perhaps the technical sense, the life of an adventurer is the practice of the art of the impossible, reserving the word hero, as we have agreed in the first part of this study, to his rationalized, moralized myth. By simple conclusion then, heroics is in the last resort the practice of the impossible. The capture of the impregnable, the ascent of the unscalable, the logic of the illogical; wild sounding phrases, exactly, for that is just what adventure is. In it are mystery and absurdity, without which even ants could not live—if, as I suppose, they have some sort of consciousness, for these are the basic components of hope. Just as every yard of the King of Denmark's position was guarded but one—that was the "Flinterend," the unnavigable part of the channel of the Sound—so the possibilities of human life are impregnably walled, to an intolerable minimum, by natural law, by the clockwork of determinisms of all sorts—except just where the adventurer breaks through. Where common sense is horrified, where the sign "impossible" is raised in warning, kindness or spiteful joy, there is your exit, exactly there, prisoner; there is the door of adventure. There is a trick in the world; did you imagine it was solid all through? Expect the unexpected, for it is hard to find and inaccessible, said the deepest of the pre-Socratic Greeks, not wilfully hermetic, but struggling to convey a secret which tied his tongue.

It was then across the Flinterend that Charles descended on his victim. He had first to conquer his own admiral, a sound, expert, dutiful man, and that was another impossibility accomplished. The Flinterend was unnavigable, the wind was wrong, Charles was only eighteen, so they landed safe, without a shot, four miles north of Copenhagen, which the victorious Swedes in the great days of his grandfather had never even attempted.

The impossible, the rule of heroes, is extremely fascinating to achieve. But it is somewhat fatiguing to read about; and there are massive strokes of it to come. Therefore we will leave this first instalment with the summation that in a fortnight, Charles had imposed peace, restitution, apologies, and tribute on his first enemy. If he had wished, he could have annexed Denmark; and ended a thousand years of war and history. But Charles had no weaknesses; now and thereafter he was behaving out of a book. The first maxim of Alexanderism is never to stop; Charles continued.

But not of course in the same condition as heretofore. There is a miraculous bonus in the hunt for the miraculous, as you have noticed before in all these heroes; at every turn of the impossible road is waiting an impossible good, unearned; a present. Charles had conquered an invincible enemy with a mediocre, unconvinced army. He now possessed, suddenly, an incomparable company of demi-gods. His Swedes were henceforward as incredible as himself, out of a book. Every nation has a legend of invincibility about its soldiers at some point in its history, but to me, the archers of Crécy, or the Old Guard, or any of all the others who have been illustrated in colors by national vanity, cannot compare in the facts of their deeds with these men of Charles.

Such is the arithmetic of adventure, in which two and two no more make only four than that Euclid rules in the Universe of Einstein. Nothing or a million; a fool's death in the Sound, or the leadership of an army that would have scattered the Greeks at Thermopylae at the first charge. Like the absurd maps of Columbus, the absurd rules of Alexanderism had led him straight.

In first consequence, this success immunized him from the criticism of others, and from doubts he could possibly have had of himself. Some have tried to find and sometimes to persuade themselves they have succeeded in finding a deep plan in what followed. But in himself there was no trace of sensible politics. He had finished the first part of a revenge; he now henceforward, right to the last stage, added chapters to the same schoolboy story. He fought with Augustus and Peter, not with Russia or Poland. He aimed at full apologies, not conquests. He no more intended anything deeper and wider than Quixote was plotting revolution against the government of Spain. His country, his army, therefore, are nothing more than weapons to him; in him, as in his model, there is here the pure antisocial egotism of the boy who runs away to sea or to fight Indians. He is sending the world spinning round himself as the pivot. Military, economic, political consequences of his actions—nothing but overtones of a tune he is whistling.

So, this campaign of Narva, unique in the military history of the world, is inwardly nothing but a terrific thrashing, administered to some insolent bully, Czar Peter. Incited by the noble Patkoul, Peter began an invasion of the Swedish possessions on the Baltic before the news or the significance of the news from Denmark arrived to him.

With him he brought one of those swarming multitudes that are an Asiatic tradition of war: eighty thousand Russians, with one hundred and fifty cannons—a Somme armament for the times—and rolled on as far as the Swedish fort of Narva, where a garrison of one thousand Swedes despairingly entrenched themselves. Peter himself conducted the operations in the highest of spirits and after his own patent. He first appointed himself to the rank of simple lieutenant, from which at every moment he stepped out to give advice, orders and energy to his commander-in-chief. Like Bottom in the play he took all the rôles; stood at attention to a captain to show what real discipline was, then rushed off to cuff a general for making a crooked trench. He knew everything, enjoyed everything and did everything.

In the midst of this horde of warriors from the obscurest and most picturesque corners of the world, Kalmuck archers, Cossack rough-riders, slant-eyed Siberians from the burial grounds of the mammoth, armed with everything that could hurt, from the most modern muskets of Holland and France to clubs studded with nails, and jagged spears, the energy of their emperor burned like a fever. With a machine-gun battalion, evidently, one could comfortably dream of facing such a mass, but equally or very nearly equally armed, they would be as formidable as a herd of a million buffaloes, at least. They were divided by language, by separate traditions of fighting which no teaching could unify. But their religious love and respect for their despot, Peter, made them contemptuous of death, and all were mad for loot, which secular tradition promised them in a march towards the west, and a fight with western men.

When Peter, who had thoughts as well as instincts, had his secret despatches about the strange evolution of his enemy, he set about arranging for an absolutely riskless victory. He knew that Charles was bringing with him only twenty thousand men, yet he put himself on the defensive. In front of his hordes he had deep ditches dug, lined with pointed stakes on the latest and most approved system, and an intricate arrangement of outworks, trenches, glacis, was thrown up quickly and competently. In front of this bristling porcupine was a rocky ground of little stony hills. To take advantage of the least slope twenty thousand picked troops, sharpshooters and artillery, were disposed here. Still apparently not content, after all this, Peter went himself to fetch up another army of reinforcements. If one fails to remember his character, all this preparation might seem exaggeration, or the mark of a great fear. It is more probable, however, that, while no doubt extremely impressed with Charles's first stroke in Denmark, Peter was merely indulging, with the enthusiasm peculiar to him, in one of his hobbies.

Even the twenty thousand men with which he had landed on the coast seemed superfluous to Charles. Leaving most of them to follow him in forced marches, without stopping one day, he dashed off to the death trap at Narva, with about four thousand horsemen and the same number of grenadiers. It was already winter. The roads were frozen. But in three days and nights he had arrived at the outposts of the Czar. Having passed by the impossibilities of strategy and even geography, the hero now smashes out of his way those of physiology—the need of sleep, the need of rest. Such is the superhuman power of the nonsense in his head. Without a pause then, Charles proceeded with such of them as could move to a frontal attack. The white Russian sharpshooters behind the rocks were certainly not expecting them, these tattered, haggard ghosts on horseback, led by a spectre. They loosed off a ragged volley. One of the bullets ricochetted and the spent ball dropped in his cravat. Another killed his horse. "These…give me some exercise," said he.

His Swedes were soon up to them, and most of the Russians dropped their guns and ran back, dodging their own fears among the rocks, into the camp of the twenty thousand, "carrying with them the greatest confusion." It is not necessary to believe that this picked outpost division was undisciplined or incompetent; it was precisely the best-trained part of Peter's army. But the better the training, the greater and more detailed the preparation, the more men are at the mercy of the impossible. Everything natural had been prepared for. Every possibility had its instructions—but the time, the very smallness of numbers, the idiocy of the whole thing, threw everything out. The Swedes rushed them. At the first screams, the whole organization melted into a struggling mob, through which the pallid giant and his men ran panting and killing. "All these outposts were broken in, and that which in other histories would have counted as three victories did not delay the progress of Charles for one hour."

So, at last he appeared before the main position of the Russians, behind which stood in a fever of excitement eighty thousand men brandishing their arms, yielding their war cries. Tomtoms and war drums, savage music from central Asia, and Peter's fine fife and bugle band, trained by Germans, mixed in a symphony of frenzy and enthusiasm. And in the middle of this, came first a snow storm, and then, in the midst of it, like spirits riding on the wind, the new berserkers and Charles.

How they passed the deep trenches, the steel spikes, the cannon-swept glacis, none, so far as I know, has left a clear account of. In its greatest moments, memory seems to desert human beings; only tiny ordinary events leave clear detailed trace. Probably none at the pitch of exaltation which Charles and his men had reached had any remembrance of what happened; we can be supermen only on condition of going into a trance. The result alone is related; that after half an hour they had taken the first trench with the bayonet. After three hours they were in the centre of the fort, where the slaughter heaped up and Swedes, mad with victory and fatigue, struggled with Tartars and Turcomans, spear against bayonet, on the heap. A panic started in the mass of the Russian troops, who, jammed together, could hardly see what was happening for the thick snowfall, and only heard the screeching of the massacre. It exploded among them, and they ran, throwing aside their guns, bows and greatcoats. Charles's three thousand cavalry pursued this mob of fifty thousand and glutted their appetite for killing as far as the river. A single bridge crossed here. It was too weak for the weight of the rout, and suddenly collapsed, filling the water with drowning men. When finally all this terror had worn itself out, the survivors came in in a rabble to surrender to Charles.

This, perhaps the greatest and noblest butchery in the military history of Europe, ended in perfect character play by the two leaders. Charles, I need not say, was superb in the rôle of classic magnanimity, ordering, with an impassive wave of the hand, the release of all but the generals; to these sending handsome presents and polite enquiries and apologies for keeping them captive. Peter, after ordering the bearer of the news to be strangled, was excited, then amused, vastly interested. His dominant passion for learning had food for months in minute questioning of the survivors on the minutest particularities and incidents of the fight, as far as they could inform him, and in the speculative hunt for its technical reasons. His final judgment on the catastrophe was "By force of beating me, Charles will teach me to beat him."

To console the less rational feelings of his people, he spread the report that the Swedes were warlocks and magicians, news very comforting to the Russian mind, and ordered searching prayers to be offered to Saint Nicholas, the patron of the country, to send reinforcements of angels. And then, he was off to consult with his uneasy partner, Augustus in Poland.

This meeting lasted fifteen days, and during it, the two consumed several hundred bottles of good wine. Voltaire, like all rationalists, squeamish at heart, judges it so: "These northern princes frequent each other with a familiarity that is unknown in the south. Peter and Augustus passed the fortnight together in pleasures that became excessive, for the Czar, who tried to reform his nation, could never check in himself his dangerous leaning to debauch."

Now, while these two men of the earth were thus taking counsel, our Plutarchian hero made preparations for part three of his romance of revenge. In the spring he appeared on the Dwina. The Polono-Saxon army, drilled, European, competent, waited for him on the other bank. Patkoul, the patriot whom Peter had discarded after Narva, and a hot little band of Livonian nobles, who had sworn to die where they stood, were included among them.

Charles was helped by the wind. He made great bonfires of wet hay, which a stiff breeze carried across in the face of his enemy. Under cover of this he trotted his horse into the water in another frontal attack. The old, experienced, unsuperstitious German general, von Stenau, met him (Charles was fourth across) with a charge of heavy German dragoons, who broke the Swedes' order and threw them back into the river. In the shallows, in the smoke, Charles rallied his troops. You know the result, as perhaps secretly and unconsciously the stolid German troops had forecast it in their hearts. The marvelous and impossible again appeared. Charles chased them all as if they were a herd of bison and not the most reputable troops in the world as far as the walls of Mitau in Courland.

And so begins the strangest campaign in military history: a competent general and a seasoned army of eighty thousand men chased like deer, in their own country, by an invader who used his vastly smaller forces more like a pack of hunting dogs than men; laying them on the scent rather than mapping routes, caring no more for their feelings, their fatigues, their lives, than a hunter who is rather fond of a good dog. Up and down the map of East Germany they ran, hunter and hunted, in an Alexandrian zig-zag of the best manner. The only strategical question in Charles's science was "Where are they?" Never, "How many? How entrenched?" At last Charles had made war into what schoolboys dreamed it ought to be.

In this tally-ho, the situation of Augustus the Strong was not only painful but slightly ridiculous. He bore it with the humor that is a virtue in his sort; harried mercilessly through the deep forests of Poland, across inaccessible mountain passes, up and down precipitous ravines, without respite for his high blood pressure. Never has a mortal suffered such a hallucinatory chasing, more like the nightmare of De Quincey, fleeing through "all the forests of Asia from the wrath of an idol." And in his fitful dreams, as he lay on the uneasy cushions of his coach, or in a shakedown bed in a lost inn, the stout bon vivant must often have had the vision, the absurd mixed with the terrible, of a tall, bald boy with a ridiculous grin, dressed "in a riding coat of coarse blue serge, with copper buttons, jack-boots, reindeer gloves that came over his elbows, riding or running like his infantry at the stirrups," on his track.

Charles never caught him. He turned his dominions upside down, decorated all the roads in northeast Europe with skeletons, and at last, disappointed but steadfast, had Augustus solemnly dethroned in Warsaw by his own people. In his place Charles put a young man who had pleased him in some mysterious way, one Leczinsky, a bookish, mild, though not uncourageous petty nobleman. Charles witnessed this coronation incognito, from behind a pillar in the cathedral. It was his only booty, to play his Alexander-image thus, in contemptuous self-effacement.

The mad commotion of a resuscitated demi-god, running amuck after the best-known monarch of Germany through the heart of the continent, had naturally scared all Europe. In the inner circles of diplomacy and courts there was a strong presentiment that the human race was near one of its cyclic disasters; that bad days were coming, and the race of world destroyers had reappeared in this

Charles. So besides a host of genteel adventurers who flocked to offer
their services at his camp, there was a continual flux of graver and
more serious personages, half diplomats and half scouts, come to
peep into the crater. One of these was the great Marlborough himself, sent by his government. His experience was particularly interesting.

Charles received him without the slightest sign of interest before
the fire, in a bare mess room, flipping at his jack-boots with his rid-
ing-crop. He listened to a long compliment from the victor of
Blenheim in Marlborough's best French, which was bad, without
interruption or reply. His chancellor, Piper, was in the room. Charles
remarked to him in Swedish, "Is this Marlborough?" The Englishman,
who was a great diplomat as well as a soldier—what an interesting
war the two could have made together—took no notice of this rude-
ness. He had come to prospect the intentions of Charles towards the
French and the Anglo-Austrian coalition, and even if Charles had
thrown his jack-boot at his head, it would not have disturbed him
from his mission. Marlborough was a slow negotiator. He was never
in a hurry to make propositions or ask questions, preferring under
cover of a banal conversation to use his extremely acute faculties of
observation, and his art of unravelling other men's motives, as it
were, sideways. The ablest diplomat will never boast of understanding a man, but only his intentions. It was not long before a word in
Marlborough's flow brought a strange reflection, a spark into
Charles's icy look, that struck his explorer; and following this up
deftly and smoothly, he soon learnt that he might safely keep his own
proposals and fears back, without going into them further. For the
word was the name of Peter. Without Charles having opened his
mouth once, the wily Englishman had completely understood that
"the ambitions, passions, designs of Charles were exclusively directed
eastward, to Russia, and that the rest of Europe had nothing, for the
moment, to fear or hope from him." With this brilliantly managed
discovery, he took his leave, and made his report.

The comet was indeed headed in a direction wide of the western
world. The reason is sufficiently simple—two of the enemies who

had basely attacked him at the beginning of the story were now out of the way. But Peter was still on his throne; still, in spite of Narva, cheerful and lively.

If anyone should say that his victories had had no effect on the character of Charles, he is wastefully embroidering a true story. Your cold, calm young hero is peculiarly liable to grow peevish with success, which mood is one of the main breeders of cruelty. To this, rather than to any sort of sadism, or policy, should be attributed two disgusting actions which belong to this period: the killing of Patkoul, whom Charles very basely extorted from Augustus, and the cold-blooded butchery of two thousand Russian prisoners of war, scouts who had been captured by his outposts. Of another sort, and more in the character he was playing, was the incident of his trespassing on the territory of the Austrian Emperor. In one of his chases after Augustus, the frontier of this mighty state lay in his path, and he cut across it without excuse or hesitation. It was this same Emperor, who, being reproached by the Pope's legate for allowing Charles to treat him in this unheard-of fashion, replied: "How lucky it is Charles did not order me to change my religion, for really, your Eminence, I do not know what I should have done."

And so Charles decided to recommence his punishment of Peter. On the march eastward, he passed at the head of his army, as was his custom, some miles in front of it, practically alone. His road lay quite near Dresden, where Augustus now reigned in peace, trying to forget his lost Polish possessions. The idea came to Charles to visit him; out of sight of his officers round a bend of the road he galloped off across country to do this. At the gates of the city a sentinel presented arms and asked the solitary rider his business. "My name is Charles. I am a dragoon. I am going to the palace." The guards of the palace themselves were taken by surprise, and he rode his horse up the main steps, swung himself off, and with a clatter, entered the hall, and walked up the staircase. Augustus, greasy, unshaven and liverish, for it was still early in the morning, was pottering in his dressing gown in the first salon he entered. They conversed for a short while—about trivial things. The quality of the cloth of Charles's uniform, his jack-boots, which he said he had never taken off, except to sleep, for three years—Swedish leather. Then they went out to look at the view from the terrace. A Livonian majordomo prayed Augustus in a whisper to intercede for his brother in a Swedish prison. Augustus did this heartily and good-humoredly. Charles refused coldly and abruptly, looked at his watch, and then called for his horse and departed as he had come. Immediately he had gone the State Council was convened and passed the afternoon deliberating what they ought to have done. Meanwhile Charles's army, in the most agonizing apprehension and doubt, had begun to deploy itself for a siege of the city. Without any explanation he ordered the march eastward to continue.

And so this young man left Europe, as a master leaves a house that belongs to him, so far removed from realities and so involved in the progress of his own inner novelette, that his tyrannies themselves were usually nonchalant and disinterested, more like the absent-mindedness of a god than the insolence of an invincible conqueror. He set out to hunt Peter—the third villain of his piece—and afterwards, perhaps, to conquer Asia. Alexander did.

Until its very end, in fact, this Russian campaign was a hunting of the Czar; all incident, no plan. Every month Peter lost an army and a city, escaped and raised another, to be caught and thrashed again. One or two of Charles's monstrous military dicta have been preserved. Thus, "It was his habit never to ask anything of his scouts but to tell him where the enemy was." "Charles used to reckon that one Swedish grenadier was the equivalent of fifty Cossacks." So deeper and deeper into Russia and winter, the doomed adventurers pursued their fatal victories.

An adventure as hopeless, splendidly futile as life itself, which by whatever roads our appetites and vain plans push us to take, converges inward inevitably to death. At the end of every possibility, impossibly achieved by Charles and his troops, whether he had preserved his lines of communication—as he did not; whether he delayed in some fortress over that winter, the worst in the memory of man, when even the crows dropped dead from the air, through which he rushed after his White Whale, the great Czar: at the end was Pultawa. And he would not have lost Pultawa, but gone on to some later catastrophe, if the pitiless or pitiful gods had not so contrived that here in an immense marsh, surrounded by the endless hordes of Mother Russia, he had not for the first time been put out of action, half killed, and entirely stunned by a cannon-ball. Two or three of his officers carried him off out of the massacre, while the rest made the last stand.

For a time yet, while he lay unconscious and was shifted like a dead-weight from horseback to stretcher, to a rickety coach found by accident stranded, across rivers, through quagmires, while the wolves and the Cossacks hunted them, Charles was in the strongest current of adventure that even he, the high priest of the cult, had ever found. The hunting of Augustus and Peter were two epics; the hunting of the body of Charles to the Turkish frontier was superior to them both. At last they got him there and to safety. Now carefully observe the reason of his next extravagance. A fixed will has logically and pathologically its own inherent disability. It is subject to a locking of motive, to an inhibition of turning; Charles's was iron. He had set out to chastise Peter; now when every motive of sense and opportunity, ruined, exiled, armyless and penniless, told him to postpone his end, he refused to budge, probably could not.

For whole years he stayed in the small Turkish village, leaving his conquests, leaving even his patrimony to fend for itself and be gradually eaten by the return of his enemies, obstinate and silent, with no thought in his head but to finish somehow his quarrel with Peter.

These years, psychologically a sort of trance, catalepsy self-induced by the very power of his will, were occupied outwardly in the strangest, most persistent intrigues with the Sublime Porte in the attempt to get the Turk to give him another army.

In the end, instead, the Sultan determined to expel him. The result of this was that famous incident, that makes the deeds of Achilles and King Arthur seem adult and unromantic. Charles refused to leave. He had a stone house in the village. The Pasha of Bender was ordered to expel him by force, and to avoid trouble by a show of force. He had the idea of using the whole troops at his disposal, who were at manoeuvres, to parade with him on his mission. Charles not only refused abruptly to go, but actually opened fire from his window on this host of thirty thousand men. Artillery had to be brought up, which finally, after some time, set fire to the house. Even then not conquered, the hero and his little band sallied forth into the street, which was crammed with a regiment of Janissaries, and started to hew their way through them. The Pasha's voice was heard, cracked with excitement and wonder, offering a hundred gold pieces to anyone who could lay hands on the giant King and survive to bring the proof. At last in this wild mêlée, in which the Swedes killed several and wounded a great number, the spurs of Charles's jack-boots, those famous jack-boots, caught together. He tripped and fell, and was frog-marched off to prison; "his features," says Voltaire with a keen flight of imagination, "still preserving their accustomed composure." The truly noble must have a dash of the idiotic in it to put it out of the reach of baseness, which is nothing but the commonest of common sense.

After this, with the suddenness of the resolutions of an infant, Charles was freed in his will. He accepted his expulsion, and set off with one companion on horseback to traverse Europe and return to his own country, which he had not seen since he set out for Denmark. The will, turned aside into a new channel, now rushed with the velocity of a torrent. He rode across Europe as if he were late for a wedding, and on the 11th of November, 1714, having shed his companion by the wayside, alone, ragged, grinning, in the dead of night he knocked at the gate of the Stralsund, the only fortress of his empire still to fly his flag on the south coast of the Baltic.

That fortress he saved, as a heap of ashes. His awestruck country received him again, as a race of poor savages would receive another avatar of their tribal god, after an earthquake which had destroyed him. No one dared to reproach him, nor even to question him, and he himself, with the same grin, the same uniform, took possession of his ruined kingdom, as if nothing in the prodigious years had happened out of the ordinary.

Yet this broken man possessed the offensive as inalienably as his boots. Until he chose to move, the north of Europe was like a church.

Armies on the move towards his defenceless dominions stopped and entrenched themselves, on triple urgent messages from their over-lords. The coalized kings, ceasing all action, hurried into conference and laid down the lines of a vast defence.

Charles meanwhile mildly surveyed the situation. The hero-ico-comical episode of his expulsion seems to have released some cog in his thoughts. For the first time, in all appearance, he now felt free to think out a general plan of the conquest of Europe. The lines of his attack were, you will be satisfied to hear, of an unheard-of audac-ity. The prospects of its success, but for one thing, which happened, no one seriously can doubt. Here was the most formidable peril to which modern Europe has ever been exposed. Charles decided first to attack the inaccessible regions west of him, Norway, possessed by Denmark, where no Swede before him had ever dared to march in arms. This would be a surprise in the nature of his first descent on Copenhagen; no mere exploit or moral gain, but with the motive of gaining the open sea and the coast. From there, he fixed coldly, he would attack England, mistress of the seas—his plan, deeper than Napoleon's, just started here.

But to attack England, he must first have a fleet. Perhaps, once landed, the project was easier than it now seems. For we are now in 1717. The Old Pretender was still active, and Charles was in negoti-ation of alliance with him and his still considerable party. But the transport? Here is your Charles. He had heard, by the general rumor of the world, of a huge settlement of pirates in Madagascar, well armed, well shipped, fighters, and to them he sent an embassy to propose to hire them for their services as a ferry in return for his leadership and the unrestricted plunder of the English ports he would capture.

From this and one of history's most formidable possibilities, we were all saved, very unfairly, that is, miraculously, by his death. In some small siege, nearly over, Charles was in the front parapet. A ball smashed his head.

VIII.

Napoleon I

THERE IS ALMOST AS much book behaviour in Napoleon as in Charles. He said himself, "I am the Revolution," and the core of the French Revolution was so literary, that it sometimes looks like a plagiarism, rather than an original event. All its actors were book-conscious. They lived autobiographies, and when they were executed they were all careful to have a balanced phrase, ready composed, like a Greek epitaph—often imitated from one. They took their feelings from Jean-Jacques, their motives from Voltaire, their attitudes, and seriously I am tempted to think even their faces, their facial expressions certainly—from the copperplate illustrations to the current library editions of Plutarch.

So, much of the Napoleon Myth, all perhaps of his popular attributes, the reminiscent aptness of his sayings and gestures at the right moment, the too obvious Plutarchianism that has dazzled his long succession of historians down or up to Emil Ludwig, is decorative and not structural. Whenever Napoleon reminds of Cæsar, or Alexander, whenever he behaves Roman, he is behaving out of a book. It is stupid to allow this conventional ornament to disguise a character and a plot it was intended deliberately only to embellish.

We have first then to perform a slight osteopathic operation on the backbone of history, if we are not only to admire but understand. It is a matter of restoring his spinal motive to its right position, rescuing him from legend and restoring him among humanity.

That central motive is no mystery. Its records and evidences are in even the shortest and most pious of his biographies, though they are always detailed simply as more or less pathetic and sympathetic eccentricities. I mean his relations with his family, his attitude towards religion and laws; his own conception of life, which at bottom, and perhaps that is another reason why it has been resolutely ignored, was not very different from that of any other Corsican of his class and breeding within the last two or three hundred years.

That class was not low enough to have lost all reasonable grounds for ambition. The Bonapartes were not serfs, or shopkeepers. They were in the ambiguous between class our studies have often indicated as the most apt to produce adventurers, the shabby-genteel. They may really have been cousins of titled people in Italy; sometimes they, especially Napoleon himself, believed it. Now there is hardly more than one form which the ambition of an Italian can take. The Corsicans are a provincial sort of Italians, when all the romancers have finished talking. By Italian I mean simply any human beings who have had a history like the Italians have had. This ambition-form is fixed for them by that history; it is a highly concrete, vivid, splendid and pictorial vision of wealth and power, accompanied inseparably by a title of nobility. No Englishman dreams of being King; his history denies the possibility; his poetry denies the desirability. His tradition is that court life anyway is dull; dull as that of some American millionaires, which with its restricted call to own a private golf course on Long Island, to have a private doctor, and a box at the Metropolitan Opera House, is incidentally the stingiest ideal that has ever invited youth to desire it. The Englishman, when (as he sometimes is) he is ambitious, sees a country landscape of lawns and low hedges, a red coat, a full stable, misty autumn mornings, John Peel blowing his horn, and Mr. Jorrocks coming up the drive.

But to an Italian, especially a provincial Italian, and especially a Corsican, and most of all to a Corsican between two classes like our man, there is only one possible scenery in his dreams: a palace, a crown, a coronet, or tiara, and a dazzling court at banquet or gala. They have never forgotten the Renaissance. They all are for civilization; their ambition is essentially social, luxurious and possessive.

It is for an interlocking reason that such ambitions are never solitary, but invariably contain the Family. Mark Rutherford, who studied slave psychology in the back streets of London, makes one of his deepest characters state that "no one but a slave can understand what marriage means." No one who is not a member of a highly social, possessive race, who have suffered conquest and revolution so often that the very list is confused, who have turned the whole hunger of their hypertrophied and exasperated desire for polity, ownership and stability towards this institution, in despair, can understand what more than normal, traditional and religious feeling there is in an Italian family such as the Bonapartes. When they are poor, each still owns the other members, more than anything except the food actually passing down the throat can be owned. When they are rich, the use, the savor of prosperity is in sharing it with others. In short, like the mythical caveman, the unit of that part of our race is not the individual but the family.

We may take all the nobility of this for granted; each may easily apply all the pretty things he thinks of such a relationship for himself. Then he should notice that the basis of such a peerless compendium of the virtues of mother-, father-, sister-, brother-, son-love is strictly the blood relationship. The remarks of Napoleon, adept of the cult, which are recorded by Roederer, on the discussion of adoption in law before the State Council show this from a beautiful oblique.

"What is adoption? an imitation of nature, a sort of sacrament. By the will of society, the offspring of one human being's flesh and blood is supposed to become the offspring of another's flesh and blood. Can any action be more sublime? Thanks to it, two creatures between whom there is no tie of blood, become inspired by a natural mutual affection." Whence must this action come? "Not from a notary," said Napoleon, but "like the lightning, from on High."

One can hear all the italics the Emperor put into his astonishment and admiration. He had the best mind in Europe; a lesser man of his class and race would have simply refused to believe that anyone could give family love where no blood tie existed. It is to him a rare, possible, sublime case bordering like saintship on madness. For the essence of the Italian family is that they feel one body and one blood, "a sacramental relationship." They love each other like themselves, because they think of each other as detached portions of themselves. A pair of Siamese twins the moment after some necessary operation that separated them, after a lifetime of four legs, two heads, one arterial system, would know and may illustrate the real nature of family affection as a Napoleon understood it. The members are limbs of the same being; family hate would be physical amputation; he loved his family as himself; because he felt it was very literally and materially himself. In all this elemental part of his character, the solid unity of egotism.

So far we may look inside the head of that romantic young figure, brooding on the future in the well-known cottage in Ajaccio, and find nothing but what is admirable; and nothing that distinguishes him. An Italian dream-palace, court, throne, and all the family enjoying it together. But in any case later on there is a development which is very tragic, and a little idiosyncratic. Whether as a result of the wild and often unnecessary expenditure of energy he made to progress towards his goal, or whether it was really congenital with him, Napoleon fell into the situation that is the misery of many men of action, and lost the power of enjoying things directly, by himself. It is a weakness, a gustatory impotence which is felt the whole length of the moral ladder, from the saint to the voyeur. It is the secret inspiration of much philanthropy and of much vice; shared by a Napoleon and by the tired cook who has lost her appetite over the stove, and can only get pleasure from the good things she has made vicariously, watching the other eat. It may even be that it was accompanied, as a result of the same years of prolonged nervous strain, late hours, study, and mental concentration, by another impotence even more painful to an Italian (above all men); in his quarrels with Josephine in the pre-Imperial period, in the queer retorts of the mistress in Egypt he reproached with barrenness, in his recorded taste for "gentleness" in women, there may be some sort of underlying sexual secret we will very properly forever remain in ignorance of.

This disability, whatever its extent, certainly existed and had the necessary result of increasing his feeling for family above even the norm we have explained. Not only were his brothers and sisters part of his own body, but they were the only parts in which he could feel and enjoy. They were his palate, his eyes, his ears, and his inflamed appetite for life could only be satisfied through the canals of their enjoyment. Do you remember when in the midst of the pomp of his consecration in Notre Dame, with the Pope himself standing behind him, his wife at his side, a crown on his head, the Emperor suddenly nudged the Uncle Fesch he had made a Cardinal of, prodding his sceptre in his back? A puzzle to historians, for Napoleon was awkward but not in the least *sans gêne*. It must have been simply that he wished to see Uncle Fesch's face, to get his share of the fun he could not feel directly.

But this complexity of meaning in Napoleon's family-love is not yet complete; he looked to blood relationship to satisfy the most subtle and profound of all desires—Immortality. His impelling, insistent, mastering longing for an heir of his body is too important to be discussed in terms of mere sentiment, or glossed over affectionately as "paternal instinct." It was one of the key aims of his career; part of the indivisible prize-money for which he fought to a standstill. He loved his family like an Italian. He longed for a son, an extension of his body in time as well as space, somewhat, as it is said those other primitives, who have made a mystical religion of common sense, the Chinese, do. A son, a dynasty. This was the exclusive form in which this rational man, who believed only in his instincts, conceived life long enough to satisfy his everlasting appetite for it. The mode of his motive can be intellectually understood. But its real affinities are with the blind urges of some multicellular, pre-sexual, pre-terrestrial organism of the deep seas. A little good nature therefore, and Napoleon, the most destructive of adventurers, might be displayed as preeminently a good family man by anyone who possesses the casuistry necessary in any debate on the vice and virtue of men. Call him that, or a monstrous, crippled egoist, or merely a perfectly primitive anachronism; they are all true. The importance is to avoid seeing him as any of the fictions self-indulgent romancers have told: "the incalculable genius," the "Plutarchian Hero," the "misunderstood dreamer," and so forth. He was neither mad, mythical, nor romantic. His aim was that of all adventurers: to satisfy at the expense of destiny the utmost possible of the appetite he felt for life; in the only way he knew, as a child knows the way to its own mouth, that it could be done. Health, instinct, upbringing, forced him to have a multiplicity of bodies. He had to drag a family with him in his single combat with Fate; but it was not a physical battle, and this retinue of enjoyers would only be a physical handicap outside the metaphor.

His mother was a remarkable person, who plays the human interest in most of the stories. I find it impossible to feel sentimental about her; this hawk-eyed, greedy, handsome woman, Letizia, who wanders through the splendours of his success, saying pathetically, *"Pourvoo que ćlà doure."* To a Frenchman, a comical mixture of "Well, that's all very well," "Do be careful, Johnny" and a stage country-wife's accent. I will say at once that I do not believe that Letizia Bonaparte ever thought that her son's career was a failure at all. If Leipzig and Waterloo had left but a skim gain of a thousand dollars to the family, she would have counted it. Exquisitely adapted to the scale on which she brought up her family, she never expanded, and most of the easy pathos of her figure is misunderstanding of this. Just as Napoleon needed his family to enjoy life with, so his mother had the good natural idea of children as investments; safe receptacles of her emotional superfluity, where it would not be wasted, but earn interest. Money and position earners, reasonably expected to return handsomely for their upkeep in infancy. The rest of what she had to spare she banked in heaven, in the sure and certain hope of seventy times seven per cent, on the last day. If Napoleon, basically a family man, was an egoist, so was Letizia, the normal human mother; their faults are not separable from the general indictment against the institution of the family that Plato is blamed for making.

The father, Carlo, seems also to have been a healthy normal; he shared Letizia's hopes of the young stock they reared, and put on them the weight of accomplishing all his ambitions. These ambitions to the whole family, except Napoleon, at the Corsican stage were: enough money to cut a respectable figure in Ajaccio, perhaps the freehold of a house. Possibly a real title to replace that which they vaguely claimed, and in which even themselves did not always believe. Good jobs, in short, and the respect of the neighbors. Out of this narrow ideal Letizia, and it is probable Joseph, the eldest son— Fesch, the uncle, at any rate—never stepped. It made their lives very happy. For them all the magnificence of Napoleon was sheer surplus. Letizia did not, as her traditional cue shows, take it too seriously. She salted down three quarters of her allowance, when she became Madame Mère, enjoyed meeting the Pope—the Bishop of Ajaccio would have sufficed. Even at St. Helena, her son, Napoleon, was "someone"—who would have thought that one of the Bonapartes would ever have a whole island devoted to his residence and a whole fleet to guard him?

At what stage the marvelous boy first felt and gave signs of the titanic intensity of his want we do not know. It would be interesting because it is this, most likely, that is the ultimate element of genius. Given the power and the quality of the life desire, according as it is more or less tainted with contradiction, that is, then human force which in its highest degree we call genius might be calculated. Thousands of little Italian boys to the present day wish to be kings, and their brothers to be dukes. No one has ever pulled the picture towards them, sucked this destiny out of the universe towards them with the same centripetal longing as Napoleon. We cannot know even as much of the cause of this attractive will as whether it is physical or spiritual. But we can suspect, and name, several factors that would exasperate it, like blowing a fire. First among them is the ambiguity of the family's social situation, the unsubstantiated claim to be of better birth than its neighbors. The shock of discovering sooner or later that no one believes it, may make the boy laugh, or be angry, or cynical. If he is immoderately vain or sensitive or obstinate, (three names for the same thing) it will give an exacerbated definition to his ambition. Here is obviously what the military academy that he was sent to, may have done to Napoleon. Surrounded by

genuine little marquises and viscounts, he learnt to conceal his own
family claims to be one of them; and even affected a democratic
contempt for all such things. Injured vanity leans naturally on politics for ease; it was the same cause that opened the eyes of the young
Robespierre to the rights of the canaille. And I should not be surprised that back in Corsica, watching the rich, disdainful French
officers made the whole Bonaparte family determined nationalists,
and rebels. Poetry and vanity make the sincerity of all oppositions;
just as vanity and self-interest do for all conservatism; they are only
intolerable when they are unconscious.

This was not the case with young Napoleon. While indulging the
full force of his hatred, he found place to stand and look at it, and
wonder at it; and study it. He learnt the power of nationalism and
tuft-hunting, principal arms of his later technique of ruling men
from the inside of their hearts.

As oxygen for the fire, those were the times. The Revolution came
when he was twenty. For years before there had been an excitement
like that of the last day of term in a school. Even the aristocrats knew
that the days of privilege were ending. It was supreme, fashionable to
admit it. In that complex expectation each saw the fulfilment of his
wish: Napoleon's was simply and unalterably to get on. On the whole
this was the preponderant view of what was going to happen and
what the leaders deliberately tried to produce; not a better world, but
a world of free chances. The impetus behind the Revolution is not
the philosopher but the bourgeois. Not the Rousseau spirit, but the
Napoleonic.

The instinctive weapon of the bourgeois, the reading and writing
class, is the book. Whenever he is in a state of danger or hope he
starts furiously to learn. So Napoleon, the typical and perfect bourgeois hero, spent these excited years in a furious autodidacticism. He
read and tried to memorize a mass of uncoordinated stuff outside his
military studies (which suffered from the competition) about Plato,
the history of England, of Tartary, of Persia, of Egypt, China, Peru,
the Incas, the Popes, everything. "There is extant a whole series of
copybooks containing Napoleon's notes, penned in an almost illegi-

ble handwriting. The contents of these reprinted fill almost four hundred pages. Here we find a map of the Saxon Heptarchy with a list of the kings for three centuries; the varieties of foot-races in ancient Crete; lists of the Hellenic fortresses in Asia Minor; the dates of twenty-seven caliphs, with a note of the strength of their cavalry, and an account of the misconduct of their wives." His miscellany is so scattered that there is even a note on the situation and climate of St. Helena.

In such a ragbag anyone can find pretty much what he wants to make coincidences. All we need trouble to see is the deep coloring in the two predominant tastes of the day; the attraction of two book worlds, Plutarch's Greece and Rome, where everyone lived in heroic anecdotings, and the East of the Arabian Nights. Both moulded his imagination. The rest was mostly waste of time.

This wild, instinctive preparation for he knows not what, took up most of his time. Like most people of his temperament, though sociable, he disliked company in which he would have to appear merely as one of the crowd, even if not definitely as an inferior. He did not know and never learned how to mix on equal terms, though, provided he was assured of some special position, definite social hostility did not make him feel awkward.

All this is behind his Paris Cadet School Report: "Reserved and diligent, he prefers study to any kind of conversation, and nourishes his mind on good authors. He is taciturn, with a love of solitude; is moody, overbearing and extremely egotistical. Though he speaks little, his answers are decisive and to the point, and he excels in argument. Much self-love and overweening ambition." If these considerations are true, then the large phases of Napoleon's life become both intelligible and connected. We have no need of most of the sedative commonplaces of most of that vast library that sedentary men, to whom the most active career in history makes an irresistible appeal, have made about him and we gain the advantage of ceasing to look gawky, every time he strikes a pose, or makes a Plutarchian speech. Thus for the Revolutionary period: I dispense with the explanation "that he was young and enthusiastic" in the matter of his attitude to the Revolution in its beginnings, so opposed to the rest of the cadet officers, all royalists, with whom he was being educated. Reason enough why young Napoleon Bonaparte, shabby, jealous, out of it, should "belong to the Club of the Friends of the Constitution at Valence" where he was stationed as a cub lieutenant in the south of France; take the oath of obedience to the Constitution when "most of the others refused," put down a riot in the interest of the new party, and so conduct himself in all the acts of the Jacobin stage of his career. Show me a mystery, show me young Napoleon, penniless, greedy, taking the losing side, that of the men who barred his way.

And so let us pass without stumbling through the thicket written round the Corsican adventures. Everything at the school going very nicely to hell, he asked for leave of absence, and returning to Corsica joined the rebellion of Paoli. Why, later, break with Paoli? and go back to France and the French cause? Do you, peaceful and innocent young apprentice adventurer, imagine that in rebellions, nationalist rebellions or otherwise, all conspirators are brothers because they risk the same death? That there are not cliques, inner groups, class hatreds of those who "own the movement" and detest and are detested by outsiders within the cause—yes, a paradox—worse than the villainous oppressors themselves? Join then a noble uprising, if you have a taste for bitters, and find out. As Napoleon, the unwarned, unappreciated, frozen out, found with Paoli; and so very reasonably and angrily acted upon in returning to France.

So much for the Corsican episode. And then came Toulon. Where his royalist collegians and their great families had let in the English and the Spanish forces. Bonaparte had his chance there, and took it. "Never," said the report of the victor, General du Teil, when it was over, "can I find words to describe the merit of this Bonaparte; so much science, intelligence, and bravery. Reward him."

Then, in 1793, he has the rank of Brigadier-General. It may mean much or little. In the last war many brigadiers made their fortunes. One, at least, afterwards went back thankfully to his job as a traffic police-officer in Cardiff. It depends. To a Bonaparte it represents what Jacob Astor meant when he said, "The first hundred thousand dollars are the most difficult." It is the beginning, the possibility of a fortune, not a fortune itself. With it, Bonaparte, the greedy little soldier, could go to Paris and begin the story.

Still it took him three more years to win Josephine. That luscious and aspiring heroine married him in 1796, after he had made himself extremely useful in Paris in police work—the famous "whiff of grapeshot" that hoisted the middle-class revolution out of a logical difficulty with the mob. So many tears—so many hearts have throbbed for this lady, that my own will not be missed. Their match reminds me, alas, only of the seaside romance of a young store-hand and a milliner, each deceiving the other that it is a rich match. Josephine, the perfect type of between-worlds and between-ages woman who rarely fails by heart failure, and the pushing young striver much too ambitious to be a gigolo, who is dazzled by his idea of a real lady. Through Josephine, Bonaparte obtains the Italian chance.

Did he know that his wife's influence was a physical one on certain of the new great of the new order—Barras, for example? If so, no hard names. Certainly he never allowed himself to admit it to himself, in the most secret places of his heart that consciousness may reach to. And he loved her—with the exalted and romantic intensity that a social climber gives to a woman whom he thinks superior to his own class. Napoleon was convinced at that time that his wife was a great lady, a great beauty and a society woman: this was the only poetical material he could digest.

But after the sneers, admire the great man. Never did he have a chance and waste it; if you read his life coldly and critically, and above all forward, not backward, as you would a novel not knowing the end, you will be everlastingly astonished by the few chances he actually had, and the extraordinary use he made of every one of them. That enigmatic croupier who hides behind the shadows dealt him poor cards; everyone he finessed with. This Italian job—a poorish thing, at that time, in those circumstances. Which, with a ferocious singularity of will, so strong that it gave him originality as it does in the rarest of cases, he so used that he made out of it, with a ragged army, against a superior enemy, the campaign of Italy, which is incomparably more studied to this day than all the semi-divine feats of, say, Charles.

Studied, certainly, as a work of art, and not as an achievement in that pretended science of war, the vain belief in whose existence has destroyed more armies, and generals, than any incompetence or cowardice.

The wars of Bonaparte are works of art, and so they escape the uncompellable bias of everything that is merely scientific to oblivion and the out of date. Specifically, they are masterpieces of will, electrical displays; the opposite of all that is static, and so at the other pole of the spirit's delights, from architecture.

This masterpiece immensely advanced him; yet only to a fork, not a goal, where two great causeways of possibility branched off. On the one hand, as always, fate made him an offer to stop; to cash in. The Directory in Paris, that is, now accepted him as a great man, and tried to make him one of their greatest servants. They offered and pressed on him the command of a projected expedition against England, which if he had been in the least dizzy, or tired, could have appeared to him a very gorgeous reward. Such are the hardest moments of adventure: to rise a winner. We have learnt their supernatural danger.

Instead Napoleon went to Egypt. Why Egypt? The political excuse was to attack the British East; very feasible and practical in spite of the look of it. For the British fleet was out of the Mediterranean and, more, rotten with mutiny. Two personal reasons, concerning us more. First, the touching one of romance, and reading, the exotic Alexanderism of his book-days. Second, that trick of opportune temporary effacement, which is commonly practised by all politic ambitions.

It is vain to set down this campaign as a failure, for the value of the structural episodes of such a life is not in themselves but in their function in the whole. On the half debâcle, half apotheosis of Egypt, Napoleon built the next step to the Consulate. I can dimly perceive that its scale, its atmosphere clinging to him when he landed at

Fréjus, in 1799, picked him out against the whole background of possibilities. For, intersecting and counterplotting the private adventure of Napoleon Bonaparte, was the even vaster and higher soaring adventure of the middle class, that had made the Revolution. At this time, not to get lost in the fascinating intricacies of their position, they were seeking a king of their own, to give them their three wishes: a court, plausible legality, and a police.

The route of Napoleon's adventure was in the satisfaction of the whole of this, and it is the same through all the set landscapes of his dramatic ascent to the imperial power. Napoleon imposed himself on France, and later in legend on Europe, as the Messiah of the new middle class. As to legality, he resolved for them the dilemma Robespierre had posed them of choosing between the King of France and the King-Nation—a mob of kings—by buying out the latter's rights with the plebiscite. The emperor of the French held the power of attorney of four million kings by divine right of Nature. As to police, every Corsican is a born policeman, and the vast structure of the Code Napoléon still is in working order today.

The court of Napoleon Bonaparte, in short, summed up all the spiritual wants of the class that made the Revolution. It was perhaps as poetical as a Victorian oleograph is artistic; that is to a certain limited degree. It is rarely noticed that besides the Utopian dream, which certainly existed among a small fierce minority, the emotional drive of the Revolution was the desire of the French bourgeoisie to share in the aristocratic life. Every feature of it attracted them, least, perhaps the subtle and evasive ideal, æsthetic, of course, rather than moral, which nevertheless was its chief charm and importance, even to a majority of those who shared in it by right of birth. The French burgher coveted the posts of profit under the government and the commissions in the army for his sons; his wife dreamed of invitations to court balls for her daughters. And this younger generation were Napoleon's chief supporters, for he gave them all their will, a vast system of safe, honorable jobs in an immense civil service and a huge army; and a court which for sheer dimensions surpassed anything hitherto seen in Europe. It was Napoleon, who, from the secrets of the aspirations of his own soul, invented that paradoxical ideal of the life of the adventurer assured of a pension, with all the glitter and the danger, the uniform, medals, titles, shine, but without the normal ruinous penalties of adventurer's failure. His men were soldiers of fortune, paid regularly by the month. Every young man, in the south of Europe at any rate, to this day dreams of the life Napoleon provided for his chosen young men. Not to be a Napoleon but to serve one. A thousand novels have propagated the attraction of the life in his garrisons, especially where the young officers of an all-conquering army dazzled high-born foreign beauties with their uniforms and their prestige. The goose-step, let us say, to a waltz tune, and pass me the anachronism.

Without assenting whole-heartedly to the criticism of the exiled "authentics" that the glamour of Napoleon's court was rather like that of a pirate's cave, when business has been good, and the girls of the islands have arrived, one is allowed to think of it as a little tawdry, slightly grotesque and faintly vulgar; as most of his furniture must have been when it was brand-new. It was in fact, and had to be, a court of arrivers, and the qualities, brilliant, as they undoubtedly were, which had brought his companions, generals and courtiers to this height, were not such as make agreeable company. Still, anything less highly colored than this assembly of brand-new unlettered dukes and twenty-year-old generals with their taste in women, dress, manners, and arts would scarcely have had such a world-wide or lasting appeal.

Magnificently, however, as Napoleon rewarded the investment of the life-thirsty middle class in him by giving them in profusion laws, adventures, titles and civil service careers, this did not absorb the whole force of the man. It was all almost a by-product of that terrific will, accidental bounty, for like all true adventurers he kept all his motive firmly personal. Thousands of asteroids, small and big, were drawn along in his huge parabola by this comet of adventure. They were welcome. But it was not to serve them he rushed across the sky. This man, and it fixes his altitude in our history, elected and determined not only to rule the world, but to enjoy it. This, as you saw recently, was only possible to him through his family, used as a complex organ of taste. For it to be worth while to him to be the Emperor of the French, every member of his family had to have a throne. There were a great many of them. But none too many for that appetite, even if they had all wholeheartedly lent themselves to this queer, yet apparently enticing service. Like a dyspeptic caliph of the Arabian Nights, Napoleon convoked the whole crew to his feast, and only asked of them to enjoy themselves. But we may have a natural suspicion that there was a drawback; that Napoleon's king-making was, in a homely and popular figure of speech, rather like that of a father who gives his son a mechanical toy but does not allow him to work it himself. That may account for the constant attempts of various members of the family to quit their thrones and dominations, and live their own life. Then there is the case of Lucien, the finest of all of them, the best brain and heart, and so presumably, as the one capable of the greatest enjoyment, the most prized for the Emperor's purposes. It was Lucien, who, at a certain hairpin bend in his brother's career, righted the vehicle; it was Lucien, more than Napoleon, who gained the first *coup d'état* at St. Cloud. But Lucien married beneath, not the Bonapartes indeed, but the Napoleons (if you will excuse the phrase) and Lucien remained a good, that is, anti-napoleonic democrat. For this (and any other explanation of the fact is improbable) his brother, disregarding all other claims to his affection, cast him off and disowned him; as much as he ever could one "tied to him by blood."

Therefore, the respectable myth that the doom of Napoleon arrived because there was no other issued to his adventure, that to keep his power in France he was obliged to go on conquering in Europe, I am obliged in large part to reject as excellent drama but poor fact. Along with that may go such details as that Napoleon was betrayed by Talleyrand into certain of his most damaging adventures. The Spanish War; a large part of the other wars that followed the period when his French Empire was steadily established; all had, however complicated their motive, a core of the acquisition or preservation of kingdoms, principalities and dominions, by which through members of his family the vicarious ogre sought to enjoy his power.

To this set undoubtedly belongs that raid on Moscow, which quite incomparably repeated the strange adventure of Charles, in the preceding chapter. When set over his expedition to Egypt, underneath the superficial and inglorious resemblance of their ends in a desertion, it will easily be seen that it differs in a fundamental absence of romantic, or book feeling. No more Roman speeches; here and now we see a man who has virtually ceased to be an adventurer at all, and is merely, if desperately, trying to protect his gains. The arches of the demi-god's feet have given way. He is now on the earth, where I think, in spite of Victor Hugo, he ever afterwards remained.

This phase, which curiously enough our earlier fancy of a "ballistic law" of adventure would again explain, dates, I think on purely psychological grounds, from the time of his divorce, his remarriage, and especially from the birth of his son in 1811. The fate of Josephine is as classic a subject for sentiment, as Leda for sculpture. The wife, indeed, and not the mother as earlier or the lover as seldom, except in the highest art, is the sacred cult of the whole century that followed, and has lasted well on into our own times. You either feel such things or you do not, for there is no compulsion of the intelligence or the heart in them. The unilateral rights of a woman, deriving from marriage, have never seemed to me beautiful, sacred, or indisputable. So the divorce of Josephine, richly alimonied, her loss of the position of Empress which she received from a husband to whom she never gave a son, nor even faithfulness, has made many good people weep, but not me. In her place, Napoleon put the Archduchess, who, at any rate, had youth, manners, breeding, a stupidity that was not pretentious, and in a short time she gave him the goal of his whole fortune, the child whom he made promptly King of Rome.

I will not return on the analysis of Napoleon's philoprogenitiveness, as the phrenologists call it, except to repeat that children of his own body represented to him the possibility of immortality—if he could found a dynasty, then an immortality of kings, the vicarious rule of the future. He had parted with Josephine with much more emotion than was reasonable; this new wife enchanted him. So much so that he is actually reported to have given orders during her accouchement that if a choice was necessary, the wife and not the child was to be saved. No doubt in his mind there was the thought of having more children by her, very likely, many more, a race of kings for the whole world; still it was a fine and unlikely thing for such a man to do.

But that fatherhood secretly was the end of the adventurer in him. The sacrilegious moment had come for counting and preserving; and the gods are insulted. Everything after this moment goes mysteriously awry, as heretofore it had gone mysteriously right. The luck has shifted, like the wind on a voyage.

Henceforward—post or propter—comes Russia, Leipzig, Elba. France received back the old frontiers and the Bourbons. Marie Louise is separated from him with the boy, in the same spirit of obedience or indifference as she showed when she was married to him. Though the fortunes of the family had suffered considerably from his fall—all was by no means lost. The Bonapartes were and indeed have since remained one of the greatest and richest families in Europe. So then we have to ask, why Napoleon could not, content with this rich booty, stay quiet in the queer situation, in which the banal idealism of the Russian Emperor, it appears, had left him?

Here we have, it seems to me, a phenomenon of an incidence so regular in the lives of successful men of action that it might be treated as a law. They, whether steel kings or Bonapartes, cannot, after a certain age, endure solitude. For it is the solitude, even though strictly relative in the majority of cases, that kills them, or sends them on the road to Waterloo. The deprivation of the band, the audience, the ambiance, which, originally only the tonic of their will, has grown to become a drug without which life is intolerable. There is as much action in the rule of a tiny kingdom like Elba, or there could be, as in the Empire of the French. As much mental, physical, nervous energy is demanded by the ideal organization of a farm as in manœuvring the Curb. Only the excitement, strict function of the social interest in his doings, lacks. Who can enjoy acting in an empty theatre? And not because such dependence in fact on the presence of the crowd, perfectly co-existent with a theoretical contempt for it, is an evident ignominy, an euphoric drug habit, the adventurer especially, whose essence is individuality and independence, even to opposition, should watch himself all his life against acquiring it. Napoleon left Elba simply because he could not stand being deprived of public opinion.

Therefore, I find the episode of his return pitiable, even painful. I know they have poeticized it into a sort of return of Arthur. But Arthur and Barbarossa stayed in their trances. Except only in the conduct of a battle, Napoleon was no artist, and had no taste.

This, by the way, may explain by a hidden affinity the worship his memory has received by seemingly quite incongruous admirers. There is a core of vulgarity somewhere in Napoleonolatry, as there was in the whole Napoleonic decoration, which by no means escaped the attention of those intimately mingled in it even when, like Talleyrand, they were also men of taste.

Because of its enormous and still openly or derivatively existing influence, on the ambitions and ideals of the world, it is useful to make a little summary of this Napoleonic ideal here. I have already mentioned the fundamental difference in that earlier "Imitatio Alexandris" which the Imitation of Napoleon practically superseded: that after the Corsican, young men dreamed of being officers, not leaders. Conjointly, in their vision, with the pay, the regulations, the relief of responsibility, was that amazing system of medals and rewards that has so powerfully influenced the whole mode of ambitions. Napoleon taught the world, or perhaps only satisfied a latent longing and gave it shape and hope, to want to be rewarded, visibly, definitely, let us say inorganically, for its deeds. It is the ideal of schoolchildren who have been accustomed to an examiner, to the allotment of marks, to the roster at the end of the term where all are placed in numerical order of merit. Curiously enough, this mode of thought is even commoner among women than men; the postulation of an infallible judge somewhere, somehow, who will examine work done and measure it exactly and register it in a stepped list of rewards. The sigh, "for recognition." But instead of Napoleon, with his big bag of ribbons, stripes, and rank warrants, you may if you wish place either a judging god, or the newspaper critics, according to your convictions.

The Legion of Honor was perhaps Napoleon's prettiest invention in this line, and it endures all the vicissitudes of change of governmental form. It was one of the most substantial payments made by Napoleon to the bourgeoisie he found sitting forlorn by the side of the success they did not know what to do with. As an institution it is connected with that imitative, largely literary, longing for "birth" with which they gazed after the aristocracy they had destroyed. In almost every middle class—why not say all?—this is observable, and even to be specified more closely. For your middle-class burgher, if he is French, or English, or American, it does not matter, not only longs for rank, which is a metaphysical synonym for birth, but still more: to find that he is the descendant of a good family. I think, trying to find an expression of a very subtle feeling, your truly Napoleonized bourgeois would prefer to discover he is the collateral descendant of an extinct nobility, some second son who ran away three hundred years ago to Baltimore, than to be regularly in line for a peerage. A whimsical combination of the love of the ledger, and the minor poetry of snobbism; as it were a sentimentality about bad debts which prescription has touched.

Connected with this, undoubtedly, is the conception of nationalism which Napoleon, if he did not invent it, at least introduced into the modern world. Byron, that excellent Napoleonist, certainly put increased vigor of emotion into it, but let us apportion fairly the credit of the strange movement that ended in the doctrine that has converted the world. Here again the emphasis, the romance, that is, or the poetical feeling is concentrated on the younger obscurer branches. A few feel it a pride to be a Jew. But oh! the millions who went wild when they were told by archæologists they were Slovaks; and the millions there must be, whose comfort and secret inspiration is that their great-grandmother was a Gipsy. This at bottom is poetry, middle-class poetry, the fascinating charm of old ledgers, the mysticism of carrying forward old entries, old claims forever and ever. Like the great system of the bookkeeping of honor, the first social register, the golden book of the Legion of Honor, this was one of Napoleon's principal and most ingenious social methods, and legacies to us all.

It was in such senses that may lie the deepest truth of Napoleon's confession, "I am the Revolution." For the revolution is the middle class, and Napoleon was its prophet, seer and messiah. He was for long its trusted employee. When his expense account grew too big, they were forced to part with him—reading Chateaubriand, that appears the fundamental reason of his downfall. When he returns from Elba, like a stock broker who has tired of golf, he speaks indeed to the French soldiers, not like a Plutarchian hero, but with the wheedling of a returning manager. "Will you shoot your old General? Do so. I am ready." So he said at Grenoble, and they had not the heart.

Is that not respectable and pathetic? Certainly, to my mind. The end of Napoleon, with its aggravations of being beaten by a Wellington and guarded by a Hudson Lowe, seems to be as tragic as a bankruptcy, as the failure of an old firm, and, thanks to Balzac, we know that that can be equal in dramatic density to the death of a king. But he had long ceased to be an adventurer, long resigned from our company, that is, and emigrated from our subject. So, a stout gentleman who has fallen on hard times, in the hands of ferocious creditors, we must leave him.

IX.

Lucius Sergius Catiline

THE ORDER HITHERTO FOLLOWED has been only loosely chronological. Once more for the purposes of the theme a great breach must be made in it. Just as palaeontology is used in comparative anatomy, so in the rare case of Napoleon it is natural to consult that vast, as it were, fossilized, collection of human types, the classical epoch of Rome, to find an elucidating contrast. That is the reason why Catiline, one of the most interesting possibilities of the history of the world, stands here.

As a matter of fact, he continues and develops rather than precedes the study of political adventure: it is so often the case that the characters and types of the Old World, when you turn them up, instead of appearing archaic, and contributing a sort of antiquarian foot-note, are astonishingly, even alarmingly modern—to say the least. Between Napoleon and Catiline, for example, it is not the two-thousand-year-old Roman who is old-fashioned; nor his times; nor his city. The adventure of Catiline, if it could scarcely be set anywhere at this definitely present day, could quite possibly belong to the future. Let us say in America, where the resemblance to pre-Christian Rome to those who are not baffled by merely sumptuary differences, who do not find a planetary distance between life with and without a telephone, grows every ten years more striking. To say that the present United States is the historical counterpart of old Rome is too far-fetched. To say that it will be extraordinarily like it in a hundred years is an intelligent probability.

There, then, the ruling class was on the whole immensely rich, and had begun to be immensely dissolute, without any apparent loss of the energy, the genius for organization, the daring, the hardness which had brought them to the mastery of the known world. Behind these patricians was a semi-poetical genealogy of well-born but impoverished emigrants from the other shore of the Mediterranean. They, too, possessed somewhere in reserve for orators, a countrified moral ideal, an agricultural list of virtues, in which frugality and honesty were put at the top.

As a rival to their power, there was principally a newer middle-class, which was still puritan, composed of country squires, and city merchants, and below that again was the elemental embryo of a monstrous proletariat, composed of slaves and the descendants of slaves, captured in the wars, who were already being used in an early factory system, landless soldiers, peasant serfs, and a dangerous underworld that had grown up around the gladiatorial shows. Some years before Catiline, this same underworld had embarked on the enterprise of Spartacus. This was a Thracian slave who escaped from a gladiators' training school, with seventy others, and in an incredibly short time was at the head of an army of seventy thousand runaway slaves, impoverished peasants, smugglers, broken soldiers and brigands of all kinds. The Republic had great difficulty in wiping him out.

And so in the overgrown city, the greatest, most picturesque contrasts existed. On the hills stood the gleaming palaces of the millionaires, "so rich," said Catiline once in a speech, "that they squander fortunes in building over seas, and levelling mountains, in joining mansions together and in the purchase of pictures, statues and embossed plate, and though lavishing and abusing their wealth by every possible method, yet cannot with the utmost efforts of caprice, exhaust it." Around them was an endless and complicated entanglement of thin streets, broad walks, public gardens—every conceivable variety of street-scape that the concentration of the power, wealth and industry of the world could create in untold centuries of building and decay. Roman population was immense and overcrowded, and socially as well as topographically, the highest world and the lowest, interpenetrated each other. In such a city the greatest scandals were always breaking out; huge cases in which the highest names were involved, not only of bribery and extortion, but of murder, and vice. Many of the great ladies mixed in the story of Catiline had intimate dealings with the scum of the underworld, thugs, blackmailers, whores, poisoners, abortionists; but, as I have said, in all this festering a curious character of hard energy prevailed. Old Rome sinned, more and deeper than Athens, or Alexandria, or Memphis, or any other great city of the past, but there was no sort of softness in its degeneration. It was still rather a boiling melting-pot than a cesspool.

Such a pace, naturally, not all could keep up. Many of the patrician familes, though retaining all their prerogatives of power, and usually the bare shell of their houses, were already utterly ruined. The great plague of the times, to all except the moralists, was debt. The credit system was in its youth. Some of the greatest families were not only utterly penniless, but endebted for more than they had ever possessed.

Fifty years before, such situations were still reparable. A good governorship, obtained by the family prestige, could be made to yield, out of the subject population, enough to start again in Rome, within a few years. But this game was showing signs of being worked out. First, because of the growing likelihood of prosecution, in which the inveterate enemies of the patrician class often won through the talents of the great lawyers they notably produced, Cicero, and the rest. And then, those families who had managed to preserve themselves, were more and more inclined to keep all the plums for themselves. The upper class had begun to concentrate, and to shed off to the ground those of its members who could not keep up with it.

Among these, in incompletely realized danger of being squeezed out, was the ruined Catiline. His life had been typical of the fast young society man of the epoch; that is, he had squandered madly, became mixed in several unsavory cases, borrowed up to and beyond the hilt, so that at thirty his only hope was in a rich post of governor, of the sort that were now becoming extremely difficult to acquire. Besides he had already had one, and had been impeached, convicted and dismissed. Indeed, this did not absolutely bar his prospects of another—Rome was not squeamish—nor that he was strongly suspected of having killed his brother-in-law, or, even, that during the *coup d'état* of Sulla, he had shown himself one of the cruelest in persecution of the defeated party. Perhaps the thing that Rome held worst against him, queerly enough, was his seduction of a Vestal Virgin, who happened, too, to be the sister-in-law of the great Cicero. The Vestal Virgins were practically the only sentimentality Roman society allowed itself; and that too is typical.

But though his reputation was below even the current standard for a young man of his class and time, still there was not enough in that, in itself, to distinguish him from scores, very likely hundreds of other dissolute young rake-hells. For that, the prime cause of his notoriety and interest, we must search carefully into his character, and find a name, if possible, for one extraordinary feature of what we find there.

This ruling class at Rome, the patricians, a rich, intelligent, vigorous oligarchy, was perhaps more like the group that has decreed its own membership in the Social Register of New York, than any of the European peerages.

It contrived, ingeniously, to be firmly anti-monarchical; at the same time jealously keeping to the hereditary principle. I do not think that the term aristocratic even in the corruptions of its many meanings could easily be applied to it. An aristocrat is usually the descendant of a long and illustrious line; he may be a person of taste and honor; yet these qualities do not cover the inner sense of the word, but rather only likely deductions from it, or perhaps vital consequences. Let us start at the other end. The natural man, if he is rich and powerful, is still ruled by the desire both to add to his possessions, or to preserve what he has. This underlying policy of his character underlies most of his reactions to social life. And if he is poor, even if he has nothing to preserve (and this is extremely rare even among gipsies or tramps), at any rate he feels continually an urge to acquire, which is only kept in order by his lack of intelligence, his fear of the law, moral or penal, and perhaps most usually by a certain sluggishness. Therefore, in this general majority there is a fundamental similarity, which may be opposed to that of an infinitely smaller group in whom this double instinct is either absent, or so deeply modified that it seems to be. For, while the instinct for property seems universal and invincible, there is another force just as natural which may be opposed to it, the force of habit; the effect of constant usage, which blunts every single human desire, perhaps even, as G. B. Shaw devoted a trilogy of plays to proving, that for life itself. That is to say, it is possible, though it is not common, that a man can be so used to the things which the rest of mankind hungers and thirsts to gain and keep: place, power, position, wealth, that he has completely lost his appetite for them. He cares no more for them than banqueters for food when they have come to their dessert.

It is this vital attitude for which I think we should reserve the name of aristocratic feeling. It is a spiritual satiety, obviously unlikely to occur in a man who had built his fortunes himself, who, as is said, "knows the meaning of money"; but perhaps natural to a descendant of a long line who have never lacked or stayed unsatisfied of any desire or ambition. In the special case of a great hereditary name, furthermore, there is obviously something, and that very considerable, which the holder can never lose: the title itself, and its indelible, inalienable prestige. Whatever happens to the fortune of an English duke, one thing remains that he can never squander, and which will always be envied and respected in him; and this, to the purists of the eighteenth century would, of course, make such a claim to pure aristocratic feeling suspect. But abandoning these niceties, I fancy that the commonest stigmata of aristocracy, the languor, the disdain, the boredom, as well as the code of honor, excluding a lie in a man who can feel no possible motive for one, since he fears nothing and desires nothing very much, are all explained by the analysis. Then, Aristocracy, in this reserved and I think useful distinction of meaning, is primarily a spiritual quality; an immaterialism, which might well, if carelessly compared to the way of life of a saint, seem equal or superior. An absence of desire, against a conquest of desire.

But though this curious consequence adds a certain attractive brilliance to the true aristocrat, a faintly supernatural glitter about his conversation and frequentation, it is much more shrewd to see in him a great danger. A gorged tiger, indeed, is much pleasanter to meet than a hungry one. I, for one, would prefer to be governed by a tired grand seigneur, rather than by a famished socialist newcomer. But in social life, the aristocratic possibility is by no means always ornamental, or reassuring, as you will see in the case of this perfect aristocrat, Catiline.

He and his likes in that old Rome were, beside the rest of the citizens, free, incalculable, unserious, uninfluenced by the great connexus of wholesome feelings by which the human pack is kept together in peace and trembling.

The personality of Catiline attracted round him a suitable milieu. In it were young men in his own station of life—Cneius Piso, "a young patrician of the greatest talents and daring"; Quintus Curius, who had been expelled from his hereditary seat in the Senate, as a blackleg gambler, and profligate; gentlemen like Publius Autronius, like Catiline convicted of graft in a public office; Lucius Cassius Longinus—an enormously fat man who had run for the consulate against Cicero himself; and scores of others, besides many of lesser or no rank.

Though without any regular source of income to pay them, for he had long ago exhausted both his own and his wife's money, and was inextricably in debt to money-lenders, he was surrounded, everywhere he went, with a small army of hangers-on from the lowest and most criminal class, fugitive gladiators and pugilists, men under a cloud, who both protected him and were protected by him in everything they did.

Since his trouble in the courts, Catiline had continued to play politics; he had even announced his intention of running for the consulate against Cicero, as the candidate of the "people's party." He had become entangled with a celebrated woman of the town, Aurelia Orestilla, "in whom no good man, at any time of her life, commended anything but her beauty," Sallust severely remarks. Nevertheless, or therefore, she had become possessed of a large fortune, and he actually married her; his enemies said, after poisoning his first wife and his son.

The young men whom he had drawn to join him, he initiated, by various ways, into evil practices. From among them he furnished false witnesses and forgers of signatures. "And he taught them all to regard with equal unconcern as himself honor, property and danger, and to be, like himself, gratuitously wicked and cruel."

The elections having resulted in complete failure, with the new funds of Aurelia at his disposal he began to organize his big idea. Probably, as an idea, the sack of Rome by the criminal classes had probably been in his head for a long while. Such characters often enough seem actually to have an affection, as much as they are capable of, for the poorest and vilest of human beings as a class. Not I suspect, through anything remotely resembling pity, or compassion, but through some obscure common term that exists in their desperation and his indifference. The underworld amused him. The prospect of letting them loose in a night of fire and blood on the respectable citizenry, the shops of the plodding bourgeoisie and the palaces of his own kinsmen and acquaintances, tickled him still more. You may, if you like, look for self-interest in the plotting of such a man; it is not hard to find, for one of the chief planks in his extraordinary "program" afterwards betrayed to the government by a kept woman in the secret, was "the total remission of all debts." And Catiline owed more than most. But at the bottom, the whole plot was a sinister drollery, the simple delight of stirring up great crowds to die and kill, of one who could not be swayed by anything himself; the anticipation of the spectacle of fear by one who was terrified at nothing. The vice of a man who had become inhuman by losing his human greed.

However crazy the project sounds, it was not at all impossible, in theory. The underworld population which he proposed to use was very large in size at Rome, very wicked, very desperate, and very devoted to him. The most serious combative elements in it were seasoned, and soured, veterans of Sulla; who had spent the grants they had been given for their services: terrible veterans, who could at any rate be counted on not to be merciful in a massacre. With them would move gladiators, professionals of the death struggle, the runaway pugilists, whose very servitude showed they had been picked out by connoisseurs of brutal ferocity, for their arm was the murderous Roman knuckleduster of hide and steel. With them, within the city, were an uncountable flock of men whose origins very likely were honest, members of the oppressed races which the Roman legions had crushed out by superior discipline: brooding, revengeful aliens, with memories of better times to correct any thoughts of mercy or compassion. Then there were the hordes of gentlemen, and tradesmen of all sorts, who had lost their way, their homes, and their hopes in the boom times which had enriched their rivals. A huge flock of beastly Asiatics, who sinned by religion, would follow these shock troops, doubtful, no doubt, in their general allegiance and courage, but a powerful accessory if things went well.

Outside Rome, in the vast estate of the Empire, circumstances were possibly even more favorable. I do not speak of those far provinces where the rapacity and heartless corruption of such men as this very Catiline, quite apart from the sufficient motive of revenge for their conquest itself, had made all men of spirit implacable enemies in Asia, in Africa, in Gaul: wherever the Roman standards were imposed, there were whole populations of born warriors restrained only by fear and lack of a leader or opportunity. That friend of Catiline, Piso, had actually managed his own appointment as governor of the Spains, with full military powers. He was deep in the plot with Catiline. Another, one Publius Sittius Nucerinus, another patrician, governor of Mauritania in North Africa, was accomplice in his plans. Catiline had engaged vast complicities in the background of Italy: in Etruria especially, where the pre-European population, embittered, revengeful, poor, had every reason for seeking the least opportunity of revenge on their conquerors.

With all this—and the genius of Catiline, who well knew how to work and was in no way inferior to the extraordinarily high general level of organizing ability in his class and roll, had fitted it painstakingly into his plans—there were large and dark complicities. It is said, and it is not incredible, that Marcus Livinus Crassus himself, one day to be, with Pompey and Cæsar, a member of the first triumvirate, the rulers of the world, had been let into the secret, Crassus, perhaps, but hardly Cæsar himself, though it is known that he was overheels in debt through his largesses to the populace, and his many enemies claimed to believe he too at least guiltily knew of the plot in its green state.

Sallust professes to be able to give notes of an actual speech made by Catiline at a meeting of the principal conspirators. Whatever its authenticity, at any rate it lights up the mood of those young patricians who listened to him. Catiline said, "Since the government has fallen under the power and jurisdiction of a few, kings and princes have quitted the habit of paying tribute to them all over the world; nations and states pay them taxes. But all the rest of us, however brave and worthy, whether patrician or plebeian, are looked upon by them as a mere mob, without importance or to be reckoned with, and under the heels of those whom, if things were right, we should be able to frighten out of their minds. Hence all influence, power and profit are in their hands, in their gift. For us they reserve only snubs, threats, persecutions, and poverty. How long now, you high-spirited fellows, are you going to put up with this? Is it not better to die trying to change the situation than to live tamely putting up with their insolence in a wretched and uninteresting condition of poverty and obscurity?

"But I swear success will be easy. We are young, our spirit is unbroken. Our oppressors, on the contrary, are only worn-out old millionaires. Therefore, we have only to make a beginning, and the rest will come about by itself."

But just as his statement of motives to this outer circle of conspirators was incomplete, leaning on the mere hope for a reshuffling of honors and posts of profit, and made hardly any mention of that inner malice, that desire to destroy stability itself because it bored him, so the aristocrat Catiline seems to have hidden from all but a chosen few the full program he intended. Which included not only the total abolition of debts, a proscription of all wealthy citizens— that is, the posting of a list offering a reward for their heads—and "a new sharing out of offices, sacerdotal dignities, plunder and all other gratifications which war and the licence of conquerors can afford," but, secretly, the firing and the sack of the whole city.

This young man in fact was using them all, from the young patricians who listened to his talk of ambition and debt-remission, to the lowest ruffian, to whom he promised loot and rape, as the tools of his own real design to civilization itself, like a bored, vicious boy, who might turn to burning the expensive toys he had lost interest in, just to amuse himself with the sight of the faces of those who gave them to him. The aristocrat has become an anarchist, from the opposite direction and the opposite motive by which extreme idealists and philanthropists sometimes arrive there. They would destroy government and burn Rome, because they believe in the goodness of the human heart: he, because it would be fun to see all, good and bad, art, morals, wealth, poverty, laws and police and criminals, go up in one great blaze together. We have here the adventure of Neronism: the instinct for destruction that comes smiling in, when all that men usually blame, greed and avarice, have withered out of the human heart.

And now, going back to the adventure of Napoleon, it ought to be clear that under their outward similarity of two *coups d'état*, two plots, two usurpations, there is a difference of exact opposition: Napoleon's vast passion for life, his timelessly insatiable want, is supremely conservative, constructive. He offered himself to the men who had, to save them, and their possessions, from the anarchy of mob-kings; and, driven by his own greed, he fixes and ruins himself in an attempt to build up a universal dynasty of kings. That is his end, and enough remained of its fragments to build the new Europe. So, his was the adventure of life, though it led millions to death. Catiline's, the adventure of death, led incidentally to the Roman

Empire, through Cæsar. Having easily counted Catiline's forces, we
have to turn now to the other side, much less simple to reckon. For
who can describe a weight? Yet it was mainly a weight that suffocated
him and his gangsters; the dead weight of the centre of gravity of the
Roman people, which had long ago shifted unperceived from his
fellow-patricians to the new middle-class, the new men. There was
little, indeed, aristocratic about these Roman burghers and squires:
horse-sense, liking for work, love of bad art, good morals, mon-
ey-making, and sententious speech-making. They built solidly, believed in paying and collecting debts; and if you visit the Vatican
gallery of Roman busts you can see what they looked like, and how
in their clean-shaven, rather obtuse dignity, they astonishingly resembled the sort of business man who makes good in Minneapolis
to this very day. Their leader at the time was that "glorious nonentity," Marcus Tullius Cicero, or, in translation, "Chick-pea." A hard,
indigestible plate for a man like Catiline to digest.

This Philistine, this predestined barrier against the adventure of a
ferocious bohemian, had more than his due honor, in the Middle Ages,
when the Latinists made a god of him—possibly because his literary
work that has survived is easy to construe—but rather less than is right
in our own times. It has become the fashion, launched by the English
schoolmasters, to despise him; to dig out the many traces of vanity,
and pompous vanity, both in his speeches and correspondence, and to
pin them together as a portrait of a ridiculous, puffy old fellow. All this
is inadequate. He was, of course, middle-class, a little excessively, perhaps, which is called prosy. But at great moments, the commonplaces
of honesty, virtue, justice, and the like are very big words indeed. His
life and his death prove that he actually believed in them. For the rest,
if on a horse in white armor in the Campus Martius, he was not in his
place, why, he was not a soldier at all, but a lawyer. With a pike in his
hand on the great evening, coming down a blazing street with other
burghers, his peers, he might well have impressed differently such evil
gladiators, rabble of pimps and thugs of Catiline that would not give
them gangway.

It has been said that Catiline was defeated by talk, by Cicero's speechmaking. There is this true in it, that for a long time after it was generally known that Catiline and his friends were preparing some sort of stroke against the regular government, there was even more apathy than the wide underground sympathy we have measured up. Even among the solid peaceful class, who, though they did not know it, were doomed in the secret thought of Catiline to pay most of the expenses of his amusement. It was a time of grumbling; no one was satisfied with the government of the patrician Senate, and practically everyone contemplated the mere idea of a change with pleasure. Crassus and Cæsar were, as we have seen, supposed generally to be mixed in it; only Cicero seems clearly to have seen that here was not a mere political disturbance, but the intention of a monstrous, almost lunatic, crime. The first step, therefore, obviously was exactly that which he took; that is, propaganda for what he knew. To get a higher platform for his denunciations, when Catiline as a first step entered his candidature for the yearly consulate, Cicero entered against him. The other member of his ticket was one Caius Antoninus, one of the moderates. So moderate, that in the revelations later it appeared that Catiline had secretly had negotiations with him for his neutrality. The meetings of the campaign were naturally lively; it ended with Cicero (who does not seem to have been any too sure that right and justice would win), shutting off the candidature of his enemy by a legal trick, by which he made him ineligible and stopped him going to the polls. And now with Cicero consul, and holding full power of the police (for he had bought the goodwill of Antoninus, the other elect, by an arrangement of the spoils), the struggle between the two men, the aristocrat and the burgher, was obviously one to the death. Catiline up till this point had been so certain of success that he had carried his plot on with a certain contemptuous laziness. Now he was roused to his demoniacal energy; meetings followed each other nightly at his house; arms were bought and stored, his forces were organized for sudden action both in Rome itself and in the provinces.

At all points, the reports of Cicero's police revealed movement and activity; the underworld shivered like a web that is being shaken from the corner. A vague massive apprehension, oftener seen in those vast eastern conglomerations of humanity, where men seem to think collectively, like bees, arose in Rome. Somehow the Roman people were realizing the danger; but so far and wide were the ramifications of the plot, so impenetrable except by suspicion the decisions of its inner ring of leaders, that Cicero, daily more in possession of the goodwill and confidence of his fellow-citizens, could do little actually but spy, fear and watch.

At this point an enormous advantage fell to him and the party of law and order. A certain Quintus Curius, a patrician "of no less levity than wickedness, altogether heedless of what he said or did, a man of no mean family but immersed in vice, debt and crimes," was rather far in the counsels of Catiline, who found in him rather a kindred spirit than a useful assistant. Curius was entangled with a patrician lady, named Fulvia, who had had a large share in his ruin, and at this time was threatening to cut the connection because of his lack of money. But this Quintus Curius, growing less acceptable to her, because in his reduced circumstances he had less means of being liberal, he began of a sudden to boast and to promise her seas and mountains, "and even to threaten her that if she was not good to him, at some future time, when some great thing he did not specify had happened, he would be in a position to revenge himself as well as reward her." Fulvia, who, at any rate, had a perfectly healthy appetite for money, took this piece of information to Cicero's police for sale; the great man was informed of it, and immediately saw its importance. The charming Fulvia was paid handsomely; Quintus was secretly arrested, and after an old Roman third degree, consented not only to tell what he knew, but (for pay) to continue as a government spy inside Catiline's committee.

From that moment Cicero knew almost hourly everything that Catiline wished to keep secret. The first benefit was to scotch a plan for his own murder, for which Catiline sent a picked party of specialists to his house. Cicero, after that, formed his own private guard of vigilantes. But still the struggle was not so unequal. This was not a plan for the attack of a fortress but a fibrous growth in the very vitals of an organism, and even when located, mapped, and with the instruments ready, the utmost care was necessary for its cutting. The least false or hurried move, and those "consular personages," the great Cæsar himself, Crassus, would be forced into the arms of Catiline with all their immense influence, following, and ability. Cicero was by no means of equal importance or influence in the Senate with such giants. And yet every moment counted. The underground monster burrowed on frantically with his preparations. Even Quintus Curius could not reveal how near was his hour.

The order of events now is simple. A lieutenant of Catiline's, one Manlius, a tough old soldier, had charge of the preparations for uprising in Faesulae, that is, in the heart of Etruria, where the remnants of a once great nation were ever ready to try one more fight against Rome. Whether Manlius was over-confident, or whether local feeling was too strong for him, the commencement of a riot broke out there, and this gave Cicero the excuse, or the obligation, to call out the militia and demand and obtain from the Senate—on the whole hostile to him—the special powers granted when the Republic was decreed in danger. At the same time, according to the custom, a senatorial reward was offered for information on the conspiracy; "if a slave—his freedom and a hundred sestertia; if a freeman—complete pardon, and two hundred." At this time, Sallust goes on, "the Empire of Rome seems to have been in an extremely deplorable situation, for though every nation, from the rising to the setting of the sun lay in subjection to her arms, and though peace and prosperity were hers in abundance, yet notwithstanding these offers of the government, not one individual, out of so vast a number in the plot, was induced to give information, nor was there a single deserter from the side of Catiline."

The issue indeed seemed to totter. The city was tremendously excited and depressed; all work stopped while the citizens in gloomy or angry groups discussed the various rumors; crowds hung round the house of Cicero, either silent or uttering threats and imprecations and curses against him.

The whole situation therefore was covered in fog. The honest majority of citizens could not clearly recognize in it where were their friends, where their foes; eminently favorable therefore for Catiline. Parties, complicities, misunderstandings, compromissions had created such a vast tangle that the central opposition was completely lost. It was as if the burgher of Rome looked out and saw the street filled with a vague mob, an inextricable confusion of policemen, bandits, politicians, bystanders, in the middle of which something strange and awful was obviously going on, but what it was impossible to make out. A cloudy, boiling liquid, disturbed by all the sepia and the foam which the monster in the centre threw out around him. Only a few moments were left. Cicero had to make up his mind: no mere act of power could help him now, for it would merely add a new disturbance to the whirling storm. In this mass where friend, half-friend, democrat, criminal, lunatic, and statesman were all mixed, the only hope was a stroke, more like a chemical precipitation than a surgical cut. Or still more like a dive of the net, directed into the very centre, to bring up into clear daylight the monster himself, and as few other fish as possible, so as not to break it with their weight. Simply to arrest Catiline would be to start a gigantic riot; he must be exposed. Never perhaps was an orator more useful, more necessary. Those who despise this great art of explanation, in which the intellectual analysis, the display of facts, is made white-hot by the resources of style and voice and delivery, might meditate the case. How could a mere general, a Napoleon, a hero, now save Rome? Only a Cicero, the orator, could and did do it; and those three speeches of his against Catiline have been saved as an eternal part of the common treasure of civilization.

Their effect was of a pitiless and unwavering searchlight directed into the midst of a cavern and held there; so that never thereafter was there the least doubt possible to the most confused mind as to exactly what the darkness contained. He revealed Catiline, even to his supporters. He held him up by the ears above Rome, tortured, conquered, even (in the height of Cicero's effort), ridiculous. He made Catiline and his conspiracy actually simple; the man himself had the courage to sit in front of him and listen, and at the end, it seemed as if he had exposed Catiline even to himself.

At any rate he seemed—this man who was always cold as ice—embarrassed and ashamed when he rose to reply, and could only make a few mumbling phrases very different from his style, "that he hoped the Senate would not be hard on him and believe everything too hastily," "that they were not really to suppose that he, a patrician, whose ancestors' services had been so numerous to the state, should want to ruin it, while Marcus Tullius Cicero, a mere upstart, one of the new families, was eager to preserve it." He said no more, for a unanimous yell of hatred and contempt rose against him, crying "traitor," and "enemy." In the midst of it, screaming threats back which could not properly be heard, he left the assembly.

And Rome. From the city he hurried to the camp of Manlius in Etruria. Cicero and the police made no attempt to stop him; for their whole object had been to isolate him, to disengage him and his where he could clearly be seen, and now fought with iron.

The lieutenants whom he left in charge in Rome, were very cautiously arrested, after an elaborate police-trap had been set for them. They were Lentulus, Cethegus, Statilus, Gabinius, and Coeparius, mostly young, mostly patricians; the proofs of their guilt were documentary, and a determined attempt was made by the gangs to fire the prison and release them. Nevertheless Cicero proceeded slowly against them. Their situation exempted them from any summary jurisdiction.

He was obliged to prosecute them before the legislature. One phase of this trial shows how delicate was Cicero's situation, and how justified he was in going with every precaution. For after the evidence had been produced, and indeed they had all virtually confessed, Cæsar himself stood up; (and his personal influence over the senators was incomparably superior to Cicero's) to demand lenient treatment and subtly to discount the gravity of the affair. Had it not been for Cato, who, as grandson of the terrible old "censor" and as head of the old-fashioned puritan country squires had a great influence, at this late moment the whole business would have fallen back again into the confusion, where no doubt Cæsar for his own reasons and ambitions desired to keep it. But this Cato (years afterwards like Cicero to die a victim in Cæsar's coup) stood up immediately after the great soldier, and, without any consideration for his feelings, poured sarcasm on his "softness" and rasped out indignantly a plea for the utmost old-fashioned severity for the conspirators. Thus: "What I advise, then, is this—that since the state, by a treasonable combination of dissolute citizens, has been brought into the greatest peril; and since the plotters have been arrested, and more, convicted on their own confession of having thought up massacres, incendiarisms, and all sorts of horrible and cruel outrages on their fellow-citizens, punishment be inflicted according to old-fashioned precedent, as on men found guilty of a capital crime."

The senators, carried away, for once offended their favorite Cæsar, and passed the sentence of death. Immediately, without waiting a day for them to change their minds, Cicero's police hurried the Catilinians away to the chief prison of the city. It was getting dark. There was a place in this prison called the Tullian dungeon, which was a filthy dark cellar sunk about twelve feet under the ground. Arrived at this lugubrious place "full of dirt, darkness and stench, Lentulus first was lowered into it by a rope round his arm-pits, and down there was strangled to death by the executioners who were waiting." The rest, in their turn, had the same fate.

Lentulus had actually himself once been Consul. His family was among the greatest and most influential at Rome, and his end caused an enormous sensation. Hoping to profit by this, Catiline touched off, at last, his revolt. His Etrurian army, numerous but ragged, ranging in discipline and arms from his picked regiments of Tuscan patriots, stiffened with veteran soldiers, to the rabble of slaves and villains, many of whom had nothing but a pointed stake, a scythe or a hammer, fell upon the troops of the other consul, Antoninus himself, who had gone out of the city to meet them, with a small regular force.

Each of the combatants pursued the same tactics. They had previously seeded out the veterans from the mass of their forces, to act as shock troops, and therefore the first encounter was terrific; equally tough, equally experienced on both sides, the spectacle of the clash of these old Romans must have pleased and delighted Catiline himself. He stood under a rock, with his most devoted and sure gangsters around him, and he had put up an eagle or standard, a relic of some former war that had long been in the possession of his family. But as soon as he saw that the fight was pretty much in equilibrium, he threw himself and his companions into it, on one of the flanks of the mêlée. In the centre the fight was on. The opposing veterans early threw away their spears and missiles and came to it hand to hand with the short stabbing sword that conquered the world. Here was no place for mere gangsters and bandits, however ferocious, who therefore used their influence on the wounded on the outskirts, while then the brave but unseasoned levees of Etrurian burghers, along with the wild torrent of slaves, shepherds, pickpockets, pugilists and runaway gladiators, were launched by Manlius in a moving mass. It was apparently the Pretorian cohort, a superb regiment of heavy cavalry, who finally turned the day for the State. They had not the habit of being resisted by any foot soldiers alive, even Roman veterans, and driving with hardly any loss of impetus through the frantic light troops of Catiline, that famous army of the underworld which had long terrorized the imagination of peaceful citizens, as if it were a mere pack of wolves, they arrived in a charge on the deadlocked centre and dissolved it. Manlius, Catiline, all his principal lieutenants on horseback almost simultaneously disengaged themselves, and leaving tactics to look after themselves, rushed to meet them in this whirlpool. There they all died.

There was a great slaughter on that day. It is recorded that no single freeman of Catiline's forces survived, and the conquerors lost all their bravest men. The survivors of the rebels were hunted for sport afterwards by the regulars, and when the army was withdrawn a great cloud of police and their spies descended on the district to probe and extirpate every trace of the abscess, which a short time before had seemed to threaten the very existence of Rome, and the bed of current universal history.

This was the unparalleled adventure of Catiline and his by no means inglorious end. The rest of the conspiracy, once he was gone, squibbed here and there, in Gaul, in the slums of Rome; but it was rather easily extinguished. The most important part of it, except the force of Catiline himself, was the complicity of Piso, the new governor of Spain. But on the very threshold of an attempt to lead his troops in the wrong direction, this ambitious young man was assassinated by them; a curious thing, for Sallust says that never before or after were Spaniards known to mutiny, being a patient as well as a dour people. Perhaps the hand of Cicero's secret police can be seen in this, too.

And so, I think the adventure of this young aristocrat one of the most surprising of all. He was conquered no doubt mainly by the momentum of established society, which I see (and not mere chance), showing itself in the various accidents which worked against him. Even more than its character of the unusual, this attack on a republic, one might well say, on a whole civilization, has its interest in the extraordinary likelihood of its being one day repeated, once the simple factors favorable occur again. A disorganized political situation, a large underworld, and a group of aristocrats who have lost all beliefs, all sense of responsibility, and all fear of consequences: such are elements which the normal evolution of the world by no means tends to make rare. But we, who have not the slightest interest in political dangers or their prophylaxy here, who are only occupied with the study of the adventurer and have abjured moralizing even about a creature like Catiline, must treat the case as it concerns us, and can leave future republics to find or not, as the gods decide, their Cicero and their Cato.

Catiline's adventure, as we agreed, clearest when it is set alongside that of a builder like Napoleon, is the adventure of death. In a sense it was nearer suicide than murder. For what in a smoking mound, a mountain of corpses, could Catiline find for himself? No empire could have come out of the plan, in its perfect success; and long before he could have clutched the crown even of this abattoir, his own followers would extremely certainly have cut his throat and thrown him too on the pike. For as Sallust says, "Even the poorest and most abandoned did not like the idea of burning the city where they had their own homes, nor, until Cicero revealed it, did they understand that this, and not a great loot and redistribution, was in Catiline's mind." No, like suicide, this was a great adventure of world-weariness, and he who undertook it, and all those, Lentulus and the rest, who followed him in the secret of his spirit, were free from all the ordinary desires or greeds that have been the motives of all other adventurers. Yet impassionately, the same laws, the same rules of the game played with the gods of Fate seem to have been extended to them, who wanted to die, as to those who wanted to live. Catiline had no more, no less luck than a Napoleon, or an Alexander. The gods are indifferent. His trajectory, while the full force of his will and daring were in play, rose as steep as any of the others. Errors in timing, wishes to sit and count his gains, in this peculiar case the sight of the terror and confusion on the faces of his fellow-citizens, before he killed them; this gloating, when he should have struck upward and outward, lost him.

X.

Napoleon III

THE GENEROUS, DEMOCRATIC VIEW of history, which still has a following, is summed up nicely by Leo Tolstoi, in his famous description of great men as "tickets of history." By which he meant, that only the billions count. Number and poverty were thought to be the only important virtues of mankind. Nevertheless, though the theological authority for this dogma is clear and respectable (it is a corollary to the beatitudes), it is guaranteed rather by mystical intuition which I do not possess, rather than by any obvious support of appearances. The curious case, that we now can proceed with, would indeed be a trial to true believers in the automatism of history, for here was an individual and an individualist, who plainly altered the history of Europe, and not in a small way, but by deflecting its principal tide or currents until and through our own day. Moreover, according to all his historians, both the few grave ones and the mighty college of wits, he was properly not a great man at all.

But this luckily does not concern us, for we renounced all such secretly moral judgments at the beginning. He was a great adventurer; a beautiful addition to our collection.

Charles Louis Napoleon Bonaparte is said by some to have been the illegitimate son of a Dutch admiral, by others, of a music or dancing master. This is probably polemical romance, to discredit or discount him. His legal status is enough for our more objective purposes; that he was the third son of Louis Bonaparte, brother of the Emperor, and King of Holland, and of his wife Hortense, daughter of Josephine by General Beauharnais. He was therefore an integral organ of that extracorporeal extension of Napoleon's personality, whose growth and purpose we examined previously. The Emperor soon noticed the possibilities of the little boy, standing as he did to him as both uncle and adoptive grandfather, and once remarked, "Who knows but that the future of my race may not lie in this thoughtful child?"

Louis was born in 1808, so that beyond what pleasure the Emperor could have obtained from seeing him eat bonbons, Louis could not have been of much service to his vicarious appetite for life. Nor could the direct influence have been very important.

His half-brother, Charles Auguste Louis Joseph, afterwards known as the Comte de Morny, was born when Louis was three years old. There is no doubt about the identity of the father of this child of Hortense's, at any rate. He was the Comte de Flahaut, a picturesque peer, himself adulterine, with no less a father than the one-time bishop, Talleyrand, himself. Morny will come in later in the story.

After Waterloo, Queen Hortense was exiled to Florence, where she had a scandalous lawsuit with her husband, the ex-king. From there, with only little Louis of all her children with her, she wandered over Switzerland and Germany, settling down at last in the purchase of the castle of Arenenberg, in the canton of Turgau, looking down on Lake Constance. The boy was now about nine years old. Here he learnt to ride, well; and swim and fence; and received a general skirmishing education. His two tutors, one the son of Lebas, the friend of Robespierre, both ardent adepts of Bonapartism, initiated him into the arcana of that doctrine, in which the philanthropy of the revolution is reconciled with romantic nationalism, or jingoism, and the hatred of kings, with the divine right of plebiscitary emperors. Louis never developed even a rudimentary apparatus of self-criticism. The ideas he was given at this period, he retained until the end of his life. Before he was twelve years old, all of them, particularly his mother, had instilled into him that he was born to succeed his grandfather, to make everyone happy and prosperous under his own absolute rule. The Bonapartes by this time had come to believe themselves in their mission.

At the most impressionable age, Lebas took him on a tour through Italy, along the itinerary of both his grandfather's and Cæsar's victories, which ended with a visit to Letizia in her retirement at Rome; which quickened his life purpose to the sort of apostolic fervor you may imagine.

This country, for the most part in the power again of Austria, became the principal field of his life, since he was barred out of France by law. When the 1830 revolution drove out the Bourbons, all the immense clan of Bonapartes scattered over Europe undoubtedly began to hope more seriously. But the French, passing them over, adopted the mediocre solution of an Orleans, who could claim only to be related to the legitimate heirs, and to be only tacitly the choice of the people. Nevertheless in spite of the fragility of his logical position, Louis Philippe d'Orleans was in fact the nominee of the only class which matters in a modern state, the bourgeoisie; and it seemed clear to all the realists of Europe that he and probably his dynasty would last.

So, postponing any hope of fulfilling his full destiny, Louis set himself to such good works as lay to his hand. As he could not give humanity the full benefit of his benevolent despotism, he could help them to all the minor benefits of liberty. Therefore, he joined the Carbonari.

This was a secret society, of a style which a few generations hence they may find hard to understand. It combined the most merciless and gloomy methods, with the mildest and happiest ideals. The realization of an earthly paradise through private assassination and street war. It had borrowed from mostly French sources the furniture of its ideal; the bliss of universal suffrage from the Revolution, the decoration of nationalism, from, of course, Napoleon. It was extremely competent, terrible, and widespread; no one who had ever joined it could desert until the millennium under pain of death. In the Europe that was preparing for 1848, the Carbonari were near the centre of a web-work of obscurely affiliated and sympathetic societies, from Ireland to the Bosphorus.

Nor did the prince simply play at conspiracy. The secrets of the

Carbonari to this day are no more accessible than those of the Society of Jesus; but it is known there was no room among them for parlor members. In 1831 they organized a rising in the Romagna; Louis was captured after the hot little affair of the taking and retaking of Città Castellana. His mother with greatest difficulty succeeded in contriving his release from the Austrian dungeon where he was confined; high diplomacy failing, she managed to bribe the guards. He escaped in this way to France, and Louis Philippe, with extraordinary magnanimity or weakness, allowed him to stay in Paris for a few months.

Safe back in Arenenberg, Hortense induced him to rest and read for a while. He had by now become, as dreamy, round-eyed boys often do, a rather solemn young man, very serious on the subject of himself. For some reason, in fits and starts throughout his life, he was addicted to writing. To this period belongs his great work, "Political Dreamings," in which, with many quotations from his grandfather's speeches and sayings, he put into rather imprecise words, at the same time slightly pompous, with a wilful discretion about his own ambitions, the dream that you know all over the world. Every workman, burgher and farmer was to live happy, contented, and free (of any foreign yoke); in his spare time, perhaps to die gloriously for the old country, with which every man is supplied at birth; this golden age to come about by the means of a strictly disciplinarian ruler, one who could truly represent the necessary inner discipline and direction— in fact an early Fascism.

But though this book gave him satisfaction (and for years he never allowed it to go out of print, quoting from it almost up to the end), after its completion he left Arenenberg. He had not yet fallen in love; he was twenty-seven. The family funds were low. Life was calling to him. One of his first mistresses was a Swiss singer named Eleanore. He met her in the next period, his service as an artillery officer in that country. She appears to have brought him some needed funds; a phenomenon often repeated in his life. Evidently a different style from Casanova's but such as is often observable in the case of men with missions, especially when these are very personal.

With a slow even progress, the tilt of things was meanwhile shifting towards him and his ambition in France. To explain, or even to describe in detail this movement is a subtle and delicate matter, but since necessary if the further adventure is not to be left a mere miracle, must be attempted.

The growth of the Napoleon legend in France during these years is an emotional phenomenon, like the course of a love affair. But are not the strongest motives of that glorified crowd, the nation, the electorate, always of this emotional nature? In moments of indifference, interest may prevail; for all the serious affairs of war and peace, change of government, whenever the voice of the people can make itself heard, it is as hoarse as the shout of a mob, surcharged with hate, or chuckles or love.

In the engagement of the Orleans king (for such it was), the responsibles were a thinking class, pursuing their interest, who imposed their will on the incurably sentimental mob by force and manœuvres. That was its only, but fatal weakness; the people, forced into a sort of marriage of reason with the Orleans family, like Madame Bovary, found it emotionally unbearable. In these circumstances, the amorous giantess looked round for lovers. Two presented themselves, the democratic dream, and the Napoleon myth. The first is none of our business, and indeed there was not a straight choice between them, for whereas the Republic excluded the Empire, the Empire offered, not certainly logically or rationally, but in the hazy, quasi-feminine mode in which the people themselves prefer to think, all the handsome traits of the Republic. We have remarked this in Louis's "Political Dreamings."

But how out of a thick, short, yellow chrysalis, the Emperor of history, the gloriously colored butterfly of the myth arrived, is a mystery of imaginative morphology. I can see, darkly, certain factors. The veterans were either dead or fallen into the story-telling age, and no old soldier ever tells how he hated the draft. Thirty years after any war, or much less, all check on soldiers' stories of their doings is buried in dusty files; the returning enemies of Bonaparte had destroyed and interdicted even these records. And so I suppose there was hardly a man over forty in any village of the land who had not been present at the most dramatic and pictorial moments of the great campaigns; who had not seen and actually been patted on the cheek by the Emperor. And Napoleon himself, in the course of this process, had recovered his youth, his romance, and his fire. The haggard yellow man in a coach of Waterloo was gone; the little corporal had put on the everlasting unchangeability of an artistic creation; he was as fixed and as real as Achilles, or Hamlet, or Sigurd.

So every fireside was a shrine of the new religion. Every youth in the land, fretted by that past of all young men, the consciousness of insignificance, heard nightly, in the resentment that has three parts of envy, some grown man telling, "When we were lined up, in front of the enemy, I remember the Emperor himself, on his horse…" Or, if he were a petty quill-driving youth, imagine the effect of that one which begins: "In garrison in Warsaw, we Hussar officers used to ride out every evening in a great park, on the outskirts, where all the fashionable society of the city used to take the air. Well, one evening…"

Then—you could fill an encyclopedia with reasons—there was the poet, Béranger. A poet, like an orator, has little influence when he utters the unpublished. But when either of them gives expression to what is struggling in the under-consciousness of all men, then he is as irresistible as the fountains of the great deep in Genesis. So this Béranger put into insolent little lilts, along with a profusion of new ways of courting women, praises of the old glory, taunts for the new regime, and these were sold everywhere and diffused as it were with the air. This, if you like, was propaganda. Strange and unlikely that Napoleon should have had a poet, and such an enchantingly light and gay one; but so it was.

In spite of all that young intellectuals could do about it, when this people of France were bored they dreamed, not of republics, but of a master, when they wept, it was not for Sieyès or Robespierre, but Marshal Ney and Bonaparte. All this emotion, this homesickness, was, as it were, unowned, like the first yearnings of a virgin. Hardly ten people had even heard of Louis; probably no single person thought seriously of his claims. Bonapartism was a feeling, a reverie reflected entirely into the past; it was not a pact, but a sigh, "O the old drums and fifes," "O the old days, the old deeds"; a music, a haunting tune, that to the words of Béranger girls hummed as they did their ironing, that street boys whistled on their errands.

It was Louis's necessity to capture this nostalgia, to condense this vapour on himself. To this he now began to set himself with a curious variety of that purified will which is the tool of all adventure; he was indeed single-minded, and imagist, he composed a momentum. All this in his own style, which was both flexible and tough, sweetly obstinate, as his mother once irritably diagnosed. Nothing could really deflect him. But at every moment he seemed to waver.

His first attempt was a failure to the point of the ridiculous. With an uneven band of friends, he worked out a conspiracy which left everything to luck after the first movement; so, with Eleanore and a Carbonarist named Fialin, one old colonel and a little lieutenant he betook himself in disguise to Strassburg and tried to bribe the soldiers of the garrison to mutiny for him. He was almost reluctantly seized by the secret police along with too much incriminating evidence to worry to take away, and without making a ripple or provoking a shot deported to America by the government.

In the autumn he returned to Arenenberg in time to see his mother, the once dangerous beauty, on her death-bed. From there he went to Switzerland again, broke with Eleanore, and from there to London.

Here he took up the regular profession, commoner then even than now, of conspirator. He dined in grubby restaurants in the foreign quarter, with seedy, fierce-looking young men, such as Fialin, Arese and the Carbonari. Years of talk across dirty table-cloths that always ceased ostentatiously when a stranger approached in ear-shot. Sometimes, since he was a Bonaparte, he was asked to the receptions of the great, where the guests eyed him as a curiosity. D'Orsay, Disraeli, and that omniscient lion-hunter, Lady Blessington, had relations with him. He is said to have enlisted on one occasion as a special policeman during Chartist troubles and patrolled the streets, for a philosophy of reasons. At last he met Miss Howard; who adored him and was very rich.

In 1839, having been delivered of another book, in which he explained that Napoleon was the first martyr of socialism and pacifism, and proved it, he tried again to seize the throne. This time thanks to a "Miss," it was a larger and more luxurious affair. He landed on the beach some miles from the quai at Boulogne, with fifty-six followers, and the party moved on towards the town. A squad of coast-guards and gendarmes came out to meet them, and Louis (or one of his friends) held out the bags of money to them, encouraging them to cry "Vive l'Empereur." Ensuing were shots; one or two of his friends fell; he and the rest were arrested.

This time the King was nervous, and a regular trial followed. With the help of the grand old advocate Berryer, who defended him, he had more personal publicity from this than he had ever had in his life. Henceforward everyone who could read a newspaper in France had, at any rate, heard of him and his claim. On the other hand, he was condemned to imprisonment for life in a fortress, one of those sentences, both savage and impracticable (for they are never carried out), which are the common faults of an intelligent and worried repression. Nevertheless, they kept him for six whole years in the fortress of Ham, where, still mildly inflexible, he gained the affections of his gaolor's daughter and wrote other books on Bonapartism.

Imprisonment has usually no other effects on such a mind, near crankiness, that is, than to confirm it in its curve, and also, very often, to add an accessory of new projects for carrying the old ones out. Back in London, with increased mildness, obstinacy, and conviction, he continued to plot and devise.

Crank or not, he was complying with the decrees of destiny; and his turn at last came. The revolution of 1848, that "spree-year of Liberty," pushed Louis Philippe and his umbrella out of France. Louis Napoleon, loaded with money for propaganda (which this time he used through a bank and not in its native bags), came back to France. A very small ripple. The astounding progress of the adventure from this point is like one of those conjurer's tricks, hard to see even when it is explained. He arrives then first of all a discredited and fantastic personage in the middle of a revolution, with a grimy fortune, and a name. No serious party welcomes him, works for him, or stands for him. His only influential friend outside the boudoirs or the gutter is his half-brother Morny, whose somewhat poetical origins we have related. Morny, also partly with the help of women in love, had made a considerable fortune in commerce and the stock exchange; a daring gambler, a shady character. With them, a third, his Fialin, once a sergeant-major, and now self-appointed Comte de Persigny, author of a book to prove that the Pyramids were the remains of the old Nile Dam, and that Egypt would be turned into a lake if they were destroyed. Catiline himself had no more commonplace inner council.

This 1848 revolution was, under all the superficialities of politics and class interest, the work of the poets; from the beginning, that is, it had no lawful owner. In this time that our trio were working, it had not been settled, who—the poets being out of the question—should inherit the power. The mob? A strong candidate. The bourgeoisie? Divided and bothered, under Thiers, who was really an Orleanist. The army of Cavaignac?—The legitimists? Hopeless. In this cauldron, the three fished, they stirred, and at last caught something.

There was no question, truly, of setting party against party, since not one of them took the slightest notice of these neo-imperialists. Cavaignac had got the mob under at last, by force; the issue thereupon narrowed down, and lay seemingly between him and Thiers. At this moment, Louis buys his election as a deputy to Parliament. Naturally, he insisted on making a speech; probably it would have contained once more the whole doctrine as revealed. But on the steps of the tribune where half the house, on hearing his name, watched him waddle, with great curiosity, his nerve failed him. He mumbled something and ignominiously retired. There was a laugh; the Bonaparte cause was over.

But Thiers had noticed him. And Thiers was in extraordinary difficulties. The party of Cavaignac was winning; his own interests, which he never neglected, were in a very poor posture. The thought came to Thiers, then, possibly at that very moment of ridicule, that here was a last home; to take this imbecile, this dummy, and work up his candidature for the presidency against Cavaignac. Unmistakably the electorate would not have a Thiers; there was the shadow of a hope they might take a Bonaparte.

And so—you will understand, not without hesitations—the bourgeoisie of the Party of Order, under Thiers and Mole, gave their support to Louis in the elections for the Presidency of the Republic of 1848. His program was excessively bizarre and excessively clever. He appealed for the votes of the mob, the revolution, first by his past of active revolutionary, his democratic mysticism. But, also, because of the party of order, he asked for Catholic votes, promising to give the church the monopoly of education, and promising his support to the temporal power of the Pope. Orleanists, like Thiers, voted for him because they calculated that he would be in their hands, or, at worst, would try some mad coup, at a later date when they were ready to lock him up and restore their King. The legitimists may have supported him out of spite against all the other candidates. The result was far out of proportion with all this mere trickery. Instead of being defeated miserably, as Thiers feared, or elected by a meagre majority as he himself hoped, he was swept up in a mighty rush to the Presidency, by 5,434,226 votes to Cavaignac's bare million and a half. Like apprentice sorcerers, his sly users had been messing with the uncontrollable forces of the deep. Most clever people who try to play chess with human beings have a similar accident sooner or later.

An inquest is hardly needed. We have already remarked the huge latent Bonapartism of France; this, like a room full of coal gas, needed only a lighted match. France, without any politician suspecting it, longed only for a Bonaparte, and the fools put one within her reach.

And so, from a catch-vote expedient, Louis has now instantly grown into a ruler, the concrete and redoubtable expression of the will of the people. Thiers, Mole, Cavaignac, all these brilliances and responsibilities fall into a mere opposition. Some vanish, some remain, to live through the next twenty-five years on a diet of pure, undiluted patience, without any admixture of the slightest rational hope of ever again feasting on power.

Having achieved the main chance, the details, hard as they were, were not to beat him and his ready-for-anything bottle-holders, Morny, Persigny, and the rest. Nevertheless he must not lose credit for a suddenly revealed genius for political manœuvre in this position of a President under a constitution that allowed him hardly any powers, and with a parliament that was openly his enemy. He outmarched, out-fought, over-reached them all, with the virtuosity of his grandfather at work on an Austrian army. At last, then, there is the 2nd of December, 1851.

This, the classic, the technical model of all *coups d'état*, has evidently many fascinating elevations. That of the resistance, only because it had an immense poet to delineate it, is probably the best known, and will outlast the interest of most of the others, for no other reason. Nevertheless, it was in sober truth, unimportant. He whom the dazzle of style cannot quite blind must see beneath Hugo's "Napoleon the Little," and "The Story of a Crime," how poor, unprepared, nearly silly, in their inadequacy were all the rushings to and fro of the resisting deputies, the sending of the fiery cross round the old working-class stronghold of the Faubourgs, the flimsy barricades and the noble, useless deaths on top of them, which was the sum of the effort to undo what Louis, Morny, Persigny, had so well conceived, and with inexorable competency carried out. So much for the first movement of the piece. The bribing of the army—the new Emperor distributed among the troops every penny he possessed the morning of the deed—the seizure of the central control of the whole machine of state by a minimum of judicious arrests, and sabotages; (just one detail: the conspirators had seen to it that even the drums of the national guard were burst the night before, so that they could not be used to raise the alarum; and every printing press in Paris was seized)—all this was beautiful in its line and impeccable. Any adventurer henceforward who directs himself towards the destruction of his nation's liberties, and the complete burglary of power must learn the plot of Louis Bonaparte by heart to the letter. Later, it was not quite so good. Two days later, for instance, there was the boulevard massacre. It was a fine Thursday afternoon. From the Madeleine to Bonne Nouvelle, the street was crowded with peaceful citizens and their wives. Perhaps because Morny, who was somewhere there in command, lost his head; or more likely, because the troops were all drunk—that was the later official explanation and excuse—a terrible slaughter, a Catilinian killing took place. The artillery and the infantry fired for ten minutes down the crowded highway. No one counted the dead.

With this ends one of the rarest adventures of Europe, and so begins another. For an adventure differs from a mere feat in that it is tied to the eternally unattainable. Only one end of the rope is in the hand, the other is not visible, and neither prayers, nor daring, nor reason can shake it free.

You may distinguish in what followed the merely picturesque, that is, the spectacle of this band of greedy and needy men composing a court of themselves and enjoying their immeasurable conquest of an Empire in their own way; or, the fate of the suffused philanthropy of Louis Bonaparte; or, the mechanism of his downfall twenty-five years later which embryologically began the day he stole the crown—to be exact, on the Thursday of the massacre. For that, as certain crimes do, brought him bad luck. It was no more difficult indeed to cover up by those who held the locks of every printing press in France, to remove its material traces from the pavement, than all the rest of the deed. But it put the Republicans irreconcilably against him; and worse still, the poets. I have heard it said by an astute politician that the worst handicap of the new regime, that finally brought it down was that all the poets, Victor Hugo, naturally in exile, in chief, were against it. It may be true in the same sense that its potential beginning was in the songs of Béranger.

And yet these almighty muses, who break and build empires oftener than the Philistines can imagine, had serious reasons to esteem the Third Empire. Paris, for example, the world city. From the champagne-culture of Montmartre to the matriarchal civilization of the Rue de la Paix, the marvellous, unchartered University of

Montparnasse, everything that the name Paris brings into mind, without racking your brains, is the demonstrable work, or any rate result, of Louis Napoleon. Quite apart from the expected tastes of the friend of Miss Howard, Morny, and Persigny, there was a policy, a pure resultant between the necessary repression of Republicans, and the theory of the Emperor that humanity should have a good time. Therefore, Paris, alone of the cities of the world, in the full centre of the Puritan-industrialist reaction that was making every other a desert of respectability, was encouraged, sometimes incited to enjoy itself in any way except in talking politics. You may have thought that the theory which combined despotism with liberty was impracticable. The Paris of the Third Empire proves your logic wrong.

Somehow, as gamblers will best understand, everything at this fortunate stage that the Empire did worked to help this scheme. For fear of any Republican revolt, the old comb of twisted streets, made for barricades and ambushes, death traps for the cavalry, natural trenches against artillery, all this had to be swept away. In the doing of it, Baron Haussmann made Paris, not only the easiest policed but the airiest and most beautiful city in the Old World. Do not forget that the Bois de Boulogne is there because Louis himself loved trees. The encouragement of a life of pleasure, the toleration of every possible means of spending money, did not beggar the citizens. On the contrary, it began that huge exodus from the great Puritan regions of England, America, and Germany, which has brought uncountable billions of "invisible exports" into France. Louis Bonaparte made Paris the first truly cosmopolitan city the world had had since ancient Rome.

And then Paris became not only sinful, but sinfully rich. A whole wing of Zola's immense and untidy master-work is the shocked celebration of this epidemic of wicked wealth by a saving provincial. Strange economic portents were seen for the first time in the skies; for example, money now brought in five per cent, instead of the Orleanist three, and yet everything became cheaper and cheaper. A Fordian circle of consumption and production, whirling the whole community along in its ascending spirals, had been accidentally entered upon, to the dizzy despair of moralists and republicans alike. To this very day in the remotest suburbs of Lancashire and Ohio old wives still pray for the destruction of Louis Bonaparte's Paris. Now, at the summit of this Babylonian revel of cake and circuses, was the singular court of the Tuileries.

It was highly likely that the Emperor, Morny, Persigny, and the rest of the circle of good friends, would not deprive themselves when everyone else was feasting at their invitation. But they were not mere pirates to practise absolute liberty of amusement—they had a philosophy, a program, and even a tradition. So therefore in their revels there was a deep underlying framework of etiquette. The Emperor, he announced, wished to restore the "usages of the old monarchy, just as he had revived its institutions." Honored guests at these ceremonial bean-feasts have left various interesting records. "The Emperor and his court restored the fashion of knee breeches, which Louis Philippe had abolished. The dinners (at the Castle of Compiègne), were usually set for a hundred at a time. All the numerous court dignitaries were new to their office, and strict. A footman stood behind every chair, and a military band, perhaps rather too noisy, played throughout the meals." But as soon as the table was cleared away, and the lackeys dismissed, freer fun began. "We then danced to the music of a barrel organ played by one of the Italian cousins of the Emperor, Baciocchi..."

In the course of time the Emperor's romantic marriage took place. He had attempted, in vain, to induce one of the more established royal houses of Europe to provide him with a bride and an alliance. But even Queen Victoria, the only ruler to show anything but frigid politeness towards him, could not manage to do so. At last, he obeyed the "dictates of his heart" and made a regular union with a young Spanish lady, of some claims to birth, none to fortune, and many admitted ones to beauty: Eugenia de Montijo, who was twenty-six years old. The speech in which our Emperor announced his choice gives a sufficient impression, both of his feelings, and of the effect that the step must have made upon his time.

"I will show old Europe that I know a way of teaching her respect for me, not in trying to push in at any price into the family of kings, but in taking up openly the status of a *parvenu:* a glorious title, when it means that one has arrived where I am by the free vote of a great people. My chosen spouse is French by sentiment, by education, and by the memory of the military service of her father. As a Spaniard, she has the additional advantage of not having a family in France who would have to be given titles and subsidies! Catholic and pious, gracious and good, she will certainly revive the virtues of good Empress Josephine."

After his marriage, the etiquette and the gaiety became still more remarkable. Miss Howard was given a peerage—other generous friends of the past of her sex were paid off, and at least one expelled from France by force. The Empress was surrounded by four hundred beautiful ladies, hardly one of whom belonged to the old aristocracy. Masked balls were the usual form of state reception. At one of these, the old Grand Duchess of Baden, a connection of the Bonaparte family, "did not disguise her sorrow and surprise, nor her indignation." Both of their Imperial Majesties, and their intimate friends were fond of country life. At Compiègne, in 1857, according to the diplomatic Hubner, who was intimate with the family, "after a lunch under a tent, and races on the grass, we played at the taking of the fort of Malakoff; the hillock that represented the citadel was defended by the Empress and her ladies, who were attacked by the Emperor and his gentlemen friends. It was a little too gay, and a trifle too intimate." Of this last fête, the Orleanist press dared to write "that the Emperor rushed to the attack on all fours and grabbed the ladies by the feet." There is a legend, found in that ambiguous authority, Monsieur Claude, Chief of Police of Paris, in his reputed memoirs, that even livelier parties sometimes were arranged. For one of these, he says, a high enclosure was built and it is said that a choir of naked boys and girls gave a performance of classical dancing. There were also the spiritualist séances. The Empress was a convinced table-turner at one time. Home, the most famous medium of Europe, was often summoned, and showed the court many wonders. All this, says the dignified Hubner, accustomed to the ways of other and older

courts, in its alternation of "rigid ceremony and easy-going gives the
impression of newlyrich people trying to play a part too hard for
them. This luxury of costumes, of lackeys and gilding is all too new."

For a long while, then, after the bloody accident of the boulevards,
Louis Napoleon enjoyed vulgarly good hands in his game with the
gods. He had been obliged, it is true, to be harder than he wished
with the Republicans, and, especially after his marriage, more generous to the Catholics and bourgeoisie, his allies in both '48 and '51.
His ideal was, if you like, analyzable into a variation of Robin
Hoodism, a sentimental banditry. But to the fury of all right-think-
ing minds, it worked supematurally well. France became positively
bloated, *teste* Zola. The rich were richer, bread and wine were cheap.
If only there had been a little poetry mixed in it, it would be reckoned as a golden age. But as you know, Louis had banished all good
poets, and business men seldom know how to play the harp. Extra,
as the Germans say, to the cheap bread, five per cent money, the invention of the tourist industry, public works and holidays, he threw
in a victorious war, sharing with England in the beating of Russia in
the Crimea.

The Orsini affair is supposed to close this period of tranquil digestion. Never, of course, was a reign in which the under-history was so
luxuriant and obscure; "as a whole the Third Empire was a secret-po-
lice case," and no one probably ever will be able to prove he knows
the full truth about Orsini. Let us stick to the romance, the only safe
guide in the neo-Bonaparte labyrinth. This assassin then was a member of the Carbonari. He and his group were commissioned to recall
to Comrade Louis that resignations were not accepted, except from
the dead. And so, one evening in January, 1858, at the moment when
the Emperor arrived in his carriage at the old Opera (rue
Montpensier), Orsini and friends threw three bombs at him, missed,
but killed eight bystanders and wounded more than a hundred and
fifty. This was the first political use of a bomb—it was an age of
novelties.

After that message, the Emperor began to remember, and do
something for Italy. The sole reason why he had not before was his

entanglement with the ultramontanist party, who were against the Italian revolt, since its program included the annexation of Rome, and the Papal States. Their chief representative at the Tuileries was the Empress herself; after the Orsini affair apparently her opposition ceased. On the obstinate request of the Archbishop of Paris, the Emperor regretfully allowed Orsini to be guillotined. But two months later, in secret, he called Cavour to Paris and arranged with him to declare a war of Italian liberation against Austria.

A foreigner can hardly have any doubt that Louis Napoleon and the French were the real liberators of Italy; the revolutions that accompanied their victorious troops were merely an aid. But apart from the natural pride of the Italians, there are several good reasons why there is no gratitude to the man and the nation that won Montebello, Palestro, Turbigo, Magenta, Solferino. Freeing oppressed nationalities is perhaps the most dangerous of all philanthropic enterprises.

Louis Napoleon, for one thing, had to stop long before the proud Risorgimento was satisfied. Moreover, under penalty of the indignation of his own people, he had to show them some more material benefit gained than the consciousness of a good deed, well performed; and hence he annexed (of course after a plebiscite, the grand Napoleonic speciality), Nice, the Riviera, and Savoy. Also the Empress and the Catholics insisted that since he had shown himself such a magnificent Carbonaro at Solferino, he must give his Catholicism a turn in protecting the Papal sovereignty at Rome. And so the same French troops who had created the new Italian kingdom marched straightway afterwards to keep it out of its national capital. This Roman garrison lasted as long as the Empire itself.

The great ideal, the inspiration of his life, of pleasing everyone, and himself at the same time, grew more unmanageable as he grew more anxious about it. The truth was that gradually he was losing his nerve. He remained perhaps to the end outwardly impassive, but inwardly he worried; he had outgrown all the pleasures but that last and only one forbidden to the adventurer, peace. No doubt his painful and chronic illness gave this wish the quality of a physical need.

Morny died; Persigny was chased away by a court cabal of the Empress. A long string of ingenious, disastrous enterprises for satisfying the French; his sentimentalism and his interests led him from bog to marsh. He pushed in as a liberator of Poland; the Russians humiliated him and bustled him out of the matter. Perhaps the ugliest and most daring failure was his long effort to create a Latin Empire in Mexico. The unfortunate Austrian prince whom he had induced to try a coup there was conquered, captured, and shot.

Meanwhile, while the doomed gambler, all his composure in his bearing, was steadily losing hand after hand, another romantic structure, inwardly made of no more solid materials than his own empire, but painted in grey and black, the Reich of Bismarck, was steadily rising in Europe. Here too, in spite of its forbidding look, the mortar was that poetic residue, nationalism, and the framework, that impossible dream, benevolent despotism. As a mushroom displaces a large leaf in a single night, so in twenty years the ramshackle edifice of Louis Napoleon was displaced, cramped and finally overturned by the more organic growth.

In politics, where everything romantic and sentimental is folly, the converse is usually considered true, and every brutality is thought sound sense. Only on such a view was the full scheme of Bismarck a work of far-sighted genius, for with all its airs, it led direct to the ridiculous horror of 1914. But meanwhile the nonsense of Bonapartism was not a match for its illegitimate cousin, the graver, more prosy nonsense of "blood and iron." Louis, staggering from foot to foot, scratching round desperately for the impossible balance that was to please everyone, including God or at any rate the pious Empress, promising to go to the rescue of Schleswig-Holstein in the name of the rights of small nations, retiring from that promise to please the peace party at home, allying himself with the Italians to counterweight the Prussians, retreating from that alliance because it meant the abandonment of the cause of the Pope, finally actually allying himself with Bismarck, at Biarritz, shows all the symptoms of approaching ruin, long before it came. In these last years his whole policy lurches and reels like a drunken or dying man.

Still for one instant he seemed to regain his feet. He had weakened the whole repression; the republicans were allowed to return, even to have newspapers. From end to end of the country they, very properly, used this concession, this weakness, to ring round the beast, to undermine him, to goad him, to prepare his end. And yet, towards the very end, he somehow had the courage to face them all; to make one last charge in the open. You may feel it either humorous or pathetic that that act, too, took the form of trying and winning one last plebiscite. It is said to have been organized honestly enough; its result was 7,358,786 votes in his favor to 1,571,939 against. The largest majority a Bonaparte ever had.

A few weeks later, the Emperor, his dynasty, his cause and France fell headlong into the Prussian war.

And so, in a muddle of blood, ends the story. From Sedan, the extreme edge of history, with his last gesture before oblivion and obscurity engulfed him, Louis sent the telegram to his Empress. "The army is defeated and captive. I myself am a prisoner."

Poor devil, he never had much style.

XI.
Isadora Duncan

WE SHOULD NOW TAKE up again the difficult case of the woman adventurer; and indeed would long ago have done so, if examples that are not merely trivial were not also extremely rare. The matter has even a practical interest. Our own times seem half to cajole, half to bully women to search for a life of their own, and not quite to be satisfied, in many cases, when they have only found a career. The one case yet handled, Lola Montez, appeared to lead to a disappointing conclusion, or rather, suspicion. But was not the shadow of general law, half perceived, possibly only the special case of a time, place and personality? In such a doubt, the life of Isadora Duncan, of all the select groups of extraordinary lives of our time, has the most illustrative content and value. She herself thought the story of her life was "fitted for the pen of a Cervantes, or Casanova." I consider that mistaken, for almost too many reasons. It is not for the picaresque, or incidental of her life (to tell the truth, often very meagre, however padded with fine and medium-fine names of the times) that she figures here. Nor in the least because I agree with her followers, imitators, and copyists, that her contribution to art was much more than a misdirection. Many actresses of the French stage, for example, may have had lives richer in the whimsical, unexpected turns of fortune, lovers of finer quality, adventures and vicissitudes more fantastic and interesting. Nor is Isadora Duncan here because of the underlying dignity of her life, which certainly was there, and which we certainly ought not to fail to observe in its extremely precious tragic unity. We are vowed to objectivity. She has the right to stand beside all the extraordinary and sometimes illustrious people here, because she, above all women of our time, in scale, in courage, in the spirit, made the purest attempt at the life of adventure. So we can say, if you like, that she questioned the Sphinx closest on the mysteries that here interest us. And obtained a strange set of replies. The details of her early life she herself evidently considered entrancingly strange. But virtually the same family, and its way of life, appear so often in the lives of those who afterwards have earned their living by the arts, that they may well seem banal almost to orthodoxy. These Duncans of San Francisco, as she describes them, were shabby, thriftless, and intelligent. They scrambled along in a sort of gipsy opportunism, borrowing as a right, spending as a duty, and of course the mother gave private lessons on the piano. I had the closest personal experience of such people in my own youth, and out of my mixed reaction of dislike and admiration I remember I made a theory; that in reality such people were what I called "Behaving a private income." That is, and it may be, as good an explanation of all their conduct as I know now, that such people are at bottom doing nothing more wild and free than living like a good class of newly-rich bourgeois, rather wasteful, a little pretentious, with a charming surface culture. Only they have not any money. In one decisive particular alone, it is easy to see where the real affinities of their mode of life and sentiment are, and are not; their inflexible, perfectly middle-class morality. No, here are no rag and bobtail strollers, but a fragment of the rock of respectable society, economically displaced.

We must now go a little deeper into the formative influences so at work upon her young character than the somewhat tawdry romantic view she puts forward herself. The "Constant Nymphism," the "Beloved Vagabondism," or whatever you like to call the color of such a childhood, can stay by itself. I feel there are two significantly important other features. The lesser of these is the taste for books, and all the other cultural feeling and direction clustered around this, that she acquired. Such families almost by definition read a great deal, a special quality of book, and in a special way. They read, as the neighbors say, out of their station, and the children especially are only drawn towards books whose titles seem to promise them a higher, stranger, above all, unusual, world to tour. That is, for example, they are extremely seldom attracted by Shakespeare, Shelley* (not to mention accessible novels)—such names seem too common, and their magnificence is for quite a different class of child. The Brontës in their scrupulously clean old vicarage, much poorer, much more isolated than ever the ragged, somewhat cheeky little Duncans were, were haunted by the very names of Prospero, Hamlet, Lear and his Fool. Scarcely our San Franciscans, who stopped at the book-shop windows before large copies of "The Sayings of Marcus Aurelius," books with foreign mysterious names, especially Greek. But please notice that it never occurred to them to learn Greek.

It is useless to conceal that in such circumstances, besides the leaning to pretentiousness, natural and not completely a bad thing, there is in such ways inevitably a great danger of smattering, of messing with half-read books, cover-fluttering, and all the other indignities to which great books and subjects that must needs ask a moderate degree of attention are subjected by dilettante autodidacts.

Somewhere in her memoirs Isadora naïvely illustrates this. In the wings of a provincial theatre while waiting her call, she would "be deep in Marcus Aurelius." But no one noticed it, and she always felt a little peeved. Also, I would risk something that she never finished, not quite finished, the volume.

And so it may easily be likely that of all this miscellaneous reading, and general jack-daw culture, very little more than a collection of charming miscomprehensions, untargeted enthusiasms, and a general habit of skimming, remained. Perhaps also, when her ruling prejudices formed, a jealous dislike, actually, of sound knowledge and hard study, and all that can be founded upon them.

Then, in the second place in this amusing upbringing, we must observe the effect of her mother's failure in marriage. It is Isadora's

---

* The mother, by the way, read Shakespeare and Shelley to the Duncans, according to Isadora's account.

resolute rejection of the ordinary hope and destiny of women, the legal support of a man, indeed, that spiritually entitles her life to be considered as an adventure. For by a short cut through what might be a very long reasoning, let us mark out the institution of marriage as the most plausible visible reason (and quite sufficient too), why women are so rarely in any strict sense adventurers.*

The adventurer, by minimum definition, is an individualist. The life of adventure is an unsocial game; therefore in direct contrast with the married, supported life which is nuclear society itself. It may well be, or I think so, that the mere idea of marriage, as a strong possibility, if not always nowadays a reasonable likelihood, existing to weaken the will by distracting its straight aim in the life of practically every young girl, is the simple secret of their confessed inferiority in men's pursuits and professions today. If instead of looking for some obviously non-existent feminine inferiority of brain-power, educationalists would cast a look at the effect, during the training and learning years of such an underthought: "but after all I may get married," at the fiercely desperate corners where a man student or beginner passes in a spirit of life or death, they might count that in. And, in consequence, when drawing up their comparative tables, set their statistics of women's work, not against the mass of thus un-handicapped men, but against some restricted group, of those only who have some weakening third responsibility before their eyes in a crisis than straight success, or failure; such for example, as rich men's sons, who cannot be absolutely in earnest. The vast mass of men, then, have to depend on themselves alone; the vast mass of women hope or expect to get their life given to them. It is the first condition of a woman-adventurer to do as Isadora and bar from the beginning any such dependent.

Her mother was so affected by the failure of her own marriage, which ended in a divorce, that she not only ever afterwards taught the children that their father was a devil and a monster, but changed her religion. From Catholic she became in a jump Ingersollist, and an

---

* The feminine form has too special a meaning.

equally pious one in that arid form of puritanism, for orthodox athe-
ism certainly is one. But just for that reason, we are not allowed to
search for Isadora's resolution against marriage in her mother's teaching, or anywhere but in her own audacious, confident soul. A young
girl, a beauty, with all the added fascination of the education we have
criticized, but not forgotten, is more graceful and easily won than a
more serious one at her age; that she could have firmly, unreluctantly,
decided to win her life for herself, to play her own hand against the
gods is as remarkably daring as anything in this book. But it is curious, and necessary to notice, that this spiritual gesture was not complete. In place of the husbandage she scornfully renounced, as I
diagnose it, sprang up in her naturally and inevitably a social theory,
recognizable underneath its innocent sentimentality, its vagueness
and everything else, as the genuine unmistakable embryo of the
Socialism which is immanent in our times and will quite probably be
dominant in the next. She wanted no husband to look after her, support her, feed her. She was quite convinced that someone should. That
someone, when she learnt the vocabulary, was the State. But, at first,
it was the landlord, rich people, the public; not relatives, not parents—she never even thought of turning to them. Let us say, just
Society. Beautiful examples of this occur in profusion in her own
confession. After a concert in New York, where she had performed,
been applauded, paid, and praised, she does not hesitate to go back to
the giver, a rich woman, and ask her for money. "This rich woman,
with sixty millions, went to her desk, after I had explained our need
and wrote a cheque." Only fifty dollars. Think of it. The significant
incident in variations was often repeated. When she was quite small,
when there was nothing to eat in the house, "I was always the volunteer sent to the butcher, and who cleverly got the cutlets out of him
without paying… I was the one sent to get credit out of the baker…"
If, even at this age, she had discerned the least indignity in such acts,
be sure she would have refused them with indignation. It was a matter
of simple justice to her; those that have must give.

And in this, this essentially social, if not socialistic, anti-Nietsz-
chean conception of the rights of the poor, an indefinite number of

men might not concur. How many women in their hearts, I do not know. The concordance, in fact, between the form into which the modern state is undeviatingly proceeding everywhere, and the womanly, as distinct from the masculine social ideal, cannot be quite accidental. Somewhere at the end of it, is the State, the great provider, husband for every woman and father to every child; an interesting research for day dreamers. And, if it is so, or approximately, the adventurous, unsocial, masculine life is destined to take on even more rigorously the character of a revolt.

However that may be, the form of Isadora's life from its start includes a social dependence and sentiment, sincere, unquestionable, probably compensatory. It is, therefore, difficult to conceive of any other direction for it than the stage. And on that road with that beautiful floating inevitability with which large portions of her life were embellished, she began to go almost as soon as she could walk.

She has given us a very candid account of her invention of what was afterwards ineptly known as "classical" dancing. On any analogy with the use of that illustrious adjective in other arts, this abandonment to individual mood, and individual taste should surely be "romantic" rather than "classic": which name probably has been taken in allusion to some fanciful imitation of—better, borrowing from the decorated attitudes of ancient Greek potters. If anything is certain in the obscure subject, it is that Greek dancing of the heyday had no more resemblance to Isadora's than the poems of, let us say, Theocritus, to the poetical works of Gertrude Stein. At six years already she had begun to jump and caper about to her mother's playing, and other children admiring this, which must have had some unusual vigor and grace, procured pennies from their parents to pay her to give them lessons. Giving lessons was the first consequence of ideas in the Duncans' practical philosophy.

Later, her mother seems to have thought there might be some fertility in this play, and sent her daughter to learn the elements in a regular school of ballet. The master was "one of the most famous in San Francisco" which, given the low mondial ebb of the art, at the time, must mean rather queerly bad. He was such a nincompoop anyway that when the little girl confidently told him she did not like the steps he taught "because they were ugly and against nature," he appears to have been unable to answer her. This happened at the third lesson, and she never went back. Instead, henceforward she began to invent the art of dancing for herself.

Here, therefore, is an absolutely spontaneous outcrop of that feeling, theory, practice of the arts (and by no means dancing alone), whose sudden fortune in the first decade of this century has lasted, though it may be waning, right into our own days. Since it was the instrument, chart, or sword, at your choice, of her adventure, we must once more halt, to examine it attentively. From a purely academic point of view, this "free-art" theory may be ticketed as some far-off descendant of the inspirationism of the romantics, nominally, let us say, the English lyrical school; and even perhaps, still more impressively, of such wild oracles as Dionysius or Isaiah. I feel an absurd dislike for venturing, even in play, on comparisons between the dancers we are strictly occupied with and their poet-painter friends, and such magnificences as the works of, for example, William Blake. I prefer the risk and trouble of attacking the matter at its butt end. Isadora's idea, then, was, as far as I can make out, and if I am right, identical with those exploited at the same time in all the other arts, that the artist should "return to nature" and especially to himself. No more rules, no more tradition; for which things she, and they, usually have ready the word "artificial," in which they sum up all that is opposite to this "nature," and all that is trivial, false and bad. Now I consider that all this theory is a clear by-product of that puritanism she was in other affairs of life never tired of damning. The same two sentiments, one open, one hidden, are present in both theories. One, the open fear and hatred of the "artificial," the humanizing embellishment which is the very essence of civilization. She anathematizes, for example, tip-toe dancing—that exquisite and ingenious invention by which a dancer can seem to have achieved humanity's universal flying dream, and cast off the shackles of weight; exactly as a deacon condemns the lipstick, a Tolstoian, brocade, or a Quaker, church vestments and stained glass.

But this Nature, this dear, beautiful mother to which all these people invite us, wants none of us. Nature is the night, the iceberg, the uninhabitable crags of mountains, the black gulfs of the ocean, in whose unveiled presence we are dumbstruck and tremble. This giant brooding power, who will not even look straight at us, like a captive tigress, when we dare to put ourselves in her presence protected by ships, ropes, convoys, is not imitable! The suburban landscapes, the neatly growing trees, the gently curving rivers, with, naturally, a dear little cottage in the foreground, is not Nature, but artifice, the work of man. Even here, though we have painted a friendly smile on her mask, beneath the artifice (and it is thin), there is the same implacable. The nightingales, dear naturalists, do not sing for us or you. The flowers are proud, and those trees your own grandfather planted in sweat have no feelings of gratitude towards men. All animals except the parasitical dog and cat we have debauched hate us; a sparrow that will not move aside for an elephant will hide itself before the most angelic child on earth can come within reach. One night, at the height of summer, walk in the most humanly artificial park, and clearing your brain from all the kindly cant of the lesser poets (for Shakespeare never misled you), perceive first in delight the huge rustling flood of life that is playing—in the hope you would not come; and then notice bitterly how at the first sound of your step everything living and dead closes, hushes, disappears. The trees themselves, it might seem, turn their backs to you, you the wet blanket, the human, the unwanted, the horror. A strange experiment, that one of carnivorous anthropoids, killer-monkeys; the whole of Nature hopefully awaits the day we shall be extinct. It is wise and necessary to leave her awful symmetries to themselves; to build for ourselves a beauty and a world out of her ken.

Her standards of beauty, here is the crisis, are not ours. In an ancient abominable scorn, she judges us perhaps, as we find a negroid beauty, with plates in her lips. A naked woman, even Isadora at seventeen, in a forest—the commonest deer passes, and if you have not much unimaginative complacency, you may suspect the scorn of Nature for this bleached, forked, curved thing.

And now let the fondest mother remember her sweetest baby, remember the secrets of the nursery, and dare not to feel embarrassed if she hears Saint Francis *dared* to preach to unrevengeful, undestructive, quiet minds. Let us, as that old railer, Johnson, said, talk cant if we will, but prudently beware of believing it. Nature's standards of beauty, physical, moral, are outside our reach. By Nature, we are ugly. Abandoned in a jungle we would grow only into the most loathsome crawler, with this fault in addition, that we were horribly dangerous.

If what this little girl of San Francisco in a calm temerity set out to teach us were all our hope, it is a poor outlook. What is Caliban to do except live lonely and dig a deep hole? I think and hope she was mistaken. Man can look Nature in the face and return scorn with contempt, set standards against standards with a loftiness that might put that great stupid goddess out of countenance, if she had any intelligence. The noise of the open sea is not the equal of a dying speech in Shakespeare. The mere height of Mont Blanc is less than that of a Beethoven sonata. A woman, any woman, beside a fawn, says Schopenhauer, is grotesque. But let Michel Angelo dress her, put her in silk, put shoes on those feet, and the fawn may come and lick her hand. By artifice, which is the accumulated inspiration of artists, women, men and cities are as far above the natural as the clear light of the stars above the crawling life of a lagoon. The child, for all his step-mother Nature gives him, may be a horrible animal; human poetry treats him as, and will one day make him into, a god. This is the function of art: to make a supernatural world; not to imitate the natural.

In the same way that I reject her juvenile dictum about Nature, whose relative position to herself she misunderstood, so must be put out of the question the corollary that the artist, without learning, refusing the help of all the genius of the past, must only express his poor self, and be certain that that more, that that only, is worth while. To put Nature in her place is not the work of any single genius; such as appear amongst us, not every year, but in certain epochs, rarely. In practice it is in a high degree unlikely that John, or

Jean, Blank out of his own untaught nature can produce a poem, a sonata, a dance worth the meditation of an earthworm. Why should it be otherwise? Where, except in some exalted religious optimism, does this confidence in the intrinsic value of all self-expression base itself?

So much, too much, for the fundamental theory, the instrument of Isadora in her adventure. After all, she was a great personage and though she never admitted it, nor probably ever knew it, she tricked with it. To eke out her Nature, she borrowed and adopted the attitudes of Greek vases. She, the pure inspirationist, gradually constructed an intricate technique of her own, surpassing in certain few ways the old, which by *parti pris*, until it was too late, she never knew thoroughly. She taught Diaghileff's ballet many things; she could never dance in a ballet herself.

But that is in anticipation. When she set out for the conquest of the world, to a greater fame and influence than any other American woman has ever achieved, do not forget, with her family in her knapsack, the great idea is still childish, rudimentary, like a wooden sword. Powerful in a very different degree, her untheoretically real possessions, blossoming youth, a round beauty, magnificent health, simplicity and energy in a unique alloy. Not to shuffle round it, it was her bare legs more than her translation of recondite music into jumps and sways that opened her success.

That success was amazingly quick; so pure was her self-faith that it seemed to her intolerably long. Everyone on even tangential contact with her was entranced with this naïve little American girl, with her stock of impassioned abstract nouns, her unconscious and so charming pretensions, and her thoroughly novel turn. With a yard or two of Liberty muslin, a tragic expression that "everyone wondered at" she gave them Mendelssohn's Spring Song and afterwards her sister read verses of Andrew Lang's translation of Theocritus. Then one of her brothers would lecture the audience on "Dancing, and its Probable Future Effects on Humanity."

The English did not like the lecturing and the recitation so much as the bright-eyed Isadora. The coldness, the polite coolness, like an unconvinced admiration, of the various strata or reaches of London society she explored rather damped her. In London, if only because of the language, the Duncans seem soon to have dropped the verbal part of the performance. Her personal success there, however, must have been wonderful. But afterwards there seems to have been a period when the rent-bilking, and park-bench meditations, stereotyped through her youth, recommenced. There is something disconcerting in these sudden descents into obscurity and poverty, after blazing success, in the written biographies of most artists of the stage. In the intervals, the family visited museums, one of them "invented sandals," and Isadora herself dallied with platonic young poets.

Then, of course, Paris. There was a deep difference between the receptions and the applause of the two cities, which she felt and noted, but, misled by the easy nationalist formulæ which formed part of her stock of ideas all her life, she did not quite correctly calculate it. It was not because "the English are cold and unemotional," whereas the French, that lively and artistic nation, are "much warmer in their response," that the difference was one between a blind alley and a highroad. The specific differences of national characters, so unexpected and inexplicable if true—for the thousand or so years involved is a short time for such deep evolutions to sport in—belongs to the same lovely region where imagination beckons science and is snubbed, that telepathy, water-dowsing, and the theory of the Lost Ten Tribes inhabit. The realm of the unnecessary hypothesis. The English character may or may not be undemonstrative; but the English civilization certainly dislikes the new. The English, by education and the neurosis produced by it, want in art something above all to worship, to pray to in their hats as they do in church; and the first essential of the sacred is age. If today, or still safer some decade hence, Isadora could revisit London, old, lame, but an institution, she would waver in her theory of English coldness. But in France, the natural obverse of modern civilization, novelty is the essential, and the *déjà vu* inexorably hissable. They found Isadora not only new, but in the fashion. For to that same mode of the "natural," the inspirational, to which the great American puritanism in its irresistible ebb had carried her, the French obsession of originality had begun to carry all the arts. Everyone spoke like Isadora; everyone like her had begun to find the great secret by refusing to learn rudiments. The feast of self-expression was in the oven; Isadora came in with the hors-d'œuvres. Such, as I see them, were the environmental conditions that tempered and favored the public career of the brave little dancer. Every year, every month almost, at the beginning, her fame increased. Quite early she had the enlightenment to refuse a well-paid, undignified engagement for a Berlin music-hall. But there was in her the ordinary paradox of all true adventurers, that queer foresight among this people consecrated to risk, which is the moral translation of their directed will. Isadora at this speed was going somewhere; the naming of her direction haunted her thoughts. At one time it was, as she answered the German impresario, "that she was come to Europe to bring about a renaissance of religion by means of dancing." For longer stretches of time, she tried to work out a connection between her artistic ideal and the indecisive humanitarianism, the vague socialism we have noted in her before. Vegetarianism floats in and out of her scheme, the state support of poor children is mixed up with (of all things) "back to Sparta." She makes violent efforts to fix what she means. She stands hours "in an ecstasy which alarmed mother, to find out how to achieve the divine expression of the human spirit in the body" and summed up in a misty formula what she found; in her frantic efforts to prophetize there is a queer resemblance to the fabrication of the old Suras that we watched in the life of Mahomet. Leaving the cryptic results reverently to her disciples, we need only notice that, at whatever degree of intention, here was a perfectly intelligible effort to lift her art out of dependence on the attraction of her youthful body, the working of a foreboding that to be an art at all, her dancing must be something that a middle-aged woman can practise as well as a beauty of nineteen. An old ballerina may still please, at least as well as a debutante; could she not make classical dancing something more than the

charming spectacle of lightly clad nymphs, intolerable and insuffer-
able with any fading or thickening of these charms?

That, it is not my business, or competence, to decide. I mark the
depth of the problem, her concentrated attention to it, now, and to
the end of her life. Meanwhile the success curves up in a steady cre-
scendo, drawn through every capital of Europe. The city that pleased
her most was St. Petersburg, where to his own great and declared
profit she met the maker of the unofficial Russian Ballet, Diaghileff,
and Pavlova, Nijinsky.

Now as to the progress of that other life, of her private adventure,
let us call it, I can have no intention of sketching chronologically
what she has given the world in detail in her autobiography. To make
any love affairs interesting to others, is perhaps the most difficult feat
in literature; as in her admirable common sense she never hesitated
to confess, she was not a good (though she was an honest) writer. The
affairs themselves seem of impenetrable banality, except for the generosity which she put in them, which is very likely as rare as its confession. The men who figure, robed in girlish adjectives, are almost
embarrassingly awkward. They seem in their relations with this utterly disinterested girl, asking nothing (of anyone but the State), to
be reduced to the woe-begone rôle of the male among the insects and
spiders.

The result of all this incommunicable poetry was, the world
knows, two exquisite children. It knows also, with aghast sympathy,
their fate. They were drowned with their governess in a taxi-cab that
fell into the Seine. The frightful simplicity, and the stupid malevo-
lence of this accident; that also is Nature and Fate. The natural cause
of the destruction of Lisbon, San Francisco, Messina, the General
Slocum, the Titanic, and the fire at the Charity Bazaar in the Avenue
de la Seine. This, too, is at the heart of things-as-they-are, and all
optimisms must make some account of it, if they are to be more than
narcotics. Nor, unfortunately, will the appeal to a future life, with
compensatory rewards for such brutality, even if they comprised a
million years of bliss and forgetfulness absolve the agency, or put us,
the onlookers, at ease in the universe where children are drowned

and then given some bag of celestial candies to make them forget those suffocating instants. However generous the surplus of pleasure over pain on the entire operation, its horror except to those—and after all they are probably the vast majority—whose ethics are resolutely commercial, remains, staining the whole fabric, like a blood-red dye. Danger, and its emotional accessory, terror, is an integral element of the universe. Every life is therefore a desperate adventure; and, on as calm a view as anyone who is doomed willy-nilly to share in it, can achieve, it is more dangerous, more adventurous, to be born than to die. The adventurer goes out to meet the monster in the open; we that stay indoors, with the social mass, run no less risks.

Any life, the coarsest and sternest, is necessarily broken in two by such a stroke; it is far outside the limit of human elasticity. Only in a metaphysical sense can there be even continuity of personality. But this clean snap may present a different appearance, in a variety that includes even disguise. The most obvious and least beautiful response is to die, or to go mad. Then there is suicide, and there is a form of suicide known to those who have been tortured beyond the sill of endurance, which is to count oneself dead. "I died there," said Isadora to a person whom I believe. Only the formality of bleeding was unfulfilled. In such cases, to the surprise of the simple or dull, there may be a deceiving appearance of continuity. It looks like the same person and the same life, going on in the same direction and the same plan, with a smoothness that onlookers can admire, or secretly condemn as callousness according to their degree of spiritual taste.

Such a deception we will not fall into. And therefore Isadora Duncan, the one we knew, light and cloudy, a little absurd as all delightful people must be, the generous girl who misled nearly all the whole of European culture for a decade, has now ended. It is another of the same name who now uses up to its frightful and strange conclusion, like an unfinished lease taken up, the adventure of the dead girl. It is not of the same quality; there is a sensible thickening, banalization of the thread of the story and of all its details, which I fancy I notice. The dazzling little portent slips by steps into the prima donna; every year she becomes serious instead of enthusiastic about the marvellous discovery. Nothing new is added to her dance; but the technique, the gymnastic, becomes more laboured and fuller.

The naïve sparrowishness of her claims on humanity, in step, changes into a more and more definite socialism. No doubt her adherence to Leninism was never very intellectual; still the flag-waving, the red-tunicism, this was disagreeably nearer, by whatever the distance, the hysterical earnest of a woman with a cause, than to the exciting day dreaming of the other Isadora. I find the account of her visit to Russia, her marriage to Essenine, her disastrous return to America, that two of her friends have very properly and capably, as an historical duty, given us, more distressing than interesting. She moved there among people for the most part pretentious nonentities, the first crop of thistles of the greatest ploughing up of the century. Lunacharskys, Mariengoffs, Imagists, belated Futurists, all the band. And she does not always, as the other Isadora would have, make them into a grotesque supporting background to pick out her own magnificent dance of life against. Incident after incident, as set down by her dearest friends, makes us uneasy. She accepts the use of a flat belonging to an artist, a dancer (ballet, it is true), exiled from Moscow, and criticizes the furniture gleefully and without amenity. She goes to select a fur coat from the vast store of those commandeered from middle-class women, and is snubbed by the very official when she chooses one, thinking it was free of charge. The Communist conductor leads his orchestra out disdainfully when she reminds him she has sacrificed a great deal to come to "help the children of Russia."

The chief of all these disappointing happenings is her marriage with young Sergei Alexandrevitch Essenine. He was one of those literary discoveries of the new Russia, whose merit does not survive a translation. All sincere partisans of the new regime, they may be suspected of thinking of talent and genius as strictly analogous to riches and property, things which stout-hearted lads with feelings of class solidarity could take by force from their former possessors.

Genius was confiscated by the proletariat of the arts. They drank more than they wrote or knew, and were intoxicated perhaps out of proportion to the quantity of liquor. Everything in their lives was on the group system. They lived, fought, and even loved in common, and arranged the criticism and judgments on what they did strictly cooperatively. But though the general tone and choice of subjects may have been their own, or at any rate authentically national, incidents in the lives of tramps, bullies, strumpets and so on, most of their technique and theories seemed to have a genealogy. Most of what they did seemed to proceed from the Latin Quarter: the Latin Quarter of ten or twelve years before.

And so, coincidentally, these young self-expressionists, who, "led by Essenine and Koussikoff with his omnipresent balalaika, burst into the room, the calm, Isadoran temple," has some third degree of the spiritual blood of the old, young Isadora, who had tried to think out an entirely new art of dancing for herself, a generation back. With that in mind, make what you please of the rest of the account of Isadora's first meeting with her young husband.

"She arose then from her divan and asked the pianist to play a Chopin waltz that she felt would appeal to the lyric soul of the golden-haired poet. And with what rapturous joy and seductive grace she moved through the rhythms of the dance! When the music ended, she came forward with her ingenuous smile, her eyes radiant, her hands outstretched towards Essenine, who was now talking loudly to her companions, and she asked him how he liked her dance. The interpreter translated. Essenine said something coarse and brutal that brought howls of coarse and brutal laughter from his drunken friends. The friend who was acting as interpreter said with evident hesitation to Isadora: 'He says it was—awful…and that he can do better than that himself.'

"And even before the whole speech was translated to the crestfallen and humiliated Isadora, the poet was on his feet dancing about the studio like a crazy man."

So ended, for the developments of her marriage to this person virtually fill the rest of her life, the adventure of Isadora. To me it is on the whole the most tragic of all the bad ends we have related; but marriage has an interior as well as an exterior aspect. This young man, whom Isadora married "because she wanted to take him out of Russia to show him all that Europe had of beauty and all that America had of wonder," in short, to give him a good time; and which plan he instantly accepted, was a blond fellow, with the face of a spoilt child, and yellow hair, dressed advantageously over his forehead, in the fashion once common among English private soldiers—the "fascinator." As a typical false adventurer, he requires our attention for a while. He was an indeterminate number of decades younger than she, be already in chronic ill-health owing to his habits. Little conversation was possible between them, for he knew only Russian. In his general attitude towards life, besides his poetical pretensions, he claimed to be an adventurer himself, and naturally, the bravest, most disinterested, airiest of them all. He lived from hand to mouth, wasted anything he could not consume at the moment, never repaid a loan, broke anything fragile he could reach, disdained all except the members of his gang, without whom he never stirred, and yet in whose company he never ended an evening without a loud quarrel and a woundless fight. In short just as he wrote according to his idea of an improved Rimbaudism, he lived according to his idea of a gallant figure.

But this bulky package of self-expression which Isadora now encumbered herself with in a tour of half the world, turned out when unwrapped to contain an ordinary nucleus of instincts of possession and self-preservation. Certainly he accepted the proposition of being supported, aeroplanes, rides, suites in great hotels, a place of honor at Isadora's parties where there was usually very good company; all this with the most complete contempt for bourgeois scruples. In many things on the lamentable trip he outdid all the traits of his former life: thus "coming into the hotel room at the Adlon, and finding Isadora weeping over an album containing portraits of her unforgettable Deidre and Patrick (the children) he ruthlessly tore it

280 of her hands

our of her hands, and throwing it into the fire cried in drunken rage, as he held her back from saving her precious memorial: 'You spend too much time thinking about those—children.'" In fact, he carefully carried out the doctrine he summed up for his school in a letter, "Let us be Asiatics. Let us smell evilly. Let us shamelessly scratch our backsides in front of everyone." He got her turned out of her hotel in Paris by an orgy of drunken smashing and shouting, and performed many other sacrifices to his peculiar gods. But with a subtle, yet significant nuance, his hectoring always ceases as soon as the police appeared. "Bon Polizei," he would murmur, meek as a lamb, when those testy, quick-tempered fellows, the Paris police, led him off.

At the end of it all, the smashing, the spending, the bullying, drinking, the spoilt furniture in Berlin, the wrecked suite in Paris, the gala in the Carnegie Hall, the scarf-waving in Boston when they were back in Russia, Isadora and her friends found that he had stole all her underclothing, to give to his poor family. He was as fond and generous to his sister and mother as the most stolid Paris grocer-boy; everything he took he neatly folded. In his trunks, opened by force, was "a veritable arsenal for a travelling salesman in barber-shop supplies, boxes and loose cakes of expensive soaps, large and small bottles of assorted perfumes, bottles of bay rum, lotions, brilliantines, tubes of tooth paste and shaving soap, and package of safety razor blades."

In the middle of the search, in comes rushing the young husband. "My trunks. Who's been meddling with my trunks? Don't you dare to touch my trunks. I'll kill the person who touches my trunks."

Her road therefore led to a sort of marsh. The reason for the deflection of a flight that started gaily and gallantly is only our business so far as it might or might not be invariable of the adventures of all women. Moral praise or blame is out of our imposed range. Yet it is easy to see that a certain falseness of taste, "the adoption of a lie" and not a reasonless law of fate, is at work; in one small point, the character of Essenine is almost exactly the expression of an ideal she had preached all her life; she was saved from being one herself by an illogical decency, at war with her principles that kept breaking through. A true contempt for possessions and comfort, and not merely the possessions and comfort of others, is perfectly possible; but it expresses and must express itself in a life of an ascetic, a hermit. Those who love spending, breaking, wasting, the best hotels, lashings of drink, good company and the delights of the flesh must settle themselves to earn money to pay for it themselves, or be damned as parasites—with an ugly protective coloration. Nor make Bohemians your ideal, or one day you may have to go round the world with one.

But this marriage was only one feature of the sad landscape she had journeyed to, the smell of the stagnant water. Every other brittle error she had built into her universe was a weakness, that transformed itself sooner or later into a collapse. Her dancing, even, and her idolization of the uncultured, the poor, betrayed her rather horribly in Russia, which was her dream come true. A man can build on a well-constructed fiction. We saw Charles, who had swallowed a boy's-book, go a long way into Russia. But a mistake, honestly believed in, if big enough, will rot the strongest life, the most soaring adventure like a gangrene. And so if she ever consciously admitted it, the failure of the art she had invented just for them, to interest the victorious proletariat of Russia, the long and frightful trail over an immense part of their country in the steps of and just behind a ballerina of the old school, who was having an ecstatic success, while Isadora had to pretend hard even to find politeness—would have hurt worse even than Essenine. With the help of staging, masks, young and slim bodies, all the artifices of lighting and music, her dancing, or adaptations, more or less acknowledged, or mere plagiarisms, still draw audiences all over Europe, and will in obscurely traceable derivatives perhaps become an addition to the repertory of the art, which she neither killed as she hoped, nor superseded forever.

But then, to end, the tragic deflection of Isadora's life, unique in spite of everything in our day of woman's ambition, in size and fame and originality, was brought about by factors special to herself. And (which is less reassuring only to the superstitious), to that horrible, extraneous intervention of the unplumable evil. You perhaps remember that in Lola's life, too, we played with the idea that the gods are goddesses in their cruelty to the woman-adventurer.

All her life, those who have followed me so far do not need to be told, Isadora affected a loose, flowing style of dress. Flou, as the French sempstress slang calls it. So it was a trailing shawl caught in the wheel of a fast car, as if pulled suddenly in a fit of irritated spite, that killed her instantly, one night, on the Promenade des Anglais at Nice, in the middle of many new plans.

XII.

Woodrow Wilson

I T IS NOT SOME faded whimsicality that induces me to include Wilson—he has right to the simple surname—in these studies, and to end with him, but the conviction that so alone can the structure be roofed. No other life in history has the scale and extent sufficient to cover in a real unity the excessively disparate wings, galleries, and attics, with a view, which have grown up alongside the main halls and towers of this building. However novel it may be to conceive of his world-doing as an adventure, and him as an adventurer, the most soaring of them all, it is not hard to point out enough perfectly straightforward concordances with the definition. Solitude and risk were there in plenty; one of the banal reproaches against him was that he isolated himself. The repudiation of his signature was enough proof in itself that he dared everything alone, and replaces very comfortably the social disapproval we realized from the beginning was one of the surest stigmata of the pure adventurer. Naturally this stigma is purely political, and not in the slightest moral, as is more usual in our cases. But long ago we renounced blame and praise, to buy the privilege of impartiality. And in its very coloration, its grand and exciting air, the history of Wilson in its great acts is obviously related like a noble brother to some of the dubious brilliancies we have recounted, in the lives of our Alexander, Napoleon, Columbus, any name, and their world-conquests, world-discoveries, world-downfalls. Here is a man who imposed himself—ask the party bosses—as the supreme head of the conti-

nental empire of the United States. Who, further, handled that co-
lossal power as if it were a sword in his hand, sheathing it when he
wished, baring it at his own moment. With this and the power of his
thought he ends the war. And then in person he sets out to save humanity by ending war for ever. These are acts and a personage at least
the peer in romance of anything that has come about in humanity
before.

But while thus his entrance ticket as it were into the company is
perfectly in order, and while, still more to the point, the architecture
of his behaviour is unmistakable, yet there is a fundamental difference which lies, I think, in the direction of his will. His aim was just
as sure, his singleness of purpose adequate, his range even higher. But
whereas, so commonly that we may have been tempted to make it a
rule, every other adventurer has fought for himself, or at most for his
family, or indeed, as Mahomet, for his native town, Wilson adven-
tured for the whole of the human race. Not as a servant, but as a
champion. So pure was this motive, so unflecked with anything that
his worst enemies could find, except the mildest and most excusable,
a personal vanity, practically the minimum to be human, that in a
sense his adventure is that of humanity itself.

In Wilson, the whole of mankind breaks camp, sets out from
home and wrestles with the universe and its gods. That is his difference from the others, and that is why he must close the whole matter.

For I hope we have come far from thinking that only the adventurer is unsafe. The stay-at-homes, however thick their walls, however large their bulwarks, states, societies, constitutions, are
collectively on a life and death adventure, whether we like it or not.
A roof may hide the menacing, promising skies; but risk is like the
ether; it pervades all matter. This our adventure progresses with every
roll of the earth, every lurch of the solar system through dreadful
immensity. But the single adventurer stepping outside sees his risk.
We who are herded together, do not. He directs his course, aims,
soars with the strength of his will. We do not. The—only to our
individual minuteness relatively—vast group of humanity, huddled
together, is whirled hither and thither at the play of chance, tossed

up—that is progress; down—that is the dark age. Three or four times only in time has one, large and courageous enough, attempted to drag this rudderless hulk on to a course. Or rather to warp it off a barrier reef. Such an adventure may well be called the most ambitious of all; let us now express it in an elliptical formula: to make the world safe for Democracy.

Everyone, luckily, understands the immense number of postulates that is the background of the meaning of that prodigious word, Democracy; so it is only necessary to recall a few of the most important components that had a bearing on the shape of Wilson's adventure, and its issue.

Luckily, too, belief in democracy as a system of government, and as the most established hope of humanity, is practically compulsory in our days. We are therefore dispensed from any long and difficult examination of its claims. Wilson used the word undoubtedly as a synonym for the whole of mankind known to him, much as a philosopher of the Middle Ages might say "Christendom." In the smaller sense of a system of government it is based on the ground of a hope; like all human hopes, its ultimate base is a wish that every individual man is wise enough to know his own interest, and good enough to make it that of his fellowman. It is also taught that all these wills can be summed up by simple arithmetic into one single will, which is then called the Will of the People and found to be always just, right and wise.

But in practice numerous important modifications and adjustments of this simplicity have been necessary, and discovered. Almost the whole political history and the progress of political philosophy in the last age have resulted from these mending processes. Thus for example it was clear almost from the beginning that the simultaneous concourse of all citizens to add together their wills, democratically, in a chorus of thinking and expression is impracticable. Such partial attempts as that of Robespierre to carry out the theory in its purity, to collect together as many possible members of the people, in the streets and squares of Paris and to encourage them there to give vent corporatively to the just and the right, produced poor results; one of them the violent death of the theorist. Since then the English device, of canalizing and distilling this natural virtue of the people by means of election apparatus, is generally followed. But even to begin to relate the numerous ingenuities and mechanisms with which the often disappointing application of the strict theory has been corrected and improved, would be to make an outline of the history of progress in our times. Some, and the greatest, have counselled a refinement of the natural purity of the instinctive will by education, and so indirectly have given us the daily press. A large and serious school ultimately culminating in those Bolsheviks or Communists who have an acting part in the last stage of this story, have taken the opposite direction, more logically defensible, and refused any share in government except to humanity at its purest, poorest and most numerous. Oracular traditions of translating the roars and hisses of the crowd into thought-out political schemes have been invented, and their study is a deep and learned one. Too often in fact, instead of being the sum of fine instincts that are the base of human nature, completely uninfluenced vote reveals only the residue; the scum, in the shape of vanity, fear and laziness; in roughly that order. Did not both Napoleons secure several times the overwhelming majority of the people in a straight vote? It is a warning that the voice of the people needs a whole art of harmonic transcription to be understood. The people, said a great Frenchman, are always right; but you must know how to take them.

Now the mind of Woodrow Wilson, by elementary conviction, by practice, education and erudition, was the repository of the whole of this, the more subtle as rigorously distinguished from the more puritan dogma of democracy; which latter fell finally into the possession of Lenin. That is to say in his person Wilson summed up all the great moderate reformers of the preceding century, from Sieyès, or even Voltaire, to Gladstone, Garibaldi and Lincoln. He was the consecrated guardian of the principal hope of mass-humanity, the only plan of general happiness that is on the table; self-appointed, like genius, but absolutely single-minded, authentic and sure. Without a clear sight of this, the dimensions of his adventure will not appear.

Wilson is in person the doctrine of democracy. He is the deputy of all who have believed in it, dreamed with it, fought for it. He, essentially man of action, is the instrument of those great philosophers and poets you can name yourself, Shelley, Hugo and Heine, as well as Jefferson, Mill and Mazzini. In their spirit and science, he tried to rescue humanity. From what peril, and with what result, will develop, as clearly as possible, as we go.

So then, liking or disliking him as we choose, but not permitted in either case to ignore his functional position in history, we may look up his personal history. There are two highroads, I imagine, to the democratic belief in its entirety: evangelical christianity, and law. One after the other he used both. His father was a Presbyterian minister—that is, of course, one of the democratic forms of church government. It does not anywhere appear that the boy was particularly pious; but here at any rate is a sufficient possibility for the entrance into the substance of his mind, of that rooted hope, at the bottom of democracy, of a common, preordained good for the whole of humanity as a unity. From this environment, the choice of a life direction is restricted. Wilson has left a record, that "the profession I chose was politics; the profession I entered was the law. I entered the one because I thought it would lead to the other. It was once the sure road; and Congress is still full of lawyers."

At the various universities where he studied, he seems to have followed the good though generally misunderstood policy of keeping his real aim always in sight, and refusing to be drawn off his goal by the vanity or complaisance of earning prizes. He read widely, and passed his examinations just honorably. Nevertheless he "worked, prodigiously, passionately, and with a degree of concentration, which during all his life was one of his extraordinary characteristics."

Here, at Johns Hopkins, as at Princeton and the University of Virginia, his interest is so intense in his own special subjects that "he develops at times a positive hostility to his professors; his courses appear as interruptions rather than the purpose of his attendance at the university." The list of what must have been the largest part of his reading at this time has been piously preserved; it was admirably chosen, and adapted to his clearly focussed purpose, even to the complete absence of any author who might have disturbed his faith.

And from these studies and with them, after a brief hesitation, he chose the very unusual, but extremely right road to his amazing future: professorship. Except Wilson, I suppose no man has reached the Presidency of the United States from this profession. Since there is positive evidence that in thus leaving the current of tradition to go his own way, he had by no means renounced his goal, there is a typical characteristic of the adventurous, in life-technique, here also to be noted.

His literary works, beginning with "Congressional Government," and going on to "The State," published in 1889, apart from their psychological data as to the extent to which he had absorbed the true sap of democratic doctrine, are important bridges in his career, essential factors of the growing prestige. Through them, in addition to smaller performances in the reviews, came about his entry into Princeton and so his first noteworthy emergence into action.

The story of his stay and struggles there is like one of the epitomical pieces of Plutarch on the hero of a city-state. The scale and scope was in appearance merely municipal, in this case easily to be put down as the common-room squabbles of schoolmasters; but such was the real size of the protagonists, and the issues involved, political, ethical, cultural, that, like the perfect steel model in miniature of an engine, it could bear indefinite enlargement. This microcosm, in which a great world is condensed without loss of anything but dimension, is so full of detail, so luxuriant and complicated in incident that Wilson himself, when long afterwards he had become accustomed to a rôle in national politics, insisted on the difficulty of retracing even the thread of the matter.

That nevertheless, I, a complete outsider, must endeavour to do; or lose a preciously illuminating view of the personality and style of our subject.

The duality was the same as in all Wilson's adventures. He was here, too, the champion of democracy. This University of Princeton, like all the great universities of America, was in full rush of evolution towards something, which however hazy its exact definition was obviously not a "democratic institution." Without theory, all the more formidable because it was a natural growth of circumstances, a product of the natural will of its members, it was growing, rather on the social side. That is, inside the existing structure of a provincial university for the teaching of the elements of a profession, were growing fast, and encroaching on this simple purpose, clubs and private societies with a convivial, sporting object. These nuclei at first were such as occur spontaneously in any large human conglomeration of persons of the same taste and way of life, and of course their first members would be rather those who had time to spend, whose interest in their studies was not urgent necessity; in short the richer ones.

When Wilson came into power there, this process had already gone far. Club membership was prized more than any academic distinction the university could offer; "To make *a* club, let alone *the* club soon became one of the supreme concerns of lower class-men. From a fourth to a third of the sophomores knew they must be left out each year. Boys entered as freshmen with club membership set before them as one of the chief prizes of college life. Parents even came to Princeton to help pave the way for their sons into the social niche they coveted."

Mr. Ray Stannard Baker, whom I am quoting, notices moreover the irresistible tendency towards more exclusiveness, more luxury, more politics in seeking under-classmen who were known for their family connections or their money, or as athletes, or as "socially desirable."

This situation in itself profoundly displeased the new head, as an affront to the dignity of studies. "The sideshows are swallowing up the circus." But the deeper, more serious challenge to his fundamental beliefs implicit in the situation did not escape him. Here insolently under his nose the formation of an upper class was actively and obviously at work; the negation and enemy of a democratic America. A leisure class, possibly a ruling class, was germinating in these clubs, in the very apse of the temple of his ideals, the university system. His unrelenting, painstaking campaign against these clubs therefore is not a petty affair; it is a key campaign for making America safe for democracy.

The opposition had the initial disadvantage of being on the defensive. They perhaps realized as clearly as he the real nature of the quarrel, far transcending a dispute on how students should pass their spare time: the struggle between a baby aristocracy and a wary and well-armed democratic champion. As one of them, reported by Mr. Baker, put it obstinately: "No one can make a gentleman associate with a mucker." But all the phrases, all the principles, all the rules of conduct and citations were on the side of Wilson. For since the downfall of Hamilton, there is nothing avowable outside the purest democracy in America. Wilson had all the powder and shot; but they had the lay of the land. It is noteworthy that throughout his enemies made no attempt to defend openly what they were doing, made no defence of the "social rôle of a university" he attacked; never so much as brought into the conflict such potent words at their disposal as aristocracy, civilization, everything they might have thrown against his by no means philosophically impregnable conception of a university as a mere training school, or at the extreme, a laboratory; they disputed his facts, not his theory, and waited. In this reluctant, unsallying warfare, the rival chief was Dean Andrew West, apparently a naturally undemocratic, aristocratic mind. "No one could turn a better Latin inscription, or organize a finer pageant for a ceremonial occasion. He loved the outward amenities, the pomp of place, the accoutrement of things." Visits to Europe, especially to England, had "made a tremendous impression on him." The life at Oxford, imposing buildings, and striking effects captured him completely. His letter to Wilson, October 4th from that place, has pasted on it four clippings taken from a book of Oxford views. The Magdalen Tower charmed him. "By moonlight, what a dream in silvery grays and whites." Such a man was the natural antithesis of Wilson, though singularly they had much the same origins. For the artist, as West certainly was in the passive sense, and as Wilson certainly was not in any, but that of adventure and life—a single reading of his speeches would settle the matter—is the natural enemy of democracy, or if he refuses to fight, the natural butt and pariah. That, from certain aspects, democracy is the creation, the dream-child of those poets and artists, and spirited adventurers whom it can neither use nor tolerate, is another matter; Frankenstein's monster killed its master.

And yet this plain, allegorical opposition between the two men, like that between Hector and Achilles, covered a secret bond, a hidden equality without which very likely no combat can be really interesting. The Dean, the artist, throughout has to disguise, even from himself, his essential heresy. Wilson, the lone hand, the adventurer, essentially unsocial in all his tactics, as he is inflexibly social in all his aims, is also, on a far view, in an equally false situation; and so they fight, the aristocrat raising the mob, and the democrat, one against many.

For it is clear that popular feeling was with West. The whole of the alumni, the real backbone of the college, the trustees, most of the professors even, were on his side.

The details, as I say, we must relinquish. The affair concentrated round two epicentres, each concerned with West's scheme for a graduate college, which was to surpass anything in the old buildings and stand comparison with the beauties of Oxford. This building to be acceptable to Wilson had to be an integral part of the college, on the campus site. West wanted it to be placed in a magnificent landscape, rather far from the main buildings, overlooking a golf course. Under this difference was, of course, the question of its control, ideals, the style of its life; its luxury, or its service. "The real issue was Dean West's running the Graduate College as a dictator."

Now, West had found the money, some half million dollars offered by a friend in gift, to back his proposal. This large sum against any other man but Wilson in the place and time, would certainly have clinched West's victory. But at the last moment Wilson succeeded in the prodigious feat of getting his Board to refuse it, to the amazement, fury, admiration of the whole public of America. It was the first introduction of Wilson's name to the nation as a whole. He followed up this astonishing rout of the Westites by his celebrated speech, "The American college must become saturated in the same sympathies as the common people. The American people will tolerate nothing that savors of exclusiveness." But almost as soon as this taunt song of pure democracy was at its last verse, the tables were turned. West received another legacy, this time for several millions, without conditions but under his trusteeship, and Wilson abandoned the battle.

His abdication was no small thing. It had timing, motive, élan, this risk; impure adventurers boggle their jumps. As it was, Wilson pulled it off, and landed, far across the ditch waiting for him, of cranky and disappointed professor-without-a-job—now, into the main movement of his career. For, following a chain of accidents, encounters, opportunities, such as joints the stages of all adventurous lives he was first chosen candidate for Governor of the State of New Jersey; and then with a series of irresistible leaps, Governor, candidate for the presidency, and at last, President of the United States. From this immensely lofty tower, he could look down on the whole field of the world. By office, he was its most powerful ruler; as a result of his method, courage and moral strategy he was freer from the unseen control of his party than any President, perhaps, had ever been before. In fact in its essentials, his situation, in its plebiscitary force, in untied independence was outrageously comparable to that of a Napoleonic Emperor. Without contracting a single debt to hamper him, he had achieved the masterpiece of making this situation out of a defeat in college politics.

This then was Wilson when the world first saw him: the custodian of the whole traditional doctrine, as delivered through a century of preceding history to democracy's saints, by full knowledge, by full conviction, and moreover wielding power as no one of his spiritual predecessors had ever had. The mass-hope had at last its pope; and now we must recall why precisely at this moment, it needed precisely such a man.

The dogma of democracy, consisting of an entire confidence in what men have in common, or, to put it in another way, postulating that human nature is at bottom good, will naturally, in action, suffer severely from any miscalculation in this basic optimism. No mere amputation or bone-setting can hope to cure such a poisoning of its life blood. Now sometimes, it may almost appear not only to hypochondriacs, but to any objective observer, who is not in love at the time, that there is a certain exaggeration quite plainly discernible in the premise. Men have quite commonly a leaning even from extreme childhood to vanity, fear and laziness, and still graver, these tendencies are stronger and more masterful the lower you go in the scale of riches, intelligence, and education, as you approach the main mass, the "people," the seat and shrine of democracy's firmest hopes. Of these three unfortunate defaults, laziness affects mainly the economic part of the democratic hope, fear perhaps the moral, and vanity is the most dangerous of all, as it is the strongest and most general, because it tends always to lead to war.

The question of war has become the main preoccupation of humanity. Before democracy this was by no means the case; the exploits of Alexander, Charles, and their likes, except on exceptional occasions spaced by tens of centuries, was not fractionally so great a worry, as, let us say, the plague. Following such sublime deceivers as Victor Hugo, there has come about certainly a contrary illusion, whose prompt dissipation by facts is the first shock of any student of history. War has not only become more destructive and common, but vastly greater in the scale of those it touches, along with the very unequal but very general growth of democratic government. This concordance has not, of course, escaped the most enrapt believer in progress, and there is a brilliant, circumstantial legend, known to all, that the real reason is some international conspiracy of rich men, armament companies, newspapers, and perhaps beautiful wicked adventuresses, who steal plans from young attachés. Besides this folk-poetry, there is a more matter-of-fact charge, that the progress of science is the cause. I prefer (but you are, of course, not obliged to) the more ingenious theory that Napoleon is to blame, by his invention (rather improvement) of the levee en masse. Kings used to be cautious about asking anyone but the vagabonds and tramps, and those spiritual vagabonds and tramps—the romantic younger sons of aristocracy—to murder and be murdered for them. Conscription, apart from small and unimportant precedence, is a democratic institution; do not forget that Napoleon was Emperor by the expressed will of the people.*

Moreover, quite apart from the habit this great and stern teacher of democracy imposed on it, of going in hordes to get killed, instead of hiring victims from the surplus population, democracy received from him a tremendous encouragement to organize itself in just the way to make these mass slaughters more likely and frequent. Nationalism, the forming of states on a linguistic and historical—that is, really literary if not poetic and archæological—basis is recognized even by democrats to be a dangerous excitement of this war-spirit; for it makes all its appeal to the irrational, strongest part of the abysmal vanity of mankind. But democrats have a special sort of nationalism, diluted, lukewarmed, which they consider not only harmless but beneficial; which I am willing to believe if I could only distinguish exactly between the noxious "My country right or wrong," and "The right of every nation to dispose of themselves."

As things are, infidels must go on believing that large-scale mass warfare is a typical activity of democracies, that nothing excites the enthusiasm of an undoctored vote like a proposition to fight, that never yet has mankind joined with an entirely united will and effort in any other enterprise. And that, as Wilson gradually saw, unless this propensity could be cured, or dammed, or extirpated, either democracy or humanity must die.

It is unnecessary, then, to insist that the last war, with which we are concerned in this account, was a thoroughly democratic affair. England, after a heart-breaking attempt to keep the old monarchical system of sending only volunteers to get killed, adopted the full democratic institution of conscription. The only country in which the war was not absolutely overwhelmingly and openly the will of the whole people was, significantly enough, Russia. In Germany, the

* Lord R. Cecil, the English Liberal, learnt with obvious astonishment that conscription, in France, was supported by the Republicans; a small mercenary army on the English model, one of the program planks of the Royalist Reactionaries...

only completely popular act of the regime was, besides perhaps workmen's compulsory insurance, this war.

And in America, for a long while, Wilson was in opposition to the will of his people, in keeping them out of it. For two or three years, in fact, he was plainly guilty of the grievous sin of benevolent despotism. How he squared his conscience for this is a curious and difficult study by itself. But at length, in the long run, he decided to let them have their war.

His motives for this latter cause, however, are absolutely sure and safe. He entered the war, to kill war, and so save democracy from its recurrence, forever. The choice of sides, no doubt, was made for reasons of nationalist interest—the object, every one of his acts, speeches, and his whole life proved to have been the purest altruism, the love of democracy as the total and only hope of the whole of humanity.

The course of his intervention, the sudden and startling cutting of the bloody knot which every victory and defeat, before America entered, only tightened and swelled; this is, I hope, in every Schoolbook in every country of the world. I fancy, not with entirely pure motives, but rather for the vanity of minimizing the military part played by his troops, it is general to attribute the largest share of the credit in this world-triumph to the speeches, and especially to the Notes, Points, Particulars, Principles and Ends, which he personally emitted. If in this view is included the enormous and absolutely necessary moral encouragement to the Allied troops, which I can bear witness to as an ex-soldier, as well as the disintegratory propaganda effect on the Germans, there is some justice in it.

There are two features of these documents especially noteworthy; in the first place their absolutely plain intention to put future war out of possibility for the sake of democracy. And then again a certain rather ominous indecision of expression. It is not only that the fourteen points, for example, rather overlap each other in places, that the logical expression of his thought is not absolutely clear, and that there is a considerable stress on a doubtful theory of the ultimate cause of war, in "secret diplomacy"—however flattering that may be

for the democratic faith. The Ten Commandments themselves have
similar defects. But the weakness of the too many "as far as possi-
bles," "lowest consistents" is a grave matter; it looks (after the event),
as if this was already a subtly different, less daring man than the
magnificent Wilson of Princeton and New Jersey. A Wilson, let us
say, who was suffering already from the ailment, dangerous to adventurers, of a too clear consciousness of the difficulties ahead. He did
not speak like that to West. The thought underneath, however, is
simple and grand. War is to be prevented forever, mainly by three
self-denying measures; the first national self-determinations only
asked from the Central Powers, the other two more timidly, as I say,
from the whole world. Democracy in all her children. That is, first,
the abolition of armaments—the freedom of the seas as a corollary—
second, universal free trade. But both, mark, only "as far as possible."

This extent, so far as it depended on the will of mankind in its
peoples—all that Wilson could care about—can never of course be
exactly determined. And yet on an estimate of that great possibility, all
estimates of the mighty adventure, now brought to a crisis by his personal embarkation for Europe, must wholly depend. It can never be
disproved that for a terribly short time—a month, a fortnight, more
likely, only one short week all limits were withdrawn. As far as possible, it became in England, in France, in Germany, by the immense
repentance and love of the whole common people for the man who
had saved them, absolutely possible. If Wilson stepping off the boat
had announced, in the tone he once possessed, world-disarmament,
British fleet and German, French army, and Italian submarines,
Gibraltar, Malta, Aden dismantled, and with that the abandonment of
all the tariff barriers of the world—those of his own country first—as
his unalterable terms, I am at perfect liberty to believe that he would
have won through, and, with a larger destiny than any human being
who ever lived, opened the doors to a new and fascinating prospect for
the whole of his fellowmen. The common people wherever he walked
screamed for him to do it; there was certainly a scream.

No one has ever had such cheers; I, who heard them in the streets
of Paris, can never forget them in my life. I saw Foch pass,

Clémenceau pass, Lloyd George, generals, returning troops, banners, but Wilson heard from his carriage, something different, inhuman—or superhuman. Oh, the immovably shining, smiling man.

To be sure, it would not have gone easily, this total humanitarian adventure. Singularly enough, the resistance of the two most obvious barriers, Lloyd George and Clémenceau, was quite doubtful. Both were at a tremendous pitch of relief and joy; for, remember, both were great orators, a breed who have nerves. And both were in their different ways almost mystically exalted democrats, sincere demagogues. Clémenceau, in addition, through his whole history (and often it hurt his career) an almost boundless, blinded admirer of Anglo-Saxon institutions and leadership; Lloyd George, a humanitarian much more by fanaticism than even by calculation. There was, in that week—that is understood—just that trembling, maddening chance; and such is the very material of adventure. If Wilson had just been, at that instant, a little crazy; if, when the British Prime Minister started, in his sense of duty—for he was a small man—to push perfunctorily against the keystone of the Wilsonian arch; the freedom of the seas, the usual rigmarole of "never used except for freedom and justice"; never for a moment expecting that his hero would hear him out; and then surprised with a queer secret disappointment, discover that he, Lloyd George, England, the status quo, and common sanity, as he put it to himself in the car home, had won the day. Technically, in short, the pressure of England came first, then the pressure of France. And then it was unnecessary to take up the third matter of world free trade.

The world would have resisted; the intelligent sane middle-class would have let him go home, and tried to quell the revolutions. In America, in all certainty, he would have had to resign; the Princeton issue all over again. But on the London platform, waiting for the train to take them to the boat for Russia, the English Guards threw down their arms; a little unrecorded, historical anecdote. And practically every town, almost every village in France had once a Rue Wilson. Did you know that? It was not because of, or after his share in, the Treaty of Versailles; the naming took place in a moment when everyone seemed to be crazy with Wilson; in those early hysterical times of the peace. Since then the plaque has in most cases been taken down. But sometimes still in odd corners of the country, in towns where they contented themselves with taking it from the chief street, the boulevard they are proudest of, nailed up over a side-alley, you may still come across this uneasy nudge of what, wild and unexpected, might have happened: if only Wilson in that one sole week had been a little crazy.

But he was sane; conscious all the time. And now, leaving all the relief to those who feel it, we must briefly examine the causes of the strange metamorphosis of the fourteen points into the Treaty of Versailles. And immediately, that great safeguard of failures, that insurance which the great and their friends claim in case of disaster—bad advice, evil counsellors; that excuse must be ruled out. The important part of the entourage of the great President was, if possible, more daring than himself. The heavy blanket influence of the great and banal powers of money, industry, politics from his own country if, indeed, it has not been maligned, came long after the game was lost. We would not have been occupied with Wilson here, in this company that starts with Alexander, if he had not known how to make himself and keep himself a free and lonely man. It is a rather more exclusive company than the Ivy Club at Princeton College, or than a list of the kings of England.

His acts were his own; he went through this conference with the isolated responsibility of the act of dying. All was well lost before it started. Only the rather ghastly interest of watching a killing remained. Instead of a prophet, he had been changed into a suitor, beseeching, bribing the others not to go too far. You may well believe he fought well; on his stumps, like the old hard-dying sea dog in the ballad. Even at the very beginning before they had dared quite whole-heartedly to set about him, he had forced out of them the Covenant of the League of Nations. But the blank cheque for reparations, the fulfilment of the secret treaties—every power seemed to have a boxful of them and every one was in opposition to the fourteen points—the whole savage and greedy looting of the Treaty of

Versailles was inexorably wrung out of him piecemeal. He would not even save his principle when the direct national interests of his own country were in play; thus he was forced to yield Shantung to the Japanese and receive the horrified scorn of the Chinese for doing it.

To stop even worse things, the annexation of the left bank of the Rhine, for example, he had to pay. Pay off nation by nation with alliances, promises, pawn the future of the United States, to stop these associated democracies from tearing the enemy he had delivered into their hands into a hundred pieces. Even his League—he had to pay for that by Article X., which laid down that he and his country would protect them, assure them in what they had done forever.

Such, one-sidedly, certainly (but that the outside), was the great squeezing of Wilson; whose annotated details are contained in the Treaty he signed. More, even, than the breaking-up of the Central Powers, it was the perfect partition of his own world-wide spiritual Empire, that had lasted only a few years; and he stayed to the end.

One singular incident, like a bodily convulsion, alone showed the outside world the progress of his throes. After all the great things had been sacrificed, he stuck at giving the Croatian port of Fiume to Italy. He had yielded everything to France and England; the thought of submitting to a mere Italy would have roused him, if he had been physically half-dead. Italy did not have Fiume from him; yet there was something sad, as well as noble, in his stand, at such a stage. It was as if suddenly the old, six-months buried self, in full democratic armor, "in the same figure like the king that's dead," stood up to bar the way before the aggrieved, bewildered, poor Italian couple, Orlando and Sonnino. And this towering phantom released, at last, the thunder clap. I have speculated on the effect of an appeal to the world, and its possible results, issued on his arrival. Now at last inconceivably, hopelessly, late, his cry went out! The mighty signal he had been saving; to the people of the world; and nothing but a rumbling echo answered it. The world had moved in those few months a whole century out of place.

The cause of this grand and tragic downfall, this messianic catastrophe, whose size and significance are certainly greater than the war, the occasion which it crowned, is hardly mysterious; nor in the history of adventure can it be unexpected or abnormal. Wilson went down, not because he was vain, nor because he was outwitted, nor because of any other of the small accidental reasons with which the spiteful children of his enemies sought to account for the overwhelming result of their prayers. A structural fault, nothing less, brought down that vast hope in ruins; as all great dramas end. Wilson was afraid; in that particularly deadly form, excused as it is by every moral code but not by destiny, which is called a sense of responsibility. "They held up the spectre of Bolshevism to him, and he dared not risk." Who, *They?* Clémenceau and Lloyd George? They were frightened as he was. Wilson's tragedy was no gigantic, still ludicrous version of the confidence game. He, and the world with him—for Wilson's adventure was the world's, and one day the world will know it, even the fools—were not the victims of a vulgar trick, unless the dizziness that pulls down climbers from the peak is some cunning of the Alps. We fell there because the height was too great, because he saw all the countries of the world, the bare immensity of the mass of common people which he had worshipped all his life, but never imagined until that day he knew he had them, their lives, and all uncountable, future ages of them in his own two hands. Seeing, a great vertigo leapt on him. Those days have passed more utterly from memory than if a hundred years had gone since then; but a few who lived through them, and stood near where the pedestal of Wilson was standing can remember, vaguely, as if they had read it somewhere, something of the madness, the sheer panic, mixed with exaltation, of the times. The storm has gone now. The name Bolshevism has only resonance. But those were the days in which anything might happen; Clémenceau, who contemplated quite steadily the possibility of the total destruction of Paris to get victory, used to quiver to his grey mitten tips at that subterranean Treaty of Lenin. He had been through one commune. The great killing was over: could Wilson, with its smell in the air, risk another? And so he did not risk, and so, not risking, he lost the lot. Such is the end, we have imagined, of most adventures, perhaps all adventures, though peer and probe as we might we could not find a trace of a necessity, which would set our minds at peace. For if only we could find an inevitability of failure of the game we are forced, singly, and in the whole slow moving column of humanity through the ages to play against the gods, there would be a Shakesperean release, an ease, a true tragic katharsis in it; a quasi-musical compensation, that all endeavour is predestined lost. But such, like the static dream of a fixed good in the universe attainable in time, that image of space, there is nowhere any true sign of. We are encouraged to, not absolved from, adventure by the shortest and most inadequate look at it. There is no certainty, good or bad, but an infinite resilience that makes both good and bad greater than we commonly think. The heights are further; the gulfs deeper; if it is a game, the odds are enormous.

So Woodrow Wilson, the last of our heroes, ends our biggest adventure; some people think that, like Arthur and the legendary Alexander, and many other lesser men, he left, even though defeated, a hope, a promise, that League, which is as it were a symbol of his perished flesh and blood, a fragment torn out of his heart and left with us, to serve for one who will come after in a retaking up of his adventure to put his feet on for the leap. It may be. We started by renouncing a moral, and we here end without one. But at any rate, we may be more certain now of the infinite hopeful and despairing uncertainties of things as they seem, as they are, and as they will be.

Connect with Diversion Books

Connect with us for information on new titles and authors from Diversion Books, free excerpts, special promotions, contests, and more:

 @DiversionBooks

 www.facebook.com/DiversionBooks

 Diversion Books eNewsletter

www.ingramcontent.com/pod-product-compliance
Lightning Source LLC
Jackson TN
JSHW031523131224
75386JS00044B/1710